Vocabulary Skills for the
TOEFL 3
iBT [Finish-up]

Vocabulary Skills for the
TOEFL iBT 3 [Finish-up]

저 자 윤창만, 손성균
발행인 고본화
발 행 반석출판사
2021년 12월 10일 초판 2쇄 인쇄
2021년 12월 15일 초판 2쇄 발행
홈페이지 www.bansok.co.kr
이메일 bansok@bansok.co.kr
블로그 blog.naver.com/bansokbooks

07547 서울시 강서구 양천로 583. B동 1007호
(서울시 강서구 염창동 240-21번지 우림블루나인 비즈니스센터 B동 1007호)
대표전화 02) 2093-3399 **팩 스** 02) 2093-3393
출 판 부 02) 2093-3395 **영업부** 02) 2093-3396
등록번호 제315-2008-000033호

ISBN 978-89-7172-752-2 (13740)

- 교재 관련 문의: bansok@bansok.co.kr을 이용해 주시기 바랍니다.

Vocabulary Skills for the
TOEFL 3
iBT [Finish-up]

Bansok

TOEFL을 단시간에 효율적으로 공략하기 위해 가장 우선시 되어야 할 것이 기출어휘 암기이다. 기출어휘를 많이 알면 알수록 Reading뿐 아니라 Listening이나 Writing, Speaking을 공부할 때도 학습 효과는 배가 된다. 어휘력이 늘어날수록 다른 섹션에 대한 이해도 빠르고 쉬워진다.

하지만 어휘를 공부할 때 단순히 영어 단어와 우리말 뜻을 대입하여 암기해서는 안 된다. 처음에는 효과가 있을 수 있겠지만, 시간이 지나갈수록 그 효과는 분명히 떨어진다. 이 책은 효과적인 TOEFL 어휘 학습방법을 제시하며, 과거 20여 년간의 TOEFL 기출어휘를 총정리했다.

분야별 전문용어는 지문을 이해하는 데 반드시 필요하지는 않지만 핵심적인 부분이다. 전문용어를 익히는 가장 좋은 방법은 배경지식을 제공하는 지문을 많이 읽어보며 어휘를 정리하는 것이다. 그렇지 못할 경우에는 TOEFL의 Listening과 Reading에 자주 나오는 내용을 중심으로 지문을 많이 읽어보는 것이다. 이러한 분야별 어휘 학습을 돕기 위해 이 책의 예문들은 다양한 주제로부터 선정하였으며, 문맥에서 어휘의 뜻을 이해할 수 있도록 하기 위해 연습문제를 제시하였다.

어휘 학습은 하루에 30~50개가 적당하다. 처음에는 영어 단어와 한글 뜻, 이렇게 단순하게 외울 수 있지만, 이보다는 [영어 단어 → 동의어 ▶ 영어 단어 → 동의어(Definition) → 예문 ▶ 영어 단어의 어원관련 학습 ▶ 한글 뜻 → 영어 단어] 순으로 점차 그 범위를 넓혀가면서 기억용량(Memory Span)을 늘리다보면 어휘량은 무한히 늘어날 것이다. 어휘는 문맥 속에서 적절하게 사용해야 하기 때문에 한 가지 방법보다는 여러 가지 방법으로 어휘의 본래 의미와 용례 등을 학습해야 한다. 효율적인 어휘 학습을 돕기 위한 방법의 한 예로 어휘의 뜻을 그림으로 그려가며 하는 것도 도움이 될 것이다.

TOEFL 어휘는 시험을 보는 마지막 순간까지도 지속적으로 공부해야 할 것이다. 꾸준한 학습을 통하여 TOEFL 어휘를 공부하면서 TOEFL에 대한 두려움이 사라질 수 있기를 바란다. 이 책이 부족하지만 체계적인 TOEFL 어휘 학습을 위한 길라잡이가 되어 어휘 학습량을 늘려줄 수 있다면 저자로서 더 바랄 게 없다. 모두가 큰 축복 속에 평안하기 바란다.

2014년 7월

저자 윤창만, 손성균

목차

이 책의 특징 및 공부 방법

이 책은 지난 20여 년 동안의 TOEFL 기출어휘를 분석하여 1권당 800개(20유 닛, 1유닛당 40개)를 선정, 총 2400개(총3권)의 필수어휘를 제시하고 있다.

01. Daily Checkup

필수어휘 40개를 공부하기 전에, 자신의 어휘 실력을 테 스트해볼 수 있도록 하기 위해 20개의 동의어 문제를 제 공한다.

02. Voca Bank

하루치 40개의 단어를 선정하여 [동의어 – 반의어 – 한 글 뜻 – 구문 및 예문] 등을 실었다. 구문 및 예문은 실제 시험에 출제되었던 내용을 요약·정리했기 때문에 반드 시 암기해야 한다. 자주 출제되는 단어는 별표를 이용해 서 출제 빈도를 표시했다.

03. Practice Test

Voca Bank에서 공부한 어휘를 테스트해 볼 수 있다. 틀 린 문제는 반드시 다시 한 번 체크하기 바란다. 여기에 실 린 문제들은 지면 관계상 본문에서 미처 다루지 못했던 예문을 대신하는 역할을 겸하기 때문에 문제 자체를 외우 는 것도 문맥 파악을 위해 도움이 될 것이다.

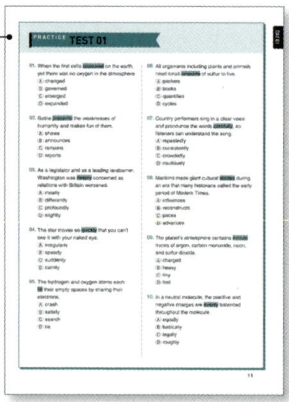

DAY 01 Daily Checkup

01. proceed to business
    - (A) concrete
    - (B) remove
    - (C) progress
    - (D) dwindle

02. Money is my motivation.
    - (A) stimulus
    - (B) learning
    - (C) obligation
    - (D) atmosphere

03. a brisk early morning swim
    - (A) energetic
    - (B) indiscreet
    - (C) negligent
    - (D) inadvertent

04. alleviate the patient's pain
    - (A) contract
    - (B) match
    - (C) abate
    - (D) form

05. made a cynical statement
    - (A) substantive
    - (B) skeptical
    - (C) pastoral
    - (D) pungent

06. periodically patrolling the area
    - (A) tingly
    - (B) randomly
    - (C) regularly
    - (D) indistinctly

07. long periods of inactivity
    - (A) assumption
    - (B) immobility
    - (C) tale
    - (D) aptitude

08. the tangible results of the plan
    - (A) functional
    - (B) impertinent
    - (C) substantial
    - (D) inadvertent

09. extract pleasure from rural life
    - (A) continue
    - (B) derive
    - (C) meditate
    - (D) lessen

10. pathetic sight
    - (A) abate
    - (B) pungent
    - (C) indiscernible
    - (D) pitiable

11. contemplate a tour around the world
    - (A) contract
    - (B) match
    - (C) plan
    - (D) extort

12. His words and actions do not correspond.
    - (A) abate
    - (B) match
    - (C) contain
    - (D) progress

13. responsible for protecting vehicles
    - (A) answerable
    - (B) acquainted
    - (C) whimsical
    - (D) mercy

14. a collection of ancient stories
    - (A) evidences
    - (B) tales
    - (C) gifts
    - (D) stages

15. for utilitarian purpose
    - (A) sarcastic
    - (B) real
    - (C) insolent
    - (D) pragmatic

16. an impudent young rascal
    - (A) impertinent
    - (B) unseen
    - (C) piquant
    - (D) feasibly

17. had misgiving about joining that club
    - (A) background
    - (B) unemployment
    - (C) apprehension
    - (D) capability

18. a piquant sauce
    - (A) pungent
    - (B) insolent
    - (C) imperceptible
    - (D) indiscreet

19. constrict the blood vessels
    - (A) lessen
    - (B) compress
    - (C) progress
    - (D) remove

20. I tried to accommodate myself to the circumstances.
    - (A) accord
    - (B) encourage
    - (C) abate
    - (D) adapt

표제어	품사	동의어와 예문	한글 뜻
1 accommodate*** [əkámədèit]	v	adapt, lodge, suit, fit, contain, hold room to **accommodate** four people 네 명을 수용할 수 있는 방	수용하다, 적응하다
2 alleviate* [əlí:vièit]	v	ease, lessen, abate **alleviate** one's sufferings 고통을 경감하다	완화시키다
3 arbitrarily* [á:rbiətrèrəli]	ad	randomly, capricious, whimsical **arbitrarily** given the present 무작위로 주어진 선물	임의대로, 무작위로
4 aware* [əwέər]	a	knowing about, acquainted with, conscious of become **aware** of ~을 알아채다	알아차린
5 blur ** [blə:r]	v	indistinct, obscure, vague, mask Camera during a long exposure may **blur** the picture. 긴 노출을 하는 동안 카메라는 사진을 흐리게 할 수 있다. **blur** out 지우다	흐리게 하다, 무감각하게 하다
6 brisk [brisk]	a	active, lively, energetic a **brisk** and humorous tale about a fox 여우에 관한 활기차고 해학적인 이야기 **brisk** about 활발히 돌아다니다	활발한, 성업 중인
7 careless [kέərlis]	a	heedless, reckless, indiscreet, negligent, inadvertent **Careless** misuse of pesticides have destroyed the soil. 농약의 부주의한 오용이 토양을 파괴해 왔다. act **careless** 무모한 짓을 하다	조심성 없는, 무모한
8 comprise* [kəmpráiz]	v	be made up of, consist of, constitute, compose **comprise** a book entirely of essays 책 전체를 수필로 구성하다	구성하다, 포함하다
9 constrict [kənstríkt]	v	compress, contract **constricts** the blood vessels 혈관을 수축하다	수축하다
10 contemplate* [kántəmplèit]	v	consider, reflect, ponder, meditate **contemplate** nature 자연을 관조하다	숙고하다, 명상에 잠기다
11 correspond [kɔ̀:rəspánd]	v	conform, accord, match I think it to **correspond** to facts. 그것은 사실과 일치한다고 생각한다.	일치하다
12 country [kʌntri]	n	① nation, state Korea is one of the mountainous **country**. 한국은 산이 많은 나라 중 하나다. ② backwoods, farmland, outback They lived on a farm in the **country**. 그들은 시골 농가에서 살았다.	① 국가, 정부 ② 농지
	a	rural, rustic, pastoral, simple, plain I want to live a simple **country** life. 나는 검소한 시골생활을 하고 싶다.	시골의, 단조로운

13	cynical [sínikəl]	a	sarcastic, satirical, sneering make **cynical** remarks 비꼬아 말하다	냉소적인
14	**diminish*** [dimíniʃ]	v	lessen, reduce, decrease, shrink, abate, dwindle **diminish** in population 인구가 감소되다	감소하다, 줄어들다
15	**environment** [inváiərənmənt]	n	surroundings, atmosphere, background a smelly **environment** 냄새 나는 환경	환경, 상황, 분위기
16	**erratically** [irǽtikəli]	ad	irregularly, unpredictably, variably, unstably Some of the ice streams are behaving **erratically**. 일부 빙하류가 불규칙하게 움직인다. an **erratic** behavior 엉뚱한 행위	엉뚱하게, 불규칙하게
17	**evidence*** [évədəns]	n	reveal, proof provide important **evidence** for the theory of evolution 진화이론에 대한 중요한 증거를 제시하다 take **evidence** 증인을 조사하다	증거
18	**extract*** [ikstrǽkt]	v	remove, extort, derive **extract** new illustration from our pamphlet 새로운 삽화를 우리 홍보 책자에서 발췌하다	발췌하다, 추출하다
19	**feasibly*** [fí:zəbli]	a	easily, readily, willingly, quickly, possibly, practicably The sun's radiant energy **feasibly** filters into the planet's atmosphere. 태양의 복사 에너지는 적당하게 행성의 대기권에서 걸러진다.	적당하게, 쉽게, 서슴없이, 선뜻
20	**forage*** [fɔ́:ridʒ]	v	feed, search the food **forage** among the villages 마을들로 식량을 구하러 다니다	약탈하다, (식량을) 찾아 다 니다
21	**hypothesis** [haipάθəsis]	n	assumption, thesis, theory **hypothesis** testing 가설 검증	가설
22	**impudent*** [ímpjudnt]	a	impertinent, insolent, shameless, rude an **impudent** young rascal 뻔뻔스러운 젊은 녀석	건방진
23	**inactivity** [ìnæktívəti]	n	immobility, dormancy, unemployment long periods of **inactivity** 오랜 휴지기	고정, 정지
24	**invisible** [invízəbl]	a	unseen, imperceptible, indiscernible Ultraviolet rays are **invisible** to the human eye. 자외선은 인간의 눈에는 보이지 않는다.	눈에 안 보이는
25	**literacy** [lítərəsi]	n	learning, education, knowledge The world **literacy** rate has risen since 1900. 전세계 식자율이 1900년 이래로 증가해 왔다.	읽고 쓰는 능력(이 있음)
26	**misgiving** [misgíviŋ]	n	apprehension, doubt, distrust, suspicion have **misgivings** about ~에 대하여 의심을 품다	의심, 걱정, 불안
27	**moreover**** [mɔ:róuvər]	a	in addition, besides, further, furthermore **Moreover**, it began to rain. 게다가 비까지 내리기 시작했다.	더욱이, 게다가
28	**motivation** [mòutəvéiʃən]	n	incentive, stimulus Money is my **motivation** to work harder. 내가 더욱 열심히 일하게 하는 동기는 돈이다.	동기, 부여, 자극, 유도

29	**pathetic** [pəθétik]	**a**	pitiable, touching, moving a **pathetic** story intermingled with comic incidents 우스운 사건과 얽힌 슬픈 이야기	감상적인, 애처로운
30	**periodically*** [pìəriádikəli]	**ad**	regularly, customarily, typically **periodically** patrolling the area 정기적으로 지역 순찰하는	주기적으로
31	**piquant** [pí:kənt]	**a**	sharp, pungent a **piquant** source 알싸한 소스	신랄한, 통렬한
32	**proceed** [prəsí:d]	**v**	advance, progress, continue **proceed** on a journey 여행을 가다	나아가다, 진행되다
33	**quarter** [kwɔ́:rtər]	**n**	district, area, mercy for a **quarter** of the price 4분의 1 가격으로	지역, 4분의 1
34	**responsible*** [rispánsəbl]	**a**	accountable, answerable, liable a **responsible** position 책임 있는 위치	책임이 있는
		n	answer, return, reply, reaction a quick **response** 빠른 응답	응답, 대답, 반응
35	**secular** [sékjulər]	**a**	world, earthly, temporal, civil ↔ religious French nobles composed many **secular** songs and poems. 프랑스 귀족이 많은 세속적인 노래와 시를 작곡했다.	속인의, 세속의, 비종교적인
36	**strand** [strænd]	**v**	desert, desolate, forsake Viola finds herself **stranded** in the country of Illyria. 바이올라는 일리리아의 나라에서 좌초한 자기자신을 발견한다.	좌초시키다
		n	filament, fiber, thread	실
37	**story** [stɔ́:ri]	**n**	level; tale the second **story** 2층 a collection of ghost **stories** 유령 이야기의 모음	층 / 이야기
38	**talent*** [tǽlənt]	**n**	aptitude, capacity, capability, gift, genius, faculty Some careers require **talent** and dedication. 어떤 경력은 재능과 헌신을 요구한다. a man of **talent** 재능 있는 사람	재능, 수완
39	**tangible*** [tǽndʒəbl]	**a**	substantial, real, concrete, substantive **tangible** evidence for the recovering of economy 경제 회복의 명백한 증거	만질 수 있는, 명백한
40	**utilitarian** [jú:tìlətéəriən]	**a**	functional, pragmatic for **utilitarian** purpose 실리적인 목적으로	실용적인

01. Because the cost of water has been cheap, people have been careless and wasteful.
Ⓐ nepotistic
Ⓑ negligent
Ⓒ negative
Ⓓ prudent

02. Shakespeare wrote his plays to suit the talents of specific performers.
Ⓐ activities
Ⓑ entertainment
Ⓒ habits
Ⓓ genius

03. Light waves become distorted, so the telescope produces a blurred image.
Ⓐ reversed
Ⓑ exaggerated
Ⓒ indistinct
Ⓓ unintentional

04. Geologists have found evidence that suggests petroleum may be present in the seabed offshore.
Ⓐ witness
Ⓑ impairment
Ⓒ proof
Ⓓ preference

05. A hypothesis is simply a tentative, unproven explanation for something that has been observed.
Ⓐ assumption
Ⓑ hazard
Ⓒ solution
Ⓓ result

06. The weight of carbon-12 is arbitrarily set at 12 atomic mass units (the unit of atomic weight).
Ⓐ remarkably
Ⓑ subsequently
Ⓒ randomly
Ⓓ exactly

07. Earlier works hinted that inefficient foraging might have been a factor in the subsequent demise of the Neanderthals.
Ⓐ searching for food
Ⓑ finding shelters
Ⓒ making fire
Ⓓ remaining records

08. Most plant cells, and the vast majority of animal cells, are so tiny they are invisible to the naked eye.
Ⓐ unable to be heard
Ⓑ unable to be seen
Ⓒ unable to be touched
Ⓓ unable to be understand

09. At the party, some students were well behaved, while the others were impudent.
Ⓐ shameless
Ⓑ pitiable
Ⓒ substantial
Ⓓ utilitarian

10. Because mountains include diverse conditions at different elevations, they provide environments suitable for many kinds of plant and animal life.
Ⓐ opportunities
Ⓑ vital forces
Ⓒ surroundings
Ⓓ requisites

11. Moreover, unlike passwords and key cards, biometric identifiers cannot be lost, forgotten, or forged.
    (A) In addition
    (B) More or less
    (C) However
    (D) Consequently

12. To accommodate the increasing number of skiers, many ski areas and resorts were enlarged or developed in the United States, Canada, and Europe.
    (A) training
    (B) reimburse
    (C) account
    (D) lodge

13. Many countries have implemented literacy programs that rely on volunteer teachers.
    (A) reading and writing
    (B) standard intelligence
    (C) current affairs
    (D) physical and mental health

14. To help keep costs low, the companies tend to locate their factories in countries where raw materials are feasibly available.
    (A) suitably
    (B) ultimately
    (C) briefly
    (D) firmly

15. Dormancy is a period of inactive growth in seeds, buds, bulbs, and other plant organs even when the appropriate environmental conditions are met.
    (A) motionless
    (B) hibernated
    (C) regular
    (D) obstructed

16. Through contemplation of sculptured images, Asian people seek to understand these divine powers and to become one with the eternal.
    (A) meditation
    (B) remembrance
    (C) complement
    (D) mean

17. According to the three-component theory, the color sensations that arise in the brain correspond to the electrical signals in a simple and direct way.
    (A) move
    (B) transfer
    (C) adjust
    (D) accord

18. Many of O'Neill's plays, especially the trilogy *Mourning Becomes Electra* (1931), include pathetic characters and a depressing atmosphere.
    (A) lethargic   (B) gloomy
    (C) woeful   (D) apprehensive

19. Protestants make up about 5 percent of Latin America's overall population, although they comprise a greater percentage in some countries more than they do in others.
    (A) undermine
    (B) depend on
    (C) revere
    (D) consist of

20. Modern Shakespeare editions show an increased awareness of the social and intellectual background against which Shakespeare worked.
    (A) delinquency
    (B) criminal
    (C) consciousness
    (D) enhancement

DAY 02 Daily Checkup

01. justify oneself
    - Ⓐ slide
    - Ⓑ verify
    - Ⓒ hide
    - Ⓓ spoil

02. bring to a crisis
    - Ⓐ prestige
    - Ⓑ depot
    - Ⓒ emergency
    - Ⓓ rogue

03. a prudent man
    - Ⓐ inexpensive
    - Ⓑ close
    - Ⓒ cautious
    - Ⓓ malevolent

04. deviate from the custom
    - Ⓐ slide
    - Ⓑ stray
    - Ⓒ testify
    - Ⓓ damage

05. receive much recognition
    - Ⓐ distinction
    - Ⓑ confederation
    - Ⓒ crisis
    - Ⓓ allowance

06. add luster to College
    - Ⓐ radiance
    - Ⓑ measure
    - Ⓒ identification
    - Ⓓ cover

07. the intermediate examination
    - Ⓐ attached
    - Ⓑ middle
    - Ⓒ exploded
    - Ⓓ executed

08. pictured proof of the break-in
    - Ⓐ affected
    - Ⓑ counted
    - Ⓒ leaned
    - Ⓓ imagined

09. small in stature
    - Ⓐ height
    - Ⓑ felon
    - Ⓒ depot
    - Ⓓ conveyance

10. acute pains in my hands
    - Ⓐ severe
    - Ⓑ unbearable
    - Ⓒ disinterested
    - Ⓓ suspended

11. affection to his parents
    - Ⓐ love
    - Ⓑ alliance
    - Ⓒ thought
    - Ⓓ enmity

12. The crowds poured into the warehouse.
    - Ⓐ thoroughfare
    - Ⓑ distraction
    - Ⓒ confederation
    - Ⓓ store

13. The river flooded the city.
    - Ⓐ confirmed
    - Ⓑ deluged
    - Ⓒ damaged
    - Ⓓ supported

14. hide one's feelings
    - Ⓐ stray
    - Ⓑ portray
    - Ⓒ conceal
    - Ⓓ depend

15. assume a disinterested attitude (toward)
    - Ⓐ intolerable
    - Ⓑ oblique
    - Ⓒ careful
    - Ⓓ impartial

16. unbearable heat
    - Ⓐ diverged
    - Ⓑ exploded
    - Ⓒ glided
    - Ⓓ intolerable

17. a busy thoroughfare
    - Ⓐ street
    - Ⓑ conveyance
    - Ⓒ union
    - Ⓓ radiance

18. a profession of friendship
    - Ⓐ expression
    - Ⓑ acceptance
    - Ⓒ vocation
    - Ⓓ concept

19. stand mute of malice
    - Ⓐ resin
    - Ⓑ confederation
    - Ⓒ spite
    - Ⓓ idea

20. a posthumous child
    - Ⓐ insupportable
    - Ⓑ after death
    - Ⓒ familiar
    - Ⓓ dispassionate

표제어	품사	동의어와 예문	한글 뜻
1 **acute**** [əkjúːt]	a	sharp, serious, critical, crucial, severe ↔ chronic Sharks are fast swimmers with **acute** senses. 상어는 빠른 감각을 가지고 빠르게 헤엄치는 동물이다.	격렬한, 예리한, 중대한
2 **affection** [əfékʃən]	n	attachment, amity, love, fondness Babies require much love and **affection**. 아가는 많은 사랑과 애정이 필요하다.	애정, 애착
3 **amateur** [ǽmətʃùər]	a	nonprofessional Only **amateur** athletes competed in this game. 오직 아마추어 선수들만이 이 경기에서 경쟁했다. **amateur** theatricals 아마추어 연극	비전문가의, 아마추어의
4 **brim** [brim]	n	rim, edge, border, margin, verge, brink be full to the **brim** 가득 차다	가장자리, 테두리
5 **carriage** [kǽridʒ]	n	vehicle, conveyance have a passenger **carriage** at the front 앞쪽에 승객이 타는 곳이 있는 **carriage** of goods 화물 수송	운반, 탈것
6 **congregate**** [káŋɡrigèit]	v	come together, collect together The workers **congregated** in front of city hall. 근로자들이 시청 앞에 모였다.	모이다, 군집하다
7 **countless***** [káuntlis]	a	innumerable, uncountable, innumerous, numberless The earth is just one of **countless** heavenly bodies in the universe. 지구는 단지 우주에 있는 셀 수 없는 천체 중 하나이다.	셀 수 없는, 무수한
8 **crisis*** [kráisis]	n	emergency The **crisis** in the Southeast Asia had passed. 동남아시아의 위기가 지나갔다. bring to a **crisis** 위기에 몰아넣다	위기
9 **criterion*** [kraitíəriən]	n	standard, measure, principle define a **criterion** for distinguishing between truth and error 사실과 과실 사이의 구별을 위한 기준을 정의하다	기준
10 **deviate*** [díːvièit]	v	diverge, wander, stray **deviate** from the original plan 원 계획에서 벗어나다	일탈하다, 벗어나다
11 **disinterested**** [disíntərèstid]	a	impartial, detached, dispassionate assume a **disinterested** attitude 담담한 태도로 임하다	공평한, 사심 없는
12 **erupt** [irʌpt]	v	explode, gush **erupt** into war between the two powerful country 두 강대국 간에 전쟁으로 폭발하다	폭발하다, 분출하다

| 13 | **flood****
 [flʌd] | v | deluge, overflow, inundate
 The river **flooded** the city. 강이 도시를 범람했다.
 a **flood** of good ideas 훌륭한 생각의 쇄도 | 홍수나다, 범람하다 |

| 14 | **functional**
 [fʌ́ŋkʃənl] | a | practical, serviceable
 functional disorder of education 교육의 기능적 장해 | 기능의 |

| 15 | **glide***
 [glaid] | v | slide, slip
 glide out of the room 방에서 조용히 나가다 | 미끄러지다 |

| 16 | **homestead**
 [hóumstèd] | n | farmstead, land
 The government's **homestead** laws gave free land to settlers.
 정부의 공유지 불하법으로 정착민들에게 공짜로 땅을 주었다. | 집과 대지, 농장 |

| 17 | **hide****
 [haid] | v | conceal, screen, cover, veil
 ↔ reveal, disclose
 hide his disappointment 그의 낙담을 감추다 | 숨기다 |
| | | n | skin of animals <br> thick **hide** of the elephant's legs 코끼리 다리의 두꺼운 가죽 | 가죽 |

| 18 | **inexpensive*****
 [ìnikspénsiv] | a | cheap, economical <br> good **inexpensive** restaurant 값싸고 좋은 식당 | 값싼 |

| 19 | **insulate**
 [ínsəlèit] | v | isolate, protect, screen, defend, shelter, shield <br> the layers of apparatus to **insulate** the contents
 내용물을 분리하는 기구의 층들 | 절연(단열)하다, 분리하다 |

| 20 | **intermediate***
 [ìntərmíːdiət] | a | in-between, middle, intervening <br> the **intermediate** examination (대학의) 중간 시험 | 중간의 |

| 21 | **intimate***
 [íntəmət] | a | close, familiar <br> play an **intimate** role to people's lives
 사람들의 삶과 친근한 역할을 하다 | 가까운, 친밀한 |

| 22 | **irate****
 [airéit] | a | angry, furious, angered, provoked, ireful <br> have received some **irate** phone calls from customers
 고객들로부터 분노에 찬 전화를 받았다 | 노한, 성난 |

| 23 | **justify***
 [dʒʌ́stəfài] | v | ① prove, confirm, verify, testify
 justify my decision to quit 그만둔다는 자신의 결정을 밝히다
 ② support, warrant, authorize, legitimize <br> information that would **justify** his decision to quit
 그만두겠다는 그의 결정을 지지한다는 정보 | ① 정당화하다, 밝히다

 ② 지지하다 |

| 24 | **league**
 [liːg] | n | alliance, confederation, union <br> the **League** of the amateur's baseball game 아마추어 야구경기연맹 | 연맹, 동맹 |

| 25 | **luster***
 [lʌ́stər] | n | radiance, brilliance, brightness <br> shed **luster** on ~에 빛을 주다
 Mineral with metallic **luster** shine like metal.
 금속 광택의 광물이 금속같이 빛난다. | 광채, 영광, 광택 |

| 26 | **malice***
 [mǽlis] | n | ill will, spite, enmity, malevolence <br> stand mute of **malice** 묵비권을 행사하다 | 악의, 원한 |

| 27 | **mar***
 [maːr] | v | spoil (by), blemish, damage
 That billboard **mars** the view.
 그 광고판이 경치를 망치고 있다. | 망치다, 훼손하다 |

28	**picture** [píktʃər]	v	imagine, draw, photograph, portrait, depict, delineate **picture** proof of the break-in 침입의 증거를 묘사하다	묘사하다, 상상하다
29	**posthumous** [pástʃuməs]	a	following one's death Emily Dickinson's **posthumous** fame 에밀리 디킨슨의 사후 명성	사후에
30	**profession** [prəféʃən]	n	vocation, calling, business, employment public understanding of the interior design **profession** 인테리어 디자인 직업의 대중적인 이해	직업, 전문직
31	**prudent***** [prú:dnt]	a	cautious, discreet, careful, wary It is always **prudent** to start. 시작하는 데 항상 신중하다.	신중한, 현명한
32	**recognition*** [rèkəgníʃən]	n	allowance, acceptance, identification, notice Many blacks have won **recognition** in sports field. 많은 흑인들이 스포츠 분야에서 인정을 받았다. receive much **recognition** 크게 인정을 받다	인정
33	**resin** [rézin]	n	sticky substance Amber is a fossil **resin** from ancient pine trees. 호박은 오래된 소나무로부터 나온 화석수지이다. synthetic **resin** 합성(合成) 수지	수지, 합성 수지
34	**sideways** [saidweiz]	ad	obliquely, laterally Whales have **sideways** tail fins. 고래는 비스듬히 꼬리 지느러미가 있다.	옆으로, 비스듬히
		a	sidelong, oblique, lateral a **sideways** glance 곁눈질	간접적인, 옆으로
35	**span** [spæn]	n	distance, length life **span** of whales 고래의 수명	기간, 짧은 시간 [거리]
		v	extend across, cover, traverse, bridge They **span** a river with a bridge. 그들은 강에 다리를 놓았다. **span** the Han River 한강의 거리를 재다	걸치다, 다리를 놓다
36	**stature** [stætʃər]	n	height, prestige She was of diminutive **stature**. 그녀는 몸집이 작았다.	키, 명성
37	**thoroughfare** [θə́:roufɛər]	n	street No **thoroughfare**. (게시 문구) 통행금지	도로, 통행
38	**unbearable**** [ʌnbɛ́ərəbl]	a	intolerable, unendurable, insufferable, insupportable **unbearable** pain 참을 수 없는 아픔	참을 수 없는
39	**villain*** [vílən]	n	rascal, scoundrel, rogue, felon He played the **villain** of that movie. 그는 그 영화에서 악당을 연기했다. You little **villain**! 이 꼬마놈아!	악당, 놈
40	**warehouse*** [wɛərhaus]	n	store, depot The crowds poured into the **warehouse**. 군중이 창고로 우르르 몰려들었다.	창고, 보관소, 도매상

Practice Test 02

01. Birds congregated in greatest numbers around the parts of the foods.
    (A) converged
    (B) limited
    (C) scattered
    (D) suppressed

02. Cross-country skiers glide over snow-covered terrain that is flat or slightly hilly.
    (A) jump
    (B) slide
    (C) walk
    (D) race

03. Philosophers have attempted to define criteria for distinguishing between true and false.
    (A) answers
    (B) inquiries
    (C) theories
    (D) standards

04. Harrison argued that people create myths in order to justify already existing magical or religious rituals.
    (A) only
    (B) legal
    (C) vindicate
    (D) simple

05. The city of Savannah, Georgia, has the world's most up-to-date systems of docks and warehouses.
    (A) harbor
    (B) storehouses
    (C) ships
    (D) equipment

06. Shark hide makes especially luxurious leather after the scales have been removed.
    (A) tongue
    (B) trunk
    (C) horn
    (D) skin

07. Irate residents protested the construction of the transmission tower.
    (A) furious
    (B) inflammatory
    (C) beneficial
    (D) dexterous

08. The five tribes that formed the Iroquois League chose 50 sachems to lead their federation.
    (A) alliance
    (B) factory
    (C) company
    (D) town

09. The leader appealed to the people to accept layoffs and other sacrifices to help recover from the crisis.
    (A) bankrupcy
    (B) emergency
    (C) depression
    (D) moratorium

10. Use of the same intermediate frequency to process many different radio frequencies simplifies the radio's design.
    (A) well-known
    (B) brief
    (C) middle
    (D) lower

11. The game was marred by a bomb that exploded in downtown area, killing 1 person and injuring over 50.
    (A) qualified
    (B) disclosed
    (C) delayed
    (D) spoiled

12. Telescopes used by amateur astronomers have about 100 times the resolution of the unaided eye.
    (A) well trained
    (B) expert
    (C) physically fit
    (D) nonprofessional

13. Adventure stories are action-packed tales about daring heroes and cunning villains in fantastic situations.
    (A) brave person
    (B) wicked men
    (C) foolish men
    (D) liars

14. Religious accounts have provided countless material for paintings, sculptures, literature, dances, and motion pictures.
    (A) innumerable
    (B) unimportant
    (C) uncalculating
    (D) interest

15. In the western part of North America, many volcanoes erupted and lava covered much of what is now Oregon and Washington.
    (A) exploded
    (B) split
    (C) roared
    (D) disintegrated

16. In Shakespeare's *Merchant of Venice*, Portia loses her affections to Bassanio but is under vow not to reveal it.
    (A) respects
    (B) concerns
    (C) longings
    (D) fondness

17. Surfaces that reflect infrared rays can insulate heat traveling by radiation.
    (A) radiate
    (B) dissipate
    (C) isolate
    (D) exhaust

18. Historians usually divide the whole span of Historic Time into four great periods: Ancient Time, the Middle Ages, the early period of Modern Time, and Modern Time.
    (A) dynasty
    (B) term
    (C) document
    (D) treasure

19. Large earthquakes beneath the ocean can create a series of huge, destructive waves called tsunamis that flood coasts for many miles.
    (A) destroy
    (B) expand
    (C) diminish
    (D) deluge

20. Color laser printers have become so inexpensive that profit margins are thin, but manufacturers still make good money from the toners.
    (A) futile
    (B) economical
    (C) invaluable
    (D) laborious

DAY 03 Daily Checkup

01. wrestle against adversity
   Ⓐ disaster   Ⓑ inattention
   Ⓒ explain   Ⓓ risk

02. Parrots imitate human speech.
   Ⓐ admonish   Ⓑ plague
   Ⓒ mimic   Ⓓ recollect

03. in combination with reputation
   Ⓐ dishonor   Ⓑ offender
   Ⓒ confusion   Ⓓ association

04. a plot to assassinate the President
   Ⓐ blame   Ⓑ bother
   Ⓒ reprimand   Ⓓ murder

05. blink one's eyes
   Ⓐ present   Ⓑ rescue
   Ⓒ wink   Ⓓ express

06. set free eight criminals
   Ⓐ woes   Ⓑ offenders
   Ⓒ inhabitants   Ⓓ inadvertently

07. horrible living conditions
   Ⓐ misfortune   Ⓑ calm
   Ⓒ energetic   Ⓓ terrible

08. Poverty is no disgrace.
   Ⓐ recognition   Ⓑ dishonor
   Ⓒ difficulty   Ⓓ merriment

09. inherent rights
   Ⓐ indisputable   Ⓑ concerned
   Ⓒ natural   Ⓓ resentful

10. come to grief
   Ⓐ flaw   Ⓑ stain
   Ⓒ anguish   Ⓓ inattention

11. outstretch one's arms
   Ⓐ whiten   Ⓑ recall
   Ⓒ spread   Ⓓ admonish

12. ornamented with jewels
   Ⓐ departed   Ⓑ decorated
   Ⓒ migrated   Ⓓ glazed

13. hurt by their indifference
   Ⓐ apathy   Ⓑ dishonor
   Ⓒ association   Ⓓ inattention

14. reprove (a person) for his bad manners
   Ⓐ exit   Ⓑ rebuke
   Ⓒ recollect   Ⓓ annoy

15. a dead calm
   Ⓐ dreadful   Ⓑ quiet
   Ⓒ innate   Ⓓ nervous

16. tease a person for a thing
   Ⓐ seize   Ⓑ cheer
   Ⓒ describe   Ⓓ irritate

17. He feels zeal for his work.
   Ⓐ inattention   Ⓑ cheer
   Ⓒ combination   Ⓓ enthusiasm

18. became fluster and tongue-tied
   Ⓐ indisputable   Ⓑ ghastly
   Ⓒ confuse   Ⓓ dreadful

19. abide in memory
   Ⓐ recognize   Ⓑ mock
   Ⓒ remain   Ⓓ bleach

20. inadvertently wrong answered
   Ⓐ accidentally   Ⓑ illegally
   Ⓒ innately   Ⓓ nervously

표제어	품사	동의어와 예문	한글 뜻
1 **abide*** [əbáid]	v	inhabit, remain, sojourn, reside **abide** in memory 기억에 남다	거주하다, 머물다
2 **accustomed to**** [əkʌ́stəmd tu]	a	used to, customary, habitual be **accustomed** to using the new device 새로운 장비를 사용하는 데 익숙한	익숙한
3 **adversity***** [ædvə́:rsəti]	n	calamity, catastrophe, disaster, misfortune Koreans showed courage in weathering **adversity**. 한국인은 기상 악재에 용기를 보여주었다.	역경, 재난
4 **amuse** [əmjú:z]	v	entertain, please, cheer **amuse** a baby with a toy 장난감으로 아이를 달래다	즐겁다
5 **arrest** [ərést]	v	seize, apprehend, capture National agency must only works to discover and **arrest** hostile spies. 국가정보원은 적대적인 간첩을 발견하고 체포하는 일만 해야 한다. **arrest** attention 주의를 끌다	체포하다
6 **assassinate** [əsǽsənèit]	v	murder, kill, slay The president was **assassinated** by a terrorist. 대통령은 테러리스트에 의해 암살을 당했다.	암살하다
7 **bleach** [bli:tʃ]	v	whiten **bleach** laundry in the sun 빨래를 햇볕에 표백하다	표백하다
8 **blemish*** [blémiʃ]	n	stain, defect, speck, spot, flaw without **blemish** 완전한	오점, 흠집
9 **blink** [bliŋk]	v	wink, twinkle, shut their eyes briefly **blink** one's eyes 눈을 깜박이다	눈을 깜박이다
10 **calm**** [ka:m]	n	quiet, concord, serenity The sound of car horns shattered the morning **calm**. 자동차의 경적소리가 아침의 정적을 산산히 깨뜨려버렸다.	고요, 평온
	v	placate, pacify, appease ↔ disturb **calm** the animal 동물들을 (흥분을)가라앉히다	안정시키다
	a	① quiet, still, tranquil, placid, serene ↔ loud, disruptive a **calm** day 조용한 날 The boats sit still on the dead **calm** water. 그 배들이 아직도 죽은 듯이 조용하게 물 위에 있다.	① 조용한
		② composed, collected, unruffled a **calm** mood 편안한 분위기	② 차분한
11 **combination** [kàmbənéiʃən]	n	conjunction, association, union A **combination** of different shapes provides variety. 색다른 모양의 조합이 다양함을 제공한다.	조합, 연계

12	**criminal*** [krímənl]	n	convict, culprit, gangster, offender	범죄자, 범법자
			criminal record 전과 기록	
		a	unlawful, corrupt, crooked, illegal	범죄의, 부정한
			lead to the conviction on **criminal** charge	
			범죄 혐의로 유죄 판결을 이끌다	

13	**deliver***** [dilívər]	v	① send, transfer, convey, present	① 배달하다
			deliver blood to the body 몸으로 피를 전하다	
			② rescue, save, set free	② 구제하다, 해방하다
			deliver a person out of danger 누구를 위험으로부터 구해내다	
			③ express, give, communicate	③ 연설하다
			deliver a speech 연설하다	

14	**disgrace** [disgréis]	n	shame, dishonor	치욕, 불명예
			Poverty is no **disgrace**.	
			가난은 불명예가 아니다.	

15	**enterprising** [éntərpràiziŋ]	a	ambitious, adventurous, energetic	기업가적인, 야심적인
			an **enterprising** spirit 진취적 기상	
			manufacturing **enterprise** 제조업체	

16	**foolproof** [fú:lprù:f]	a	infallible, certain, safe	누구나 할 수 있는, 아주 간단한
			establish one's identity a quick, simple, and **foolproof** procedure	
			빠르고 간단하고 안전한 절차로 누구의 신원을 확인하다	

17	**forfeit** [fɔ́:rfit]	v	relinquish, lose, surrender, renounce	상실하다, 몰수당하다
			A sculptor **forfeited** the statue.	
			한 조각가가 동상을 몰수당했다.	

18	**fluster** [flʌ́stər]	v	confuse	당황하게 하다
			fluster oneself 정신을 못 차리다	
		n	turmoil	당황

19	**grief*** [gri:f]	n	sorrow, woe, sadness, anguish	슬픔
			come to **grief** 완전히 실패로 끝나다, 슬픈 결과가 되다	

20	**horrible** [hɔ́:rəbl]	a	terrible, dreadful, ghastly, hideous, grim	끔찍한
			be an eyewitness of a **horrible** sight 끔찍한 광경을 목격하다	

21	**imitate***** [ímətèit]	v	copy, mimic, mock, reproduce, duplicate, replicate	모방하다, 흉내 내다
			Children **imitate** their parents.	
			아이들은 부모를 흉내 낸다.	

22	**inadvertently*** [inədvə́:rtntli]	ad	accidentally	우연히, 부주의하게
			become **inadvertently** drinks from a cup of poisoned wine	
			우연히 독이 있는 와인 한 잔을 마시게 되다	

23	**incontrovertible** [inkàntrəvə́:rtəbl]	a	indisputable	논란의 여지가 없는
			incontrovertible proof of the crime 논란의 여지가 없는 범죄의 증거	

24	**indifference*** [indífərəns]	n	unconcern, apathy, inattention	무관심
			a matter of **indifference** 아무래도 좋은 일	

25	**inherent*** [inhíərənt]	a	natural, intrinsic, innate, congenital, inborn	본질적인, 타고난, 내재된
			detail the disappointments of **inherent** loneliness	
			내재된 고독의 낙담을 자세하게 설명하다	

26	**jealous*** [dʒéləs]	a	envious, resentful, covetous	시기심 있는
			a **jealous** stepmother 질투심이 많은 계모	

27	leave* [liːv]	v	① depart, exit, vacate, migrate **leave** the area 지역을 떠나다	① 떠나다
			② quit, retire, withdraw, resign; abandon, desert **leave** one job for another 다른 사람에게 일을 물려주다	② 그만두다 / 포기하다
28	matter** [mǽtər]	n	① substance, material, medium, stuff The three forms of **matter** are solid, liquid, and gas. 물질의 세가지 형태는 고체, 액체, 기체이다.	① 물질
			② difficulty, trouble, distress, predicament **matter** in question 논의 중인 문제	② 문제, 어려움
29	mirth [məːr]	n	gaiety, merriment moment of **mirth** in this movie 이 영화의 환희의 순간	환희, 명랑
30	ornament** [ɔ́ːrnəmənt]	v	decorate, adorn, embellish, garment **ornament** with jewels 보석으로 장식하다 by way of **ornament** 장식으로서	꾸미다
31	outstretch [àutstrétʃ]	v	spread, extend, expand, stretch out **outstretch** one's arms 두 팔을 벌리다	확장하다
32	peril** [pérəl]	n	jeopardy, danger, hazard, risk Many species that have been poorly studied may be in **peril**. 거의 연구되지 않은 많은 종들이 위험에 처해질 것이다.	위험, 위기
	perilous* [pérələs]	a	dangerous, threatening, exposed, vulnerable the way out of a **perilous** situation 위기 상황에서 벗어날 방법을 찾다	위험한, 모험적인
33	predisposition [priːdìspəzíʃən]	n	sensitivity, susceptibility, inclination people with a genetic **predisposition** to rheumatoid arthritis 류마티스 관절염을 유전적 소인으로 가진 사람	경향, 성질, 소인(병에 대한)
34	regiment [rédʒəmənt]	n	army, company, force, corps Roosevelt led the famous cavalry **regiment** against the Spaniards in Cuba. 루즈벨트는 쿠바에서 스페인에 대항한 유명한 기병 연대를 이끌었다.	연대, 대군
35	reprove* [riprúːv]	v	scold, reproach, admonish, reprimand, rebuke **reprove** (a person) for his bad manners (누구를) 버릇없다고 나무라다	꾸짖다
36	shine* [ʃain]	n	beam, gleam, glisten, shimmer, glow polish to bring back the **shine** 광택이 나도록 다시 광내다	빛, 광택
		v	sheen, glaze, polish, luster The moonlight **shines** on the lake. 달빛이 호수 위에서 빛나다.	빛나다, 광내다
37	tease* [tiːz]	v	irritate, bother, annoy, plague, harass **tease** a person for a thing 누구에게 물건을 달라고 조르다	괴롭히다, 조르다
38	tense* [tens]	a	rigid, tight, strained; concerned, nervous a **tense** rope 팽팽한 줄 a **tense** person 긴장한 사람	팽팽한 / 긴장한, 부자연스러운
39	unscrupulous [ʌnskrúːpjuləs]	a	unprincipled, corrupt, crooked, ruthless, immoral George Ⅳ was an ambitious and **unscrupulous** politician. 조지 4세는 야심차고 파렴치한 정치인이었다.	사악한, 파렴치한
40	zeal* [ziːl]	n	passion, enthusiasm, fervor, ardor He feels **zeal** for his work. 그는 일에 대해서 열의를 가지고 있다.	열정

Practice Test 03

01. Some species of animals simply become extinct and leave no descendants.
    Ⓐ harm
    Ⓑ produce
    Ⓒ forsake
    Ⓓ aide

02. This scientific method requires a combination of both induction and deduction.
    Ⓐ replacement
    Ⓑ promotion
    Ⓒ simplification
    Ⓓ joining

03. On earth, matter exists in three states- solid, liquid, and gas.
    Ⓐ substance
    Ⓑ matrix
    Ⓒ equilibrium
    Ⓓ abstract

04. After the silver has been bleached out of the images, they remain as transparent areas on film.
    Ⓐ aired
    Ⓑ dried
    Ⓒ whitened
    Ⓓ scrubbed

05. People who violate criminal laws may be arrested by the police and put on trial by the local, state, or national government.
    Ⓐ conducted
    Ⓑ seized
    Ⓒ tortured
    Ⓓ disturbed

06. A nursery rhyme is a rhythmical poem that amuses or soothes young children.
    Ⓐ entertains
    Ⓑ vitalizes
    Ⓒ dejects
    Ⓓ hurts

07. Many people become easily accustomed to fast movement and rapid change.
    Ⓐ tried to
    Ⓑ habitual to
    Ⓒ dull to
    Ⓓ bored to

08. The sun gives off more ultraviolet rays as well as X rays during periods of violent activity than during calm periods.
    Ⓐ considerate
    Ⓑ hungry
    Ⓒ alert
    Ⓓ quiet

09. After World War I, race relations grew increasingly tense in the Northern cities.
    Ⓐ nervous
    Ⓑ headache
    Ⓒ brusque
    Ⓓ muscle spasm

10. All stars will eventually exhaust the energy that makes them shine.
    Ⓐ outburst
    Ⓑ crash
    Ⓒ twinkle
    Ⓓ fusion

11. About two-thirds of the people who are arrested in any year have a previous criminal record.
    A warden
    B trapper
    C chaplain
    D convictive

12. Many sea creatures have been inadvertently reduced by catching of species accidentally in nets set for other species.
    A occasionally
    B horribly
    C severely
    D unintentionally

13. No one could abide by the idea that the economic bust, like the preceding boom, could not be well understood or easily controlled.
    A tolerate
    B affect
    C intrigue
    D observe

14. Japanese soldiers believed that surrender meant disgrace, so the Allies rarely captured them alive.
    A dishonor
    B worry
    C phony
    D temptation

15. Many environmentalists and philosophers now believe that nonhuman species have an inherent right to exist.
    A a relative
    B an innate
    C a sporadic
    D an incremental

16. In the tragic play Othello, Shakespeare describes jealousy as "the green-eyed monster which does mock the meat it feeds on."
    A envy
    B incidence
    C imagination
    D eligibility

17. A flawless diamond should have no physical defects, such as cracks, inclusions, scratches, blemishes, or a cloudy appearance.
    A partialities
    B defects
    C obstructions
    D cleanness

18. Beethoven did not possess the disposition of a father and the young man rebelled against him, causing Beethoven much grief.
    A illness
    B weather
    C sorrow
    D travel

19. Conservationists have classified more than 8,000 endangered species around the world, and many other species that have not been studied properly may be equally in peril.
    A extinction
    B danger
    C preservation
    D habitat

20. Ecoinsect Co., which has built a manufacturing plant in Cheonan city, has delivered products of effective eco-friendly agrochemical materials to manage the insect population under economic threshold to major farmer customers.
    A made   B went over
    C announce   D handed over

24

DAY 04 Daily Checkup

01. at home and abroad
 Ⓐ innovation Ⓑ overseas
 Ⓒ modest Ⓓ uninterrupted

02. election frauds
 Ⓐ deceits Ⓑ nobles
 Ⓒ predecessors Ⓓ assets

03. Constant desire to innovate
 Ⓐ sort Ⓑ destroy
 Ⓒ design Ⓓ accept

04. afraid of failure
 Ⓐ humble Ⓑ scared
 Ⓒ complete Ⓓ unattended

05. try to soothe the crying child
 Ⓐ appease Ⓑ beat
 Ⓒ instigate Ⓓ provoke

06. a precursor of reformation
 Ⓐ predecessor Ⓑ dissimilarity
 Ⓒ statement Ⓓ inclination

07. assort goods
 Ⓐ insure Ⓑ depict
 Ⓒ revitalize Ⓓ separate

08. shiver with cold
 Ⓐ persuade Ⓑ sort
 Ⓒ shudder Ⓓ consume

09. revive the play
 Ⓐ separate Ⓑ delineate
 Ⓒ repeat Ⓓ rebuff

10. surpass (a person) in strength
 Ⓐ classify Ⓑ outdo
 Ⓒ consume Ⓓ concede

11. a large yield
 Ⓐ reward Ⓑ equipment
 Ⓒ product Ⓓ proclamation

12. do not guarantee growth
 Ⓐ change Ⓑ warrant
 Ⓒ deceit Ⓓ injure

13. attempt to incite a riot
 Ⓐ abolish Ⓑ persuade
 Ⓒ change Ⓓ stimulate

14. His manner is quiet and unassuming.
 Ⓐ modest Ⓑ awaking
 Ⓒ enlisted Ⓓ warranted

15. make a statement to the effect that
 Ⓐ proneness Ⓑ announcement
 Ⓒ recompense Ⓓ ruin

16. be inaugurated as professor
 Ⓐ represented Ⓑ rebuffed
 Ⓒ begun Ⓓ succumbed

17. a divergence of opinion
 Ⓐ difference Ⓑ declaration
 Ⓒ abrasion Ⓓ deception

18. haul in a net
 Ⓐ draw Ⓑ invigorate
 Ⓒ spurt Ⓓ reject

19. aberrant behavior
 Ⓐ scared Ⓑ modest
 Ⓒ unguarded Ⓓ abnormal

20. an unattended meeting
 Ⓐ enlisted Ⓑ unguarded
 Ⓒ abolished Ⓓ categorized

DAY 04

표제어	품사	동의어와 예문	한글 뜻
1 **aberrant** [əbérənt]	a	abnormal His **aberrant** behavior worsened. 그의 탈선 행위가 심해졌다.	탈선적인, 비정상인
2 **abroad**** [əbrɔ́ːd]	ad	in other countries, overseas, in foreign countries well recognized at home and **abroad** 국내외에서 널리 인정받다	국외로, 해외로, 넓게
3 **afraid of** [əfréid əv]	a	scared She is much **afraid of** snakes. 그녀는 뱀을 몹시 무서워한다. **afraid of** failure 실패를 두려워하는	두려워하는
4 **amenity** [əménəti]	n	facility, service, advance, convenience the **amenities** of civilization are left behind 문명의 시설 뒤에 뒤쳐졌다	쾌적함, 편의 시설
5 **assort** [əsɔ́ːrt]	v	separate, classify, group, sort **assort** goods 상품을 분류하다	분류하다
6 **coax*** [kouks]	v	cajole, persuade **coax** me to take language course 언어과정을 수강시키려고 나를 구슬리다	속이다
7 **deplete*** [diplíːt]	v	use up, consume **deplete** your energy 너의 힘을 모두 소진시키다	고갈시키다
8 **devastate*** [dévəstèit]	v	ruin, destroy, demolish **devastate** an enemy line 적의 사선을 무찌르다	황폐화시키다
9 **divergence** [divə́ːrdʒəns]	n	difference, dissimilarity **divergence** of opinion 견해 차이	차이점
10 **eliminate*** [ilímənèit]	v	remove, omit, expel, exclude, abolish **eliminate** waste 낭비를 줄이다	제거하다
11 **enroll**** [inróul]	v	sign up, register, enlist, accept, admit **enroll** in degree programs at college 대학의 학위과정에 등록하다	명부에 올리다
12 **fraud** [frɔːd]	n	deceit, deception protect the public from **frauds** and deceit 사기와 기만으로부터 대중을 보호하다	사기
13 **guarantee** [gærəntíː]	v	insure, warrant **guarantee** high social position 높은 사회적 위치를 보장하다 under **guarantee** of ~의 보증 아래, ~을 보증하여	보장하다
14 **gush** [gʌʃ]	v	spurt, spout Hot water **gushed** out of the tap. 뜨거운 물이 수도꼭지에서 뿜어 나왔다.	뿜어 나오다
15 **haul**** [hɔːl]	v	transport, drag, draw, pull Farmers had to **haul** large quantities of water into their farm land. 농부들은 그들의 경작지에 대량의 물을 끌어다 대야 했다. **haul** in a net 그물을 잡아당기다	운반하다, 세게 잡아당기다

| 16 | **havoc*** [hǽvək] | n | devastation, damage, destruction, ruin | 파괴, 파멸, 혼란 |

Famous player with drug addiction soon played **havoc** with his career.
마약 중독인 유명한 선수가 곧 그의 경력을 파괴했다.

| 17 | **inaugurate** [inɔ́:gjurèit] | v | begin, induct | 취임시키다, 개시하다 |

be **inaugurated** as professor 교수에 취임하다

| 18 | **incinerate** [insínərèit] | v | burn up | 소각하다 |

incinerate with the newlyt invented instrument
새로이 발명된 기구로 소각하다

| 19 | **incite**** [insáit] | v | stimulate, spur, instigate, provoke | 선동하다, 부추기다 |

incite curiosity 호기심을 일게 하다

| 20 | **innovate** [ínəvèit] | v | modify, change | 혁신하다 |

constant desire to **innovate** 개혁할 꾸준한 욕망
innovate on the present condition 현상황을 일신하다

| 21 | **means of subsistence** [mi:nz əv səbsístəns] | n | primary sustenance | 생계수단 |

work in fishery as a **means of subsistence**
어업을 생계수단으로 삼아 일하다

| 22 | **nutrient** [njú:triənt] | a | nutritious | 영양이 되는 |

the **nutrient** value of noodles and snacks 라면과 과자의 영양가

| | | n | energy source, food source | 영양분 |

Adequate amounts of the **nutrients** are provided.
적당한 양의 영양분이 제공되었다.
be full of **nutrient** 자양분이 많다

| 23 | **peer** [piər] | n | noble, aristocrat | 귀족, 동료 |

without a **peer** 비길 데 없는
peer review board of experts 전문가들의 동료 평가회

| 24 | **portray*** [pɔ:rtréi] | v | picture, depict, delineate, represent, describe | 그리다, 묘사하다 |

The characters are well **portrayed**.
인물이 잘 묘사되어 있다.

| 25 | **precursor*** [prikɔ́:rsər] | n | ancestor, forerunner, predecessor, forebear | 선구자 |

a **precursor** of reformation 개혁의 선구자

| 26 | **retrieve** [ritrí:v] | v | get back, regain, restore, redeem | 되찾다, 만회하다, 구하다 |

retrieve broken satellites 부서진 위성을 구하다

| 27 | **refuse*** [rifjú:z] | v | decline, reject, rebuff | 거절하다, 거부하다 |

refuse a person money 누구에게 돈 주기를 거부하다

| 28 | **revive** [riváiv] | v | revitalize, awaken, invigorate | 소생하게 하다, 회복시키다 |

the **Revival** of Literature 문예 부흥

| 29 | **ruefully** [rú:fəli] | ad | sadly, regretfully, contritely, remorsefully | 슬픔에 잠긴, 애처로운 |

That boy said his mistake **ruefully**.
그 소년은 그의 잘못을 애처롭게 말했다.

| 30 | **shiver*** [ʃívər] | v | tremble, shudder, shake, quake, quiver | 떨다 |

shiver in the cold wind 차가운 바람에 떨다

| 31 | **soothe*** [su:ð] | v | alleviate, pacify, assuage, appease, ease | 달래다, 진정시키다 |

↔ aggravate, intensify
The medicine **soothes** the pain.
약은 고통을 가라앉혀 준다.

32	**statement** [stéitmənt]	n	declaration, announcement, proclamation the **statement** of claim 원고의 진술	성명(서), 진술서
33	**stuff**** [stʌf]	n	① material, substance, matter; equipment all the **stuff** in the box 박스에 있는 모든 물건들 ② belongings, property, assets Let's move our **stuff** to the new house. 새로운 집으로 우리 물건을 옮기자.	① 물질, 재료 / 장비 ② 자산
34	**surpass***** [sərpǽs]	v	exceed, excel, outstrip, outdo, transcend party that **surpass** expectations 예상을 초월한 파티	능가하다, 뛰어넘다
35	**trend** [trend]	n	inclination, proneness, bent follow a **trend** 유행을 창출하다	경향, 유행
36	**unassuming** [ʌnəsú:miŋ]	a	modest, unpretending, unpretentious, humble His manner is quiet and **unassuming**. 그는 얌전하고 겸손하다.	거만하지 않은, 겸손한
37	**unattended** [ʌnəténdid]	a	abandoned, left alone, ignored, unguarded an **unattended** meeting 출석자 없는 회합	수행하지 않는
38	**unbroken** [ʌnbróukən]	a	uninterrupted, complete, intact an **unbroken** horse 사나운 말	온전한, 길이 들지 않은
39	**wigwam** [wígwam]	n	Indian lodge, lodge Many Indians built a house like the dome-shaped **wigwam** of the Northeast. 많은 인디언들은 북동쪽의 돔 형태의 원형 천막 같은 집을 지었다.	(인디언의) 천막, 오두막
40	**yield**** [ji:ld]	v	① produce, bear **yield** a good harvest 좋은 수확을 거두다 ② surrender, concede, relent, relinquish, succumb **yield** to the enemy 적을 무찌르다	① 생산하다 ② 굴복하다, 항복하다
		n	① crop, harvest, product a good(large) **yield** of corn 옥수수의 좋은 수확(풍작) ② reward, recompense, interest the annual **yield** on your savings account 저축계좌의 연간 수익률	① 작물, 수확 ② 보상, 수익률

01. Many vegetable farmers haul their produce to nearby markets soon after it is harvested.
    A cultivate
    B transport
    C advertise
    D distribute

02. A nursery rhyme is a rhythmical poem that amuses or soothes young children.
    A rears
    B enrages
    C relieves
    D attracts

03. The breakthrough technologies innovated by design and its practical conveniences have made the spread of culture easier.
    A announced
    B refreshed
    C newly invented
    D considerate

04. Nearly 100,000 gifted students in the Republic of Korea are enrolled in special programs for language education.
    A signed up
    B visited
    C educated
    D engaged

05. Primitive people take an interest in work that has to do with gathering food because they are afraid of hunger.
    A are negligible about
    B are scared of
    C are pleased with
    D are glad about

06. The space shuttles can retrieve artificial satellites that need servicing as well as launch operations.
    A accept
    B manage
    C continue
    D respond

07. The basic "stuff of the universe" is called matter; and it occurs in three states: solid, liquid, and gas.
    A law
    B circumstance
    C medium
    D substance

08. The Constitution guarantees such rights as freedom of the press, religion, and speech.
    A demands
    B modifies
    C certifies
    D insists

09. When an artery is cut, blood gushes out in spurts timed to the rhythm of the heartbeat.
    A permeates
    B coagulates
    C pours
    D penetrate

10. Graham was devastated by the failure of her marriage in 1951 to dancer Erick Hawkins.
    A extinguished
    B demolished
    C oppressed
    D destructed

11. The proved reserves of such minerals as copper, lead, nickel, and zinc may be depleted within 100 years.
    (A) exhausted
    (B) decreased
    (C) dissolved
    (D) determined

12. The development of better plant varieties and fertilizers has helped double and even triple the yields of some major crops.
    (A) storage
    (B) fertilization
    (C) dissemination
    (D) produces

13. In 1944, Goo Kim was inaugurated as the chief of interim government of Korea.
    (A) attempted
    (B) elected
    (C) inducted
    (D) erected

14. Later in 1832, South Carolina declared federal tariff laws unconstitutional and refused to collect tariffs at its ports.
    (A) exorcised
    (B) lavished
    (C) withheld
    (D) dwindled

15. Babies should never be left unattended to in their bath regardless of age.
    (A) disorganized
    (B) unguarded
    (C) incomplete
    (D) unwanted

16. Climatologists disagree about the impact that human activity has had on the climate, particularly concerning the recent global warming trend.
    (A) reasoning
    (B) phenomenon
    (C) tendency
    (D) side effect

17. As a quiet, unassuming man, he had an almost shy manner and did not seem like a leader.
    (A) talkative
    (B) wordless
    (C) uncommunicative
    (D) modest

18. Traditional customs are a mass of detailed behaviors more astonishing than what any one person can ever evolve in individual actions no matter how aberrant.
    (A) enjoyable
    (B) abnormal
    (C) virtuous
    (D) conventional

19. The conversion of forests to farmland eliminates trees that would otherwise absorb carbon from the atmosphere and reduce the greenhouse effect.
    (A) eradicates
    (B) secludes
    (C) blocks
    (D) casts

20. Throughout the play, Shakespeare portrays people at their worst, with few honorable qualities that lighten the gloom in his great tragedies.
    (A) advances
    (B) drops
    (C) depicts
    (D) patronizes

01. humane treatment of animals
- (A) hampered
- (B) burdened
- (C) sparkled
- (D) merciful

02. on site inspections
- (A) location
- (B) theater
- (C) province
- (D) vaccination

03. to abridge a 770-page novel
- (A) shorten
- (B) explore
- (C) hamper
- (D) circulate

04. without any incentive
- (A) fragrance
- (B) impulse
- (C) hostility
- (D) obstructing

05. Their interests interfered.
- (A) chased
- (B) enclosed
- (C) intruded
- (D) lingered

06. be skeptical about
- (A) dubious
- (B) compassionate
- (C) circulated
- (D) adverse

07. be incensed against
- (A) intended
- (B) spurred
- (C) beamed
- (D) sought

08. overtax one's brains
- (A) shiver
- (B) hunt
- (C) vibrate
- (D) over-strain

09. quiver with fear
- (A) shudder
- (B) intrude
- (C) intend
- (D) shorten

10. stagger across the street
- (A) install
- (B) sway
- (C) plot
- (D) roll

11. undermine one's constitution
- (A) assail
- (B) ruin
- (C) grasp
- (D) clutch

12. loiter over one's homework
- (A) clutch
- (B) shine
- (C) loaf
- (D) adore

13. be considerate of other people
- (A) dubious
- (B) antagonistic
- (C) tamed
- (D) thoughtful

14. the bulk of the book
- (A) volume
- (B) area
- (C) motive
- (D) pledge

15. further the cause of conservation of nature
- (A) follow
- (B) conflict
- (C) intend
- (D) promote

16. an exquisite critic
- (A) acute
- (B) first
- (C) benevolent
- (D) antagonistic

17. pursued the runaway horse
- (A) thwarted
- (B) chased
- (C) venerated
- (D) clutched

18. Gibbons and orangutans are primarily arboreal.
- (A) tree-living
- (B) food-seeking
- (C) leaf-eating
- (D) loiter the forest

19. a pleasant domestic setting
- (A) faltered
- (B) intense
- (C) internal
- (D) merciful

20. first and foremost
- (A) concerned
- (B) additional
- (C) leading
- (D) skeptic

표제어	품사	동의어와 예문	한글 뜻
1 **abridge*** [əbrídʒ]	v	shorten, abbreviate, condense **abridge** a long story 긴 이야기를 요약하다	요약하다, 줄이다
2 **arboreal** [ɑːrbɔ́ːriəl]	a	arboreous, tree-living **arboreal** mammals with a prehensile tail 물건을 잡기에 적당한 꼬리를 가진 나무에 사는 포유류	나무의, 교목성의, 나무에 사는
3 **assail*** [əséil]	v	attack, assault **assail** a task 과업에 과감히 맞부딪치다	공격하다
4 **bulk*** [bʌlk]	n	size, dimensions, main part **bulk** buying 생산품 대량 구입	크기, 용적
5 **considerate*** [kənsídərət]	a	thoughtful, attentive, concerned, discreet, prudent **considerate** individuals 신중한 사람	생각이 깊은, 신중한
6 **dissolve** [dizálv]	v	melt, end, deliquesce, break up Sugar **dissolves** in water. 설탕은 물에 녹는다.	녹다, 용해하다
7 **domain**** [douméin]	n	area, field, territory, province, realm public **domain** 공유지	영역, 분야
8 **domestic*** [dəméstik]	a	① internal, native handle **domestic** matters 국내 문제들을 다루다 ② tamed, trained, domesticated; home, family **Domestic** cats prey on birds and small mammals. 길들여진 고양이들은 새와 작은 포유류들을 사냥한다.	① 국내의 ② 길들여진 / 가정의
9 **encompass*** [inkʌ́mpəs]	v	include, comprise; surround, circle, enclose His repertoire **encompassed** everything from Bach to Mahler. 그의 레파토리는 바흐부터 말러까지 모든 것을 포함한다.	포함하다 / 둘러싸다
10 **exquisite*** [ikskwízit]	a	beautiful, fine, intense, acute a man of **exquisite** taste 섬세한 취미를 가진 사람	아주 아름다운, 정교한
11 **foremost*** [fɔ́ːrmoust]	a	leading, first, initial Euclid, one of the **foremost** Greek mathematicians 그리스에서 으뜸가는 수학자 중 한 사람인 유클리드 first and **foremost** 무엇보다도 먼저	으뜸가는, 선두의
12 **further*** [fə́ːrðər]	a	advance, additional I cannot go any **further**. 나는 조금 더 나아갈 수가 없다.	더 나아가서
	v	promote, encourage **further** the cause of conservation of nature 자연보호 운동을 촉진하다	촉진하다
	ad	in addition, also, besides There is no **further** news. 더 새로운 뉴스는 없다.	더욱이, 게다가

13	**gleam** [gliːm]	n	flash, beam, glimmer, glare	어스레한 빛, 번득임
			a **gleam** of hope 한 가닥 희망	
14	**headstrong** [hédstrɔ̀(ː)ŋ]	a	stubborn, wilful, obstinate, contrary, unruly	완고한, 고집 센
			He was noted for his passionate and **headstrong** temperament. 그는 그의 열정과 고집스런 기질로 유명했다.	
15	**humane*** [hjuːméin]	a	merciful, benevolent, compassionate, charitable	인도적인, 자비로운
			humane feelings 자비심	
16	**immunization** [ìmjunizéiʃən]	n	vaccination, inoculation	면역, 예방접종
			introduce antigens into the body through **immunization** 면역을 통해 몸 안으로 항원을 유입하다	
17	**imperceptibly** [ìmpərséptəbli]	ad	unnoticeably, invisibly, slowly, little by little	눈에 보이지 않게, 미세하게
			Ice melts **imperceptibly**. 얼음이 살살 녹는다.	
			Our skin is continually and **imperceptibly** renewed. 우리의 피부는 지속적이고 보이지 않게 새로워진다.	
18	**incense** [ínsens]	n	scent, fragrance	향기, 향
			fume the altar with **incense** 제단에 향을 피우다	
		v	anger, enrage, infuriate	화나다
19	**incentive*** [inséntiv]	n	motive, stimulus, spur, impulse, prod	동기, 자극
			provide an important **incentive** to encourage people 사람들을 격려하기 위해 중요한 자극을 주다	
			incentive goods 보상 물자	
20	**inimical** [inímikəl]	a	hostile, adverse, antagonistic	적대하는, 불리한
			conditions **inimical** to one's interests 불리한 조건	
21	**interfere** [ìntərfíər]	v	intrude,conflict, clash, obstruct, hamper	충돌하다, 간섭하다
			interfere in their relationship 그들의 관계에 간섭하다	
22	**loiter** [lɔ́itər]	v	linger, loaf	빈둥거리다, 어슬렁거리다
			loiter along 어슬렁어슬렁 걷다	
23	**overtax*** [ouvərtǽks]	v	heavily burden	지나치게 과세하다, 혹사하다
			overtax one's brain 두뇌를 혹사하다	
24	**pathway** [pǽθwei]	n	course	길, 과정
			trigger specific response **pathway** 특별한 반응 경로를 촉발하다	
25	**pursue*** [pərsúː]	v	chase, follow, hunt, seek	추구하다, 종사하다
			pursue one's studies 연구에 종사하다	
26	**quiver*** [kwívər]	v	shiver, shake, tremble, vibrate, quake, shudder	흔들리다
			quiver with fear 공포에 떨다	
27	**revolve** [riválv]	v	rotate, circulate, orbit, circle	회전하다, 순환하다
			The seasons **revolve**. 계절은 순환한다.	
28	**site**** [sait]	n	location, place, plot, spot	현장, 부지
			the **site** for a new school 신설 학교의 부지	
		v	locate, install, place, position, set	위치를 차지하다
			site the power plant 발전소가 위치하다	

29	**skeptical**** [sképtikəl]	**a**	doubtful, skeptic, dubious, incredulous Economists, almost to a man, were **skeptical**. 경제학자는 거의 모든 사람에 대해서 의심이 많다.	의심이 많은, 회의적인
30	**snatch** [snætʃ]	**v**	seize, clutch, grasp **snatch** chocolate bars from me 나에게서 초콜릿 바를 빼앗다	붙잡다, 빼앗다
31	**stage**** [steidʒ]	**n**	① process, phase, step, degree, point, period a **stage** in a frog's development 개구리 발달의 과정 ② platform, theater, playhouse an actor on the **stage** 무대의 배우	① 단계, 과정 ② 연극 무대
		v	plan, arrange, produce; perform **stage** a play 연극을 상연하다	기획하다 / 상연하다
32	**stagger*** [stǽgər]	**v**	sway, waver, falter The blow **staggered** him. 바람이 그를 비틀거리게 했다.	비틀거리다
33	**stumble** [stʌmbl]	**v**	trip, fall, totter, falter Troops **stumbled** blindly through the forest. 군대는 숲을 통해 가다 막다른 곳에 마주쳤다.	비틀거리다, 마주치다
34	**trim*** [trim]	**v**	cut, clip, prune, shave, shear, arrange **trim** oneself up 깨끗이 몸단장하다	다듬다, 손질하다
35	**twinkle*** [twíŋkl]	**v**	glimmer, sparkle, flash, shine Lights **twinkle** in distant villages. 불빛이 멀리 떨어진 마을에서 빛난다. The stars are **twinkling**. 별들이 반짝이고 있다.	반짝반짝 빛나다
36	**undermine*** [ʌndərmain]	**v**	ruin, thwart **undermine** one's constitution 몸을 버리다	해치다, 몰래 손상시키다
37	**vertigo** [və́:rtigòu]	**n**	dizziness, lightheadedness He had a dreadful attack of **vertigo** at the top of a ladder. 그는 사다리 상단에서 현기증의 무서운 공격을 받았다.	현기증
38	**vice*** [vais]	**n**	wickedness, evil connected with **vice** and drugs 악과 마약과 연관된 virtue and **vice** 선과 악	악, 악덕 행위
39	**vow** [vau]	**n**	pledge, promise Most couple still take their marriage **vows** seriously. 대부분의 커플들은 여전히 그들의 결혼에 엄숙하게 서약을 하고 있다. take a **vow** 맹세하다, 서약하다	맹세, 서약
40	**worship**** [wə́:rʃip]	**v**	faith, revere, respect, venerate, adore People go to church to **worship** God before any other thing. 사람들은 다른 어떤 일보다 예배하러 교회에 간다. hero **worship** 영웅 숭배	숭배하다

01. The domestic market has fewer risks than the foreign market.
    (A) internal
    (B) cultivated
    (C) implanted
    (D) reared

02. The Watergate scandal further damaged the publics regard for the presidency.
    (A) endless
    (B) additional
    (C) deserved
    (D) renewed

03. Planets shine with a steady light, while stars seem to twinkle.
    (A) faint
    (B) reflect
    (C) show up
    (D) glitter

04. Greed and laziness are not regarded as vices in modern civilization.
    (A) virtues
    (B) manner
    (C) secondary
    (D) wickedness

05. A bodhisattva is a person who has vowed to become a Buddha by leading a life of virtue and wisdom.
    (A) affirmed
    (B) played
    (C) prayed
    (D) believed

06. Sugar dissolves in water and sweetens it the entire water.
    (A) crystallizes
    (B) melts
    (C) concentrates
    (D) exists

07. On some nights, the moon gleamed like a silver globe.
    (A) fainted
    (B) faded
    (C) shined
    (D) oval shaped

08. Fiber adds bulk to food and keeps waste products moving through the intestines.
    (A) matter
    (B) assignments
    (C) texts
    (D) rest

09. Many communities have immunization programs that help protect people against disease.
    (A) resistance
    (B) medication
    (C) vaccination
    (D) vulnerability

10. Epicurus pursued happiness, not by means of a drink, but through eating only dry bread.
    (A) misled
    (B) joined
    (C) followed
    (D) identified

11. Pioneers used axes to cut away the brush, chop down trees, and trim logs.
    - (A) transport
    - (B) arrange
    - (C) cut
    - (D) roll

12. The Greek astronomer Ptolemy's theory is that the sun as well as all of the planets revolves around the earth.
    - (A) balance
    - (B) standardize
    - (C) shift
    - (D) rotate

13. Embryology is the study of the way organisms develop during the earliest stages of life.
    - (A) districts
    - (B) layers
    - (C) mines
    - (D) phases

14. The National Park System consists of 20 types of areas, including national parks, national monuments, national memorials, and national historic sites.
    - (A) locations
    - (B) elevations
    - (C) climates
    - (D) fertilizers

15. In any electronic device, a circuit provides the pathway for the electric current that operates the device.
    - (A) electronically chain
    - (B) trail
    - (C) reactor
    - (D) equation

16. City and state governments plan for many urban renewal projects and provide the incentives for private investors.
    - (A) improvements
    - (B) easiness
    - (C) stimulus
    - (D) lures

17. After the Civil War, Uncle Tom's Cabin became well known mainly through abridgments of the novel and by plays based on the book.
    - (A) compositions
    - (B) components
    - (C) digests
    - (D) greatnesses

18. In the 100's, the Roman Empire encompassed all the land around the Mediterranean Sea and extended westward to the British Isles.
    - (A) separated
    - (B) included
    - (C) replaced
    - (D) enhanced

19. During the 630's, Byzantine territories were assailed by Arab invaders carrying the banner of Islam, a religion which had been established a few years earlier.
    - (A) perturbed
    - (B) detected
    - (C) inspected
    - (D) attacked

20. Learning disabilities can interfere with the development of such basic skills as concentration, coordination, language, and memory.
    - (A) decline
    - (B) accelerate
    - (C) decelerate
    - (D) impede

D A Y 01-05 Exercise

01. a tense person
- (A) glared
- (B) blamed
- (C) innate
- (D) nervous

02. eliminate waste
- (A) quiver
- (B) remove
- (C) intensify
- (D) group

03. The characters are well portrayed.
- (A) relented
- (B) aggravated
- (C) represented
- (D) shuddered

04. follow the trend
- (A) recompense
- (B) difference
- (C) noble
- (D) inclination

05. Hot water gushed out.
- (A) declined
- (B) spurted
- (C) produced
- (D) transported

06. quit the stage
- (A) phase
- (B) plot
- (C) pathway
- (D) step

07. devastate the countryside
- (A) aggravate
- (B) pacify
- (C) demolish
- (D) outstrip

08. bulk production
- (A) inoculation
- (B) mass
- (C) impulse
- (D) scent

09. the oceans that encompass the world
- (A) revere
- (B) totter
- (C) require
- (D) include

10. in a twinkle
- (A) course
- (B) process
- (C) promise
- (D) sparkle

11. amateur program producer
- (A) nonprofessional
- (B) standard
- (C) sliding
- (D) concealing

12. forage about to find a book
- (A) cheer
- (B) search
- (C) shrink
- (D) compress

13. be accustomed to bed early
- (A) murdered
- (B) conveyed
- (C) used
- (D) terminated

14. The U.S. comprises 50 states.
- (A) holds
- (B) constitutes
- (C) adapts
- (D) abates

15. chosen arbitrarily
- (A) typically
- (B) obscure
- (C) lively
- (D) randomly

16. hide one's talent in a napkin
- (A) task
- (B) state
- (C) dormancy
- (D) gift

17. play the villain
- (A) notice
- (B) amateur
- (C) partnership
- (D) rascal

18. The volcano erupted violently.
- (A) strayed
- (B) slipped
- (C) suspended
- (D) gushed

19. amuse oneself playing chess
- (A) entertain
- (B) express
- (C) replicate
- (D) relate

20. without blemish
- (A) defect
- (B) issue
- (C) gaiety
- (D) garment

01. Although scientists recognized that Jenner's vaccine worked, they did not know why.
   Ⓐ distinguished
   Ⓑ reproduced
   Ⓒ coordinated
   Ⓓ identified

02. The fox was often pictured as sly, and the owl as wise.
   Ⓐ created
   Ⓑ thought
   Ⓒ described
   Ⓓ escaped

03. During colonial times, many Latin American painters imitated European styles.
   Ⓐ studied
   Ⓑ pronounced
   Ⓒ mimicked
   Ⓓ harmonized

04. Sherman hoped that the horrible destruction would break the enemy's will to continue the war.
   Ⓐ wonderful
   Ⓑ unforgettable
   Ⓒ colossal
   Ⓓ dreadful

05. In Italy, the popes and higher clergy lived like secular princes.
   Ⓐ gorgeous
   Ⓑ cynical
   Ⓒ temporal
   Ⓓ impudent

06. Harmony that sounds rough and tense is dissonant.
   Ⓐ erratic
   Ⓑ pathetic
   Ⓒ nervous
   Ⓓ envious

07. Cowboy hats had a wide brim to shield the eyes.
   Ⓐ coverage
   Ⓑ resin
   Ⓒ luster
   Ⓓ margin

08. The human body needs various nutrients to function properly.
   Ⓐ satisfactions
   Ⓑ health food
   Ⓒ amusements
   Ⓓ activities

09. According to deism, God regulated nature so that it would proceed mechanically.
   Ⓐ work
   Ⓑ continue
   Ⓒ stop
   Ⓓ perform

10. In general, diamonds are the most prized gems because they surpass all others in hardness and brilliance.
   Ⓐ exceed
   Ⓑ match
   Ⓒ maintain
   Ⓓ announce

11. Several Roman Catholic missionaries, especially Bartolome de Las Casas, pleaded for more humane treatment of the Indians.
    (A) ample
    (B) ruthless
    (C) merciful
    (D) fruitful

12. Psychologists can interpret the responses on these tests as expressions of an individual's personality.
    (A) reactions
    (B) warning signals
    (C) dispositions
    (D) trigger mechanisms

13. The storyteller can extract appropriate material from novels and long non-fictional works.
    (A) change
    (B) excerpt
    (C) detach
    (D) descend

14. During the 2000's, the Korea experienced periodic fuel shortages, which led to higher prices for gasoline and home heating fuel.
    (A) stagnate
    (B) irregular
    (C) sporadic
    (D) pointless

15. They made clothing from animal hides and furs and used branches and other natural materials to build shelters.
    (A) trunks
    (B) skins
    (C) tongues
    (D) horns

16. To make it coincide with Halloween, the young actor-director Orson Welles, dramatized the novel for his weekly radio program "Mercury Theatre on the Air."
    (A) relate with
    (B) collide with
    (C) occur at the same time
    (D) equalize with

17. To portray a role well, performers should know about human emotions, attitudes, and motivations.
    (A) aptitudes
    (B) intelligences
    (C) memorizations
    (D) reasons for behavior

18. The minimum educational requirement for a professional biologist is a bachelor's degree in the science.
    (A) eminent
    (B) amateur
    (C) expert
    (D) distinctive

19. Washington's portrait appears on postage stamps, the $1 bill, and on the quarter.
    (A) one third
    (B) one fourth
    (C) one tenth
    (D) one fifteenth

20. The trainer chooses birds that are in the finest physical condition and have perfect, unbroken flight feathers.
    (A) reciprocal
    (B) enduring
    (C) favorable
    (D) complete

01. The luster of a mineral may differ from sample to sample.
    Ⓐ expression
    Ⓑ distinction
    Ⓒ passion
    Ⓓ shining light

02. The male gametes vary considerably in shape and form between animal and plant organisms.
    Ⓐ above all
    Ⓑ very much
    Ⓒ in a way
    Ⓓ on the whole

03. Euclid, one of the foremost Greek mathematicians, wrote about the Elements at around 300 B. C.
    Ⓐ most difficult
    Ⓑ interesting
    Ⓒ most focused
    Ⓓ leading

04. A gem is a mineral or any other type of material used in jewelry and other ornaments.
    Ⓐ decorations
    Ⓑ medicines
    Ⓒ constructions
    Ⓓ diversities

05. In many cases, some medications diminish cell-mediated immunity as well as antibody responses.
    Ⓐ develop
    Ⓑ conserve
    Ⓒ decrease
    Ⓓ depose

06. Living at home enables people to enjoy the companionship of those for whom they feel affection.
    Ⓐ fondness
    Ⓑ longing
    Ⓒ respect
    Ⓓ concern

07. The reverse-selective filter allows molecules to dissolve into its matrix and then diffuse across it.
    Ⓐ permeate
    Ⓑ fuse
    Ⓒ break up
    Ⓓ solidify

08. Some people pursue happiness in a world that is seemingly far removed from reality.
    Ⓐ identify
    Ⓑ join
    Ⓒ chase
    Ⓓ mislead

09. A boat must have something to keep it from sliding sideways when moving across the wind.
    Ⓐ to the core
    Ⓑ to the side
    Ⓒ to the margin
    Ⓓ to shortcut

10. Many sea creatures have been inadvertently reduced in number by being caught accidentally in nets set for other species.
    Ⓐ experimentally
    Ⓑ unceasingly
    Ⓒ incompetently
    Ⓓ accidentally

11. Maria Martinez, a Pueblo Indian, revived pottery making as a fine art among the Pueblos of the Southwest.
    A recovered
    B remodeled
    C wrecked
    D inspired

12. This is a brisk and humorous tale about a fox who is convinced he is the smartest detective in the world.
    A regular
    B graceful
    C energetic
    D daily

13. Hadrosaurs, known as the duckbilled dinosaur, had hind legs that were strong and carried their tails stiffly outstretched and parallel to the ground.
    A spread
    B risen
    C torn
    D missed

14. The National Park Service repeatedly warns the public not to feed, tease, or touch any of the animals in the parklands.
    A annoy
    B imitate
    C ridicule
    D please

15. As one of the four great apes (the other three being the gorilla, chimpanzee, and bonobo), the Pongo pygmaeus is exquisitely adapted for life in the forest canopies of the Southeast Asian islands of Borneo and Sumatra.
    A entirely
    B relatively
    C uninterruptedly
    D delicately

16. A writer should always use reliable sources so that the article presents accurate information.
    A convenient
    B dependable
    C accessible
    D concise

17. As the proteins are made, they detach from the ribosomes and move through the ER cisternae into the smooth ER (which lacks ribosomes), where they may subsequently be modified.
    A saturate
    B separate
    C assemble
    D secrete

18. In Tolstoy's famous masterpiece, Crime and Punishment(1866), he explored the anguished mind of a student who commits two murders.
    A sick
    B loose
    C angered
    D pity

19. About 75 percent of precipitation falls back directly into the ocean, and the rest soaks into the earth and becomes part of the land water supply.
    A digs
    B permeates
    C falls
    D dips

20. Experts say this system is highly reliable because even people with a knack for imitating voices can generally achieve only a superficial resemblance to a person's real voice.
    A adept to
    B tone of
    C happiness of
    D difficulty of

홍수나다	- flood, deluge, overflow, inundate
망치다, 훼손하다	- mar, spoil (by), blemish, damage
황폐화시키다	- devastate, ruin, destroy, demolish
달래다, 진정시키다	- soothe, alleviate, pacify, assuage, appease, ease, lessen, abate
굴복하다	- yield, surrender, concede, relent, relinquish, succumb
요약하다	- abridge, shorten, abbreviate, condense
녹이다	- dissolve, melt, end, deliquesce, break up
떨다	- shiver, tremble, shudder, shake, quake, quiver
비틀거리다	- stagger, sway, waver, falter
숭배하다	- worship, faith, revere, respect, venerate, adore
참을 수 없는	- unbearable, intolerable, unendurable, insufferable, insupportable
익숙한	- accustomed to, used to, customary, habitual
셀 수 없는	- countless, innumerable, uncountable, innumerous, numberless
인도적인, 자비로운	- humane, merciful, benevolent, compassionate, charitable
의심이 많은	- skeptical, doubtful, skeptic, dubious, incredulous
건방진	- impudent, impertinent, insolent, shameless, rude
감상적인, 애처로운	- pathetic, pitiable, touching, moving
책임이 있는	- responsible, accountable, answerable, liable
만질 수 있는	- tangible, substantial, real, concrete, substantive
실용적인	- utilitarian, functional, pragmatic, practical
범죄자	- criminal, convict, culprit, gangster, offender
위험, 위기	- peril, jeopardy, danger, hazard, risk
악의, 원한	- malice, ill will, spite, enmity, malevolence
물질, 재료	- stuff, material, substance, matter
동기, 자극	- incentive, motive, stimulus, spur, impulse

THE ORIGIN OF BIRDS

The ❶ origin of birds refers to the initial stages in the evolution of birds that evolved during the Mesozoic Era. A close relationship between birds and dinosaurs was first proposed in the nineteenth century after the discovery of the ❷ primitive bird Archaeopteryx in Germany. In the 1970s, paleontologists noticed that Archaeopteryx shared many unique skeleton ❸ features with small ❹ carnivorous dinosaurs called theropods.

Moreover, fossils of more than twenty species of dinosaur have been collected with preserved feathers. There are even very small dinosaurs, such as Microraptor and Anchiornis, which have long, vaned, arm and leg feathers forming wings. The Jurassic basal avialan Pedopenna also shows these long foot feathers. Therefore, it is concluded that this evidence is sufficient to demonstrate that avian ❺ evolution went through a four-winged stage.

Fossil evidence also demonstrates that birds and dinosaurs shared features such as hollow, pneumatized bones, gastroliths in the digestive system, nest-building and ❻ brooding behaviors. The ❼ ground-breaking discovery of fossilized Tyrannosaurus rex soft tissue allowed a molecular comparison of ❽ cellular anatomy and protein sequencing of collagen tissue, both of which demonstrated that T. rex and birds are more closely related to each other than either is to Alligator. A second molecular study ❾ robustly supported the relationship of birds to dinosaurs, though it did not place birds within Theropoda, as expected. This study ❿ utilized eight additional collagen sequences extracted from a femur of Brachylophosaurus canadensis, a hadrosaur. The scientific consensus is that birds are a group of theropod dinosaurs.

The word that closest meaning to

1. origin	Ⓐ innovation	Ⓑ primitive	Ⓒ extinction	Ⓓ crisis
2. primitive	Ⓐ normal	Ⓑ basic	Ⓒ primordial	Ⓓ skeptical
3. features	Ⓐ recognitions	Ⓑ trends	Ⓒ criterion	Ⓓ trait
4. carnivorous	Ⓐ predatory	Ⓑ plant eating	Ⓒ polyphagous	Ⓓ decomposing
5. evolution	Ⓐ development	Ⓑ pathway	Ⓒ highlight	Ⓓ mature
6. brooding	Ⓐ staggering	Ⓑ inherent	Ⓒ aberrant	Ⓓ sitting on eggs
7. ground-breaking discovery	Ⓐ fusion	Ⓑ trivial event	Ⓒ breakthrough	Ⓓ extraordinary case
8. cellular	Ⓐ dissecting into small piece	Ⓑ relating to cell	Ⓒ classifying into a small part	Ⓓ using mobile application
9. robustly	Ⓐ healthy	Ⓑ strongly	Ⓒ professionally	Ⓓ derisively
10. utilized	Ⓐ make use of	Ⓑ devastated	Ⓒ corresponded	Ⓓ finished

새의 기원

새의 기원the origin of birds은 중생기the Mesozoic era 동안에 진화했던 새들의 진화 초기단계the initial stages와 관련 있다. 새와 공룡 간의 밀접한 관계는 원시조류the primitive bird인 아르카이오프테릭스Archeopteryx가 독일에서 발견된 후인 19세기에 처음으로 제시되었다. 1970년대에는 고생물학자들paleontologists이 아르카이오프테릭스Archeopteryx가 수각아목이라 불리는 작은 육식성 공룡들carnivorous dinosaurs이 가진 많은 독특한 뼈의 특징을 공유한다shared many unique skeleton features는 것을 인지했다.

게다가 20종 이상의 공룡 화석들이 깃털이 있는 채로 수집되었다. 여기에는 심지어 길고, 우판이 있고 날개를 형성 중인 팔과 다리의 깃털arm and leg feathers forming wings이 있는 Microraptor와 Anchiornis와 같은 매우 작은 공룡들도 있었다. 쥐라기 시대의 기본 공룡인avialan(avialae에 속한 공룡들) Pedopenna 또한 이러한 긴 발의 깃털을 보여주었다. 따라서 이 증거가 새의 진화avian evolution가 4개의 날개를 가진 단계를 거쳤다는 것을 증명하기에 충분하다는 결론을 내렸다it is concluded that this evidence is sufficient to demonstrate.

화석 증거는 새와 공룡이 속이 비고 공기가 들어간 뼈hollow, pneumatized bones와 소화계에서 위결석과 둥지를 짓고 알을 품는 행동들nest-building and brooding behaviors과 같은 특징을 공유한다는 것을 증명하였다. 화석화된 티라노사우르스Tyranosaurus rex의 부드러운 조직의 획기적인 발견the ground-breaking discovery은 콜라겐(교원질) 조직의 세포 수준의 해부와 단백질 서열을 분자적인 비교를 가능하도록 하였고, 둘 다 티라노사우르스와 새가 악어와의 관계보다 서로가 더 밀접하게 관련이 있다more closely related to each other는 것을 증명하였다. 두 번째 분자연구는 비록 예상했던 것처럼 수각류 내에 새가 위치하지는 못했지만 공룡에 대한 새의 관계를 확고하게 뒷받침했다robustly supported the relationship of birds to dinosaurs. 이 연구는 오리주둥이공룡인 브라킬로포사우루스 카나덴시스 Brachylophosaurus canadensis의 넓적다리로부터 추출한extracted from a femur of 추가적 8개의 콜라겐의 서열을 이용하였다. 과학적 의견의 일치the scientific consensus는 새는 수각아목의 공룡의 한 무리birds are a group of theropod dinosaurs라는 것이다.

1. Ⓑ	2. ⓒ	3. Ⓓ	4. Ⓐ	5. Ⓐ
6. Ⓓ	7. ⓒ	8. Ⓑ	9. Ⓑ	10. Ⓐ

01. for reasons of sanitation
   Ⓐ space   Ⓑ hygiene
   Ⓒ brush   Ⓓ seize

02. allege a matter as a fact
   Ⓐ complain   Ⓑ affirm
   Ⓒ scamper   Ⓓ magnify

03. swear a person to secrecy
   Ⓐ avow   Ⓑ rumble
   Ⓒ serene   Ⓓ quiet

04. the fusion of metal
   Ⓐ health   Ⓑ extent
   Ⓒ union   Ⓓ fight

05. mature plants
   Ⓐ bloom   Ⓑ enlarge
   Ⓒ adult   Ⓓ confuse

06. superficial measurement
   Ⓐ vigorous   Ⓑ imprudent
   Ⓒ shallow   Ⓓ peaceful

07. a verbal promise
   Ⓐ spoken   Ⓑ grown
   Ⓒ criminal   Ⓓ prevailing

08. figure the damage caused by the flood
   Ⓐ raid   Ⓑ attack
   Ⓒ count   Ⓓ intrude

09. used colloquial speech
   Ⓐ lifestyle   Ⓑ informal
   Ⓒ educated   Ⓓ desirous

10. rash promises
   Ⓐ prevalent   Ⓑ strange
   Ⓒ destructive   Ⓓ reckless

11. The skirmish grew into a major battle.
   Ⓐ examining   Ⓑ fight
   Ⓒ extent   Ⓓ bending

12. with a yawn
   Ⓐ battle   Ⓑ gape
   Ⓒ arrest   Ⓓ adoration

13. the placid water of the lake
   Ⓐ proper   Ⓑ nice
   Ⓒ undisturbed   Ⓓ prevalent

14. the wide scope for personal initiative in Academy
   Ⓐ praise   Ⓑ strong
   Ⓒ range   Ⓓ health

15. a robust frame
   Ⓐ devour   Ⓑ vigorous
   Ⓒ pernicious   Ⓓ relinquished

16. covet his videocassette collection
   Ⓐ dart   Ⓑ appraise
   Ⓒ crave   Ⓓ exalt

17. avid collector of art and history
   Ⓐ imprudent   Ⓑ avaricious
   Ⓒ odd   Ⓓ serene

18. evacuate refugees
   Ⓐ shelter   Ⓑ commend
   Ⓒ intervene   Ⓓ exclude

19. swallow one's words
   Ⓐ investigate   Ⓑ indicate
   Ⓒ write   Ⓓ gorge

20. sing one's own praises
   Ⓐ hygiene   Ⓑ acclamations
   Ⓒ blossoms   Ⓓ costs

표제어	품사	동의어와 예문	한글 뜻
1 **allege** [əlédʒ]	v	declare, affirm, assert **allege** a fact 사실을 주장하다	주장하다
2 **avid** [ǽvid]	a	greedy, avaricious, desirous, covetous, eager Bush is an **avid** fisherman. 부시는 욕심 많은 어부이다.	욕심 많은
3 **bloom** [blu:m]	n	flower, blossom, maturity cherry **blossoms** in full bloom on the trees 나무에 만개한 벗나무 꽃	꽃
4 **call for**** [kɔ:l fər]	v	ask for, require, demand, entail; summon A meeting has been **called for** Saturday. 회의는 월요일 개최되었다.	요청하다 / 모집하다
5 **cluster*** [klʌstər]	v	gather, accumulate, assemble Water molecules **cluster** around sugar molecules. 물 분자들이 당분자 주변으로 모이다. in a **cluster** 송이가 되어, 떼를 지어	모으다
6 **colloquial** [kəlóukwiəl]	a	informal, ordinary in speech write in a **colloquial** style 구어체로 쓰다	구어체의, 일상회화의
7 **covet*** [kʌvit]	v	envy, desire, fancy, aspire **covet** for popularity 인기를 얻으려고 기를 쓰다	탐하다
8 **dash*** [dæʃ]	v	① rush, hurry, dart, bolt **dash** out of a room 방에서 달려 나오다 ② shatter; depress, dismay **dash** a glass to bits 유리컵을 산산이 부수다	① 돌진하다 ② 내던지다 / 좌절시키다
9 **decent** [dí:snt]	a	right, proper, nice, pure, modest a man of **decent** character 사람다운 사람	점잖은, 순수한, 겸손한
10 **deleterious** [dèlitíəriəs]	a	adverse, bad, pernicious, destructive, evil, harmful Many **deleterious** allele have serious effect on heredity. 많은 해로운 대립유전자가 유전에 심각한 영향을 미친다.	해로운, 유독한
11 **eccentric** [ikséntrik]	a	strange, odd an **eccentric** person 괴팍스러운 사람, 기인	신기한
12 **embarrass***** [imbǽrəs]	v	confuse, perplex **embarrass** by a failing grade 승진 실패로 난처하게 되다	당황하다, 혼란시키다
13 **enlarge*** [inlá:rdʒ]	v	extend, augment, amplify, magnify, expand **enlarge** a photograph 사진을 확대하다	확대하다, 확장하다
14 **exuberant** [igzú:bərənt]	a	overflowing, luxuriant, lavish The man received **exuberant** praise as he walked to the stage to accept his award. 그 남자는 그가 상을 받으러 연단으로 걸어갔을 때 열광적인 찬양을 받았다.	열광적인, 무성한

15	**evacuate*** [ivǽkjuèit]	**v** shelter, remove, leave, abandon, desert, relinquish **evacuate** a position 진지를 철수하다	피난시키다, 비우다
16	**figure**** [fígjər]	**n** ① shape, form, outline, configuration a beautiful **figure** 아름다운 모습	① 윤곽
		② numeral, digit; sum, total, amount, price, cost calculate the final **figures** 마지막 총계를 계산하다	② 수 / 총계
		③ diagram, picture, representation, image Refer to **Figure** A in your math book. 수학책의 그림 A를 참고하라	③ 그림, 상
		v calculate, count, reckon, appraise, assess	계산하다, 이해하다
17	**fusion*** [fjúːʒən]	**n** union, coalition, unification, merger the point of **fusion** 융점, 용해점	연합
18	**grumble** [grʌ́mbl]	**v** complain, rumble **grumble** one's fill 마구 불평하다	불평하다, 으르렁거리다
19	**highlight** [hailait]	**n** climax, peak The **highlight** of the competition was women's figure skating. 경쟁의 최고조는 여자 피겨 스케이팅이었다.	가장 중요한 점, 최고조
		v emphasize, stress, underline Anthropological studies **highlighted** many differences among societies. 인류학적 연구는 사회 간의 많은 차이를 강조했다.	두드러지게 하다
20	**invade*** [invéid]	**v** ① move into, infiltrate, attack, overrun, raid **invade** the enemy camp 적군 막사에 침입하다	① 침입하다
		② intrude, interrupt, intervene **invade** a person's privacy 누구의 사생활을 침해하다	② 간섭하다
21	**mature*** [mətjúər]	**a** ripe, complete, grown, fully-developed, adult **mature** sense of humor 성숙한 유머 감각	성숙한
22	**outlaw** [autlɔː]	**n** criminal, bandit Hong Gildong was an **outlaw**, but he was the friend of poor and oppressed people. 홍길동은 무법자이지만 가난하고 억압받는 사람들의 친구였다.	무법, 불량배
		v forbidden, ban, bar, exclude **outlaw** drunken driving 음주운전을 금지하다	금지하다
23	**placid*** [plǽsid]	**a** calm, peaceful, tranquil, serene, undisturbed a **placid** temper 느긋한 성질	평온한, 침착한
24	**platform** [plǽtfɔːrm]	**n** stage, scaffold, pulpit mount the **platform** 연단에 오르다	교단, 강단
25	**praise**** [preiz]	**n** approval, acclamation; eulogy, adoration, worship give **praise** to the winner 승자에게 포상을 주다	칭찬 / 숭배
		v admire, exalt, laud, commend fans who **praise** the umpires 심판원을 칭찬하는 팬 **praised** the decision 그 결정을 칭찬하다	칭찬하다, 찬미하다
26	**probe** [proub]	**v** examine, explore, investigate Many early satellites **probed** uncharted regions of space. 많은 초기의 위성은 우주의 미지의 영역을 탐지했다.	조사 [탐사]하다, 규명하다

DAY 06

27	**rash*** [ræʃ]	a	reckless, heedless, indiscreet, imprudent do a **rash** thing 무분별한 짓을 하다	무분별한, 무모한
28	**robust*** [roubʌst]	a	strong, sturdy, vigorous, stalwart The two **robust** species formed an evolutionary side branch. 세력이 강한 두 종이 진화적으로 분파를 형성했다. a **robust** person 튼튼한 사람	건장한, 튼튼한
29	**sanitation*** [sænitéiʃən]	n	health, hygiene understand the importance of **sanitation** 위생의 중요성을 이해하다 an inspector of **sanitation** 위생 검사관	위생
30	**scope*** [skoup]	n	extent, range, space give **scope** to ability 능력을 발휘하다	범위
31	**skirmish*** [skə́:rmiʃ]	n	fight, battle, brush a **skirmish** of the general election 총선거의 전초전	작은 접전
32	**stoop** [stu:p]	v	bend, lean, bow He **stooped** down suddenly. 그는 갑자기 웅크렸다.	구부리다, 굽히다
33	**superficial*** [sù:pərfíʃəl]	a	shallow, external, outward a **superficial** analysis of the problem 그 문제의 표면적 분석	표면의, 겉면의
34	**swallow*** [swálou]	v	eat, gorge, engulf, devour Big fish **swallowed** small fishes of it whole. 큰 물고기가 작은 물고기를 통째로 삼켰다. **swallow** one's word 한 말을 취소하다	삼키다, 들이키다
35	**swear** [swɛər]	v	avow, vow, pledge **swear** a person to secrecy 누구에게 비밀을 지킬 것을 맹세하다	맹세하다
36	**trap** [træp]	n	catch, snare, seize, arrest, ensnare **trap** for monitoring of moth's population 나방의 밀도 감시를 위한 덫 a mouse **trap** 쥐덫	덫, 올가미, 속임수
37	**unprecedented** [ʌnprésidəntid]	a	unparalleled, exceptional, extraordinary, amazing, remarkable **unprecedented** international attention 전례없는 국제적인 관심	전례가 없는, 새로운
38	**ventilation** [vèntəléiʃən]	n	air circulation, air Coal mines must have a **ventilation** system to outside 석탄 광산은 반드시 바깥쪽으로 환기 장치를 해야만 한다.	환기
39	**verbal*** [və́:rbəl]	a	oral, spoken, stated, unwritten a **verbal** promise 언약	말의
40	**yawn** [jɔ:n]	v	gape, open, split People may even **yawn** when they are jogging. 사람들은 조깅할 때조차 하품한다.	하품하다

01. Adolescence means a period of 'growing-up' so strictly speaking, should apply from child birth to maturity.
    - (A) childhood
    - (B) adulthood
    - (C) demise
    - (D) adolescent

02. A lack of iodine can cause goiter, a disease in which the thyroid gland becomes enlarged.
    - (A) disabled
    - (B) swollen
    - (C) disappeared
    - (D) hurt

03. The claims section defines the scope of the invention, and may take much time to prepare.
    - (A) purpose
    - (B) title
    - (C) view
    - (D) variety

04. In springtime, gorgeous pink and white cherry blossoms bloom all over the trees.
    - (A) flower
    - (B) appear
    - (C) drop seeds
    - (D) grows best

05. Pleasurable, relaxing activities help the body to shed tension and remain robust.
    - (A) strong
    - (B) smooth
    - (C) secure
    - (D) unsafe

06. Energy is trapped within plants during the process of photosynthesis and is stored in chemical compounds.
    - (A) caught
    - (B) burned
    - (C) dirtied
    - (D) covered

07. Sessions of Congress open with prayers, and court witnesses swear an oath on the Bible.
    - (A) exploit
    - (B) employ
    - (C) pledge
    - (D) convince

08. Most mining engineer jobs call for a college degree in engineering.
    - (A) ask for
    - (B) acquire
    - (C) encourage
    - (D) summon

09. In 1966, the Supreme Court outlawed the use of poll taxes in state and local elections.
    - (A) enacted
    - (B) prohibited
    - (C) escalated
    - (D) authorized

10. Virginia militiamen drove out Lord Dunmore from the colony after several skirmishes in 1776.
    - (A) disputes
    - (B) harvests
    - (C) clashes
    - (D) gathering

11. Opera-goers have praised The Marriage of Figaro for its vivid, realistic characters.
    Ⓐ rediculed
    Ⓑ extolled
    Ⓒ checked
    Ⓓ promoted

12. For a long time the way a diamond was formed remained an entirely mysterious process; men coveted diamonds but did not know where they came from.
    Ⓐ desired
    Ⓑ hoarded
    Ⓒ costly
    Ⓓ lucrative

13. Radars, radio astronomy equipment, and space probes have been used to explore Venus.
    Ⓐ aircrafts
    Ⓑ treks
    Ⓒ illusion
    Ⓓ investigations

14. Immediately after the British evacuated Boston in March 1776, General Howe began to plan his return from Canada to the American Colonies.
    Ⓐ anticipated
    Ⓑ comfort d
    Ⓒ abandoned
    Ⓓ sheltered

15. Ski jumping is a highly specialized form of skiing, in which a skier slides down a steep track and flies off a platform at the end.
    Ⓐ slide
    Ⓑ program
    Ⓒ path
    Ⓓ stage

16. Blasting in an underground mine may produce dangerous levels of carbon monoxide if the mine is improperly ventilated.
    Ⓐ decorated
    Ⓑ circulated the air
    Ⓒ safe
    Ⓓ shine

17. In 1951, the Kefauver hearings, in which U.S. Senator Estes Kefauver and his Senate committee questioned alleged mobsters about organized crime, were televised.
    Ⓐ designated
    Ⓑ allowed
    Ⓒ cumulated
    Ⓓ asserted

18. Two physicists, Hans Bethe and Carl F. von Weizsacker, showed that thermonuclear fusion releases a sufficient amount of the sun's energy to keep the sun shining for billions of years.
    Ⓐ fixing
    Ⓑ strength
    Ⓒ union
    Ⓓ alignment

19. The Public Health Service administers work to prevent and control diseases by providing proper sanitation, conducting immunization programs, and enforcing quarantines.
    Ⓐ protection
    Ⓑ demand
    Ⓒ hygiene
    Ⓓ quarantine

20. Companies that make facial-recognition systems claim that their computer programs are intelligent enough to avoid being fooled by superficial alterations in appearance.
    Ⓐ deep   Ⓑ shallow
    Ⓒ useless   Ⓓ thorough

01. <u>award</u> a prize
   Ⓐ grant   Ⓑ revolve
   Ⓒ deduct   Ⓓ precede

02. pale <u>hue</u>
   Ⓐ joining   Ⓑ muddle
   Ⓒ union   Ⓓ color

03. repay an <u>obligation</u>
   Ⓐ intrigue   Ⓑ favor
   Ⓒ conspiracy   Ⓓ peak

04. The snow is <u>thawing</u>.
   Ⓐ acute   Ⓑ retard
   Ⓒ defrosting   Ⓓ steeping

05. <u>seize</u> a rope
   Ⓐ untie   Ⓑ release
   Ⓒ hold   Ⓓ associate

06. <u>hindered</u> the investigation
   Ⓐ deplored   Ⓑ retarded
   Ⓒ scared   Ⓓ complained

07. military <u>discipline</u>
   Ⓐ plot   Ⓑ drill
   Ⓒ project   Ⓓ tint

08. <u>lament</u> one's hard fate
   Ⓐ thrust   Ⓑ deplore
   Ⓒ superintend   Ⓓ saturate

09. a <u>devout</u> Roman Catholic
   Ⓐ consistent   Ⓑ poignant
   Ⓒ pious   Ⓓ practice

10. <u>execute</u> a person for murder
   Ⓐ perform   Ⓑ obstruct
   Ⓒ annihilate   Ⓓ bestow

11. a <u>hardy</u> constitution
   Ⓐ poignant   Ⓑ sharp
   Ⓒ epidemic   Ⓓ vigorous

12. <u>stab</u> a person to death
   Ⓐ penetrate   Ⓑ deplore
   Ⓒ superintend   Ⓓ admire

13. a <u>junction</u> station
   Ⓐ confusion   Ⓑ egoism
   Ⓒ connecting   Ⓓ muddle

14. <u>inundate</u> the valley to a depth of three feet
   Ⓐ flood   Ⓑ bemoan
   Ⓒ impede   Ⓓ drench

15. <u>protest</u> low wages
   Ⓐ grab   Ⓑ remonstrate
   Ⓒ melt   Ⓓ deduct

16. <u>soak up</u> information
   Ⓐ remonstrate   Ⓑ complain
   Ⓒ absorb   Ⓓ revolve

17. They <u>adored</u> their leader.
   Ⓐ admired   Ⓑ plunged
   Ⓒ annihilated   Ⓓ imparted

18. <u>exterminate</u> vermin
   Ⓐ object   Ⓑ impede
   Ⓒ grieve   Ⓓ annihilate

19. <u>expensive</u> to buy
   Ⓐ vigorous   Ⓑ devoted
   Ⓒ invariable   Ⓓ high-priced

20. <u>uninterested</u> in the result
   Ⓐ exorbitant   Ⓑ pious
   Ⓒ indifferent   Ⓓ robust

	표제어	품사	동의어와 예문	한글 뜻
1	**adore*** [ədɔ́ːr]	v	worship, admire, esteem, revere, venerate **adore** that kind of music 그 종류의 음악을 좋아하다	숭배하다, 존경하다
2	**agile*** [ǽdʒəl]	a	nimble, quick, light an **agile** movement 재빠른 동작	민첩한, 재빠른
3	**antedate** [ǽntidèit]	v	precede, forerun The hot weather **antedated** my departure for summer vacation. 더운 날씨가 여름 바캉스를 위한 출발을 앞당겼다.	실제보다 앞서가다
4	**award** [əwɔ́ːrd]	v	present (with), grant, give **award** a prize 상을 주다	수여하다
5	**blasphemy** [blǽsfəmi]	n	profanity, irreverence He uttered **blasphemies** against life itself. 그는 삶 그 자체에 대해서 불손한 언동으로 말했다.	신성 모독, 불손한 언동
6	**cunning*** [kʌ́niŋ]	a	clever, skillful, wily, shrewd, tricky, sly a **cunning** trick 교활한 술책	교활한
7	**currency** [kə́ːrənsi]	n	paper money, coinage, bills The bank had authority over the **currency** system. 은행은 통화 시스템을 지배하는 권한을 가졌다. local **currency** 국내 통화	통화, 화폐
8	**deceit*** [disíːt]	n	fraud, deception, cheating Trust is the mother of **deceit**. 믿는 도끼에 발등 찍힌다.	사기, 부정
9	**devout*** [diváut]	a	pious, devoted, saintly a **devout** Christian 독실한 기독교 신자	독실한, 헌신하고 있는
10	**discipline*** [dísəplin]	n	field, field of study training, drill, exercise, practice **Discipline** should be firm but just. 기강은 확고하지만 정당해야 한다.	규율, 기강, 학문의 한 분야
11	**divine** [diváin]	a	sacred, consecrated, heavenly, wonderful Jenny concentrates on God' **divine** nature. 제니는 신의 신성에 전념했다.	신성한
12	**egoism** [íːgouìzm]	n	selfishness, eccentricism ↔ altruism **Egoism** is usually seen in our society as self-centeredness. 이기주의는 자기 중심적으로서 보통 우리사회에서 보여진다.	이기주의
13	**execute*** [éksikjùːt]	v	perform, achieve **execute** our campaign 우리 행사를 진행하다	실행하다
14	**exorbitant** [igzɔ́ːrbətənt]	a	excessive, extreme, outrageous, extravagant The general contractor charged an **exorbitant** price for the new house. 일반 도급자는 새 집에 대하여 터무니없는 가격을 청구했다.	엄청난, 과대한, 터무니없는

15	**expensive** [ikspénsiv]	ⓐ costly, dear, exorbitant Marble stone is an **expensive** building material. 대리석은 비싼 건축자재이다. come **expensive** 비용이 많이 들다	비싼
16	**exterminate*** [ikstá:rmənèit]	ⓥ annihilate, destroy, eradicate, eliminate **exterminate** vermin 해충을 박멸하다	파괴하다, 전멸시키다
17	**greet** [gri:t]	ⓥ accost, salute, hail **greet** a person with a handshake 악수로 사람을 맞이하다	인사하다, 맞아들이다
18	**hardy*** [há:rdi]	ⓐ vigorous, sturdy, robust, stout a **hardy** constitution 건강한 몸	완고한, 튼튼한
19	**hinder*** [híndər]	ⓥ retard, impede, interrupt, obstruct, prevent, restrain be **hindered** in one's study 공부에 방해를 받다	방해하다
20	**hue*** [hju:]	ⓝ tint, color, tone violet **hues** of a twilight sky 반짝이는 하늘의 바이올렛 색깔	색깔, 색조
21	**inundate*** [ínəndèit]	ⓥ flood, deluge, overflow That tourist attraction **inundated** with visitors. 그 관광명소에 방문객들이 몰려들었다.	넘치다
22	**junction** [dʒʌ́ŋkʃən]	ⓝ combination, union, joining, juncture the **junction** of two lines 두 선의 접합점	연결, 접합
23	**keen*** [ki:n]	ⓐ sharp, acute, poignant **keen** competition 격렬한 경쟁 a knife's **keen** edge 칼의 날카로운 끝	격렬한, 예민한
24	**lament*** [ləmént]	ⓥ deplore, grieve, mourn, bemoan **lament** one's hard fate 자신의 불운을 슬퍼하다	한탄하다, 슬퍼하다
25	**maximum** [mǽksəməm]	ⓝ height, peak, top, ceiling the **maximum** water stage 최고 수위	최대, 최고
26	**obligation** [àbləɡéiʃən]	ⓝ requirement, duty, responsibility repay an **obligation** 은혜를 갚다	의무, 책무
27	**plague** [pleig]	ⓝ epidemic, outbreak a **plague** of unknown cause 원인 모를 역병 ⓥ bother, afflict, besiege The professor **plagued** with questions. 교수는 질문 공세에 시달렸다.	전염병 괴롭히다
28	**poison** [pɔ́izn]	ⓝ venom, potion, toxin, pollutant Romeo takes **poison** and dies by Juliet's side. 로미오는 독약을 마시고 줄리엣의 옆에서 죽었다. a deadly **poison** 극약	독, 독약
29	**protest** [próutest]	ⓥ remonstrate, complain, object **protest** low wages 저임금에 항의하다	단언하다, 주장하다
30	**refine*** [rifáin]	ⓥ purify, process, filter, clarify, improve, perfect **refine** the technique 기술을 개선하다	정제하다, 개선하다, 순수해 지다
31	**scheme*** [ski:m]	ⓝ plan, design, project, plot, intrigue, conspiracy the **scheme** of work for the last year 작년도 사업 계획 개요	계획, 설계, 음모

DAY 07

32	**seize** [siːz]	Ⓥ	grasp, grab, clutch, capture, grip	붙들다, 꼭 쥐다
			Macbeth **seized** the throne and proved a strong ruler.	
			맥베스는 왕위를 탈취하고 강한 통치자임을 입증했다.	
33	**soak*** [souk]	Ⓥ	drench, wet, saturate, absorb	흠뻑 젖다, 흡수하다
			↔ dry	
			soak up information 지식을 흡수하다	
34	**superintend** [suːpərinténd]	Ⓥ	supervise, overlook, survey, watch	감독하다, 두루 살피다
			Parents should be **superintend** the children's activities.	
			부모는 아이들의 활동을 두루 살펴야 한다.	
35	**stab** [stæb]	Ⓥ	thrust, plunge, penetrate, perforate	찌르다
			stab the meat 고기를 찌르다	
36	**subtract** [səbtrǽkt]	Ⓥ	deduct, discount, eliminate	빼다, 감하다
			subtract 2 from 5 5에서 2를 빼다	
37	**swivel** [swívəl]	Ⓥ	turn, revolve	회전하다, 흔들다
			He swiveled his hips with song.	
			그는 노래를 하면서 엉덩이를 흔들었다.	
38	**thaw** [θɔː]	Ⓥ	defrost, melt	녹이다
			thaw the frozen fields 언 땅을 녹이다.	
39	**uniform*** [júːnəfɔ̀ːrm]	ⓐ	consistent, invariable, unchanging	단일한, 변화없는
			provide **uniform** measurement standards for everyone	
			모든 사람들을 위한 일정한 측정 기준을 제공하다	
			uniform output 균등한 생산고	
40	**uninterested** [ʌníntərəstid]	ⓐ	unconcerned, indifferent	사심 없는, 무관심한
			uninterested in the result 결과에 대해 관심없는	

01. Journalists have an obligation to be accurate and to tell all sides of a story.
    (A) requirement
    (B) restriction
    (C) determination
    (D) encourage

02. Through intrigue and deceit, Rigoletto's beloved daughter is murdered.
    (A) treachery
    (B) calm
    (C) understandable
    (D) initial

03. California civic leaders and industrialists greeted the first arrival of Chinese laborers with enthusiasm.
    (A) welcomed
    (B) congratulated
    (C) addressed
    (D) accredited

04. Microwave ovens are especially useful for thawing frozen foods and heating soups, vegetables, and leftovers.
    (A) advancing
    (B) evaporating
    (C) exploding
    (D) melting

05. The art of carving is a strenuous and time-consuming process, and ties up the sculptor's money with expensive materials.
    (A) pecuniary
    (B) disadvantaged
    (C) high-priced
    (D) valuable

06. Some agile predators hunt prey by chasing after it on their hind legs or sometimes on all four legs.
    (A) slow
    (B) fierce
    (C) potent
    (D) nimble

07. Dolphins also have good vision, and the entire surface of their bodies has a keen sense of touch.
    (A) sharp
    (B) interested
    (C) enthusiastic
    (D) moderate

08. Until the early 1970's, the governments of most nations specified the rate of exchange for their currencies.
    (A) money
    (B) taxes
    (C) prices
    (D) wealth

09. All devout Muslims hope to make a pilgrimage to Mecca, the birthplace of Muhammad.
    (A) pious
    (B) formidable
    (C) tenacious
    (D) decadent

10. The substance secreted by the Diphtheria bacillus is one of the most potent poisons known to mankind: one milligram is enough to kill 3 1/2 tons of guinea pigs.
    (A) remedies
    (B) vernaculars
    (C) toxins
    (D) pollutants

11. After the artist finds a client, he or she then executes the full-size piece.
    Ⓐ lingers
    Ⓑ rejects
    Ⓒ performs
    Ⓓ groups

12. Japanese sculpture refined a style developed on the Asian mainland.
    Ⓐ thawed
    Ⓑ mounted
    Ⓒ advocated
    Ⓓ improved

13. All types of solar activity become most intense during the maximum phase of a sunspot cycle.
    Ⓐ threshold
    Ⓑ premium
    Ⓒ peak
    Ⓓ first

14. Poverty, crime, and despair plagued the black communities, which came to be known as ghettos.
    Ⓐ comforted
    Ⓑ placated
    Ⓒ besiege
    Ⓓ swamped

15. Most epics describe the deeds of heroes in battle or conflicts between human beings and natural or divine forces.
    Ⓐ sacred
    Ⓑ orbital
    Ⓒ fanciful
    Ⓓ magnified

16. Confucianism aimed to help people live better and more rewarding lives through discipline and instruction in the proper goals of life.
    Ⓐ training
    Ⓑ belief
    Ⓒ field
    Ⓓ reason

17. At the onset of the war, the Virginian government prepared to seize United States arsenal and armory at Harpers Ferry.
    Ⓐ realize
    Ⓑ capture
    Ⓒ render
    Ⓓ deliver

18. The ISO, based in Geneva, Switzerland, tries to establish a uniform size and other specifications to ease the worldwide exchange of goods and services.
    Ⓐ personal
    Ⓑ efficient
    Ⓒ practical
    Ⓓ consistent

19. Human hunters have exterminated such mammals as the blaubok (bluebuck) of Africa, the zebralike quagga, and the Steller's sea cow.
    Ⓐ trapped
    Ⓑ ensnared
    Ⓒ domesticated
    Ⓓ eliminated

20. In a uni-polar neuron, one branch connects to a sensory receptor while another branch leads to a different nerve cell where a specialized junction called a synapse occurs.
    Ⓐ connection   Ⓑ fusion
    Ⓒ distinction   Ⓓ trespass

01. give a person in marriage
    - Ⓐ point
    - Ⓑ wedding
    - Ⓒ sequence
    - Ⓓ apportion

02. gave a brief speech
    - Ⓐ short
    - Ⓑ perplex
    - Ⓒ putative
    - Ⓓ rejoice

03. gain the summit
    - Ⓐ hazard
    - Ⓑ annihilation
    - Ⓒ arrangement
    - Ⓓ top

04. rejoice over the good news
    - Ⓐ delight
    - Ⓑ categorize
    - Ⓒ fade
    - Ⓓ renew

05. resident aliens
    - Ⓐ inadequate
    - Ⓑ putative
    - Ⓒ inhabitant
    - Ⓓ recover

06. amend the club's rules
    - Ⓐ revise
    - Ⓑ chill
    - Ⓒ interpret
    - Ⓓ divulge

07. an insufficient supply of fuel
    - Ⓐ inadequate
    - Ⓑ assumed
    - Ⓒ renew
    - Ⓓ unimportant

08. a miraculous event
    - Ⓐ conclusive
    - Ⓑ compound
    - Ⓒ shedding
    - Ⓓ marvelous

09. be candid with friends
    - Ⓐ outspoken
    - Ⓑ elaborate
    - Ⓒ wedding
    - Ⓓ dreamy

10. emit superheat
    - Ⓐ arrange
    - Ⓑ interpret
    - Ⓒ give off
    - Ⓓ illustrate

11. He is restored to health.
    - Ⓐ degraded
    - Ⓑ diagnosed
    - Ⓒ ended
    - Ⓓ renovated

12. He was humiliated by their laughter.
    - Ⓐ degraded
    - Ⓑ unveiled
    - Ⓒ assembled
    - Ⓓ recognized

13. a handwriting difficult to decipher
    - Ⓐ shadow
    - Ⓑ decode
    - Ⓒ fade
    - Ⓓ revive

14. order over the telephone
    - Ⓐ unveil
    - Ⓑ command
    - Ⓒ accepted
    - Ⓓ construct

15. Someone has disclosed the secret.
    - Ⓐ constructed
    - Ⓑ revealed
    - Ⓒ pursued
    - Ⓓ faded

16. Korea today is beset with perplexing difficulties.
    - Ⓐ negligible
    - Ⓑ trivial
    - Ⓒ confusing
    - Ⓓ deficient

17. won a landslide victory
    - Ⓐ overwhelming
    - Ⓑ dreamy
    - Ⓒ inadequate
    - Ⓓ complicated

18. a submarine boat
    - Ⓐ underwater
    - Ⓑ shadowed
    - Ⓒ peril
    - Ⓓ acme

19. photographs of a far away country
    - Ⓐ poor
    - Ⓑ wonderful
    - Ⓒ distant
    - Ⓓ trivial

20. venture oneself
    - Ⓐ rupture
    - Ⓑ disorder
    - Ⓒ risk
    - Ⓓ sequence

표제어	품사	동의어와 예문	한글 뜻
1 **ailment*** [éilmənt]	n	disease, ill, sickness, disorder a slight **ailment** 가벼운 병	병
2 **amend*** [əménd]	v	revise, alter, correct, fix, modify Manufactuer **amended** the claims of the customer. 생산자는 소비자의 요구에 맞게 고쳤다.	고치다
3 **brief*** [bri:f]	a	short, transitory, transient, temporary Fable is a **brief** fictitious story that teaches a moral. 우화는 도덕을 가르치는 간단한 가상의 이야기이다. a **brief** life 짧은 생애	짧은, 일시적인
4 **candid*** [kǽndid]	a	frank, open, outspoken **candid** friend 거리낌 없이 싫은 소리를 하는 친구	솔직한, 노골적인
5 **chill** [tʃil]	a	cold, coldness, cool a **chill** in the air 쌀쌀한 기운	쌀쌀한
6 **crack** [kræk]	n	break, split, fracture, fissure, rupture, snap a deep, long **crack** in the earth's surface known as a rift valley 열곡으로 알려진 깊고 긴 지구 표면의 균열	균열, 깨진 곳
7 **decipher** [disáifər]	v	decode, interpret, solve **decipher** a code 암호를 풀다	판독하다, 해독하다
8 **demonstrate**** [démənstrèit]	v	① show, illustrate, display, exhibit Farmers **demonstrate** how crops were planted and harvested. 농부는 어떻게 작물을 심고 수확하는지 보여준다. ② prove, authenticate, validate, test **demonstrate** the scientific laws of human behavior 인간 행동의 과학적 법칙을 증명하다	① 보여주다 ② 증명하다
9 **disclose**** [disklóuz]	v	reveal, divulge, unveil **disclose** material information 물질 정보를 밝히다	노출하다, 밝히다
10 **dissipate** [dísəpèit]	v	scatter, waste, vanish To **dissipate** the crowd, she waved her hands. 군중을 흩어서 없어지게 하려고 그녀는 손을 흔들었다.	흩뜨리다, 낭비하다
11 **emit**** [imít]	v	discharge, shed, radiate, give off **emit** light spontaneously 자발적으로 빛을 방출하다	방출하다
12 **faraway** [fá:rəwèi]	a	distant, dreamy photograph of a **faraway** country 멀리 떨어진 시골의 사진	멀리 있는, 꿈꾸는 듯한
13 **frame*** [freim]	v	make, produce, construct, assemble, shape, mold **frame** a state constitution 주 헌법의 틀을 짜다	만들다, 틀을 짜다
14 **humiliate*** [hju:mílièit]	v	degrade, disgrace, shame, embarrass **humiliate** the person 창피를 주다	모욕하다

15	**identify** [aidéntəfài]	Ⓥ	recognize, diagnose **identify** handwriting 필적을 감정하다	확인하다, 간주하다
16	**insufficient**** [ìnsəfíʃənt]	ⓐ	inadequate, deficient, imperfect, incompetent **insufficient** evidence to convict 유죄를 입증할 부족한 증거	충분하지 않은
17	**internal** [intə́:rnl]	ⓐ	inner, inside, interior Emperors intruded into the **internal** affairs of the church. 황제는 교회의 내정에 개입하였다. **internal** trouble 내분	내부의
18	**intricate***** [íntrikət]	ⓐ	complex, elaborate, complicated, compound unable to follow his **intricate** directions 그의 난해한 지시를 따를 수 없는	복잡한, 세밀한
19	**landslide** [lǽndslaid]	ⓐ	overwhelming, conclusive win a **landslide** victory in the election for the mayor 시장 선거에서 압도적인 승리를 거두다	압도적인
		ⓝ	avalanche, landslip The slipping of large amounts of rock and soil occurs in a **landslide**. 다량의 바위와 흙의 미끄러짐이 산사태로 일어난다.	산사태
20	**marriage** [mǽridʒ]	ⓝ	wedding, matrimony Forms of **marriage** is very different across the ages and in all countries. 결혼의 형태는 동서고금을 막론하고 매우 다르다.	결혼
21	**massacre*** [mǽsəkər]	ⓝ	slaughter, annihilation, murder the **Massacre** of the Innocents (헤롯 왕의) 유아 대학살	대량 학살
22	**miraculous*** [mirǽkjuləs]	ⓐ	marvelous, wonderful, incredible a **miraculous** event 경이적인 사건	기적적인, 놀랄만한
23	**order**** [ɔ́:rdər]	ⓝ	① sequence, arrangement alphabetical **order** 알파벳 순서 ② decree, direction, mandate, command give an **order** 명령하다	① 순서, 차례 ② 명령
		Ⓥ	① sequence, arrange, categorize, file, systematize **order** according to last name 성명에 따라 정리하다 ② command, direct, insist, prescribe; request **order** the children to line up 아이들에게 줄 서라고 명령하다 **order** dinner 식사를 주문하다 **order** over the telephone 전화로 주문하다	① 정리하다 ② 명령하다, 지시하다 / 요구하다
24	**perplex*** [pərpléks]	Ⓥ	confuse, puzzle His strange silence **perplexes** me. 그의 심상치 않은 침묵이 나를 당황하게 한다.	당혹하게 하다
25	**putative** [pjúːtətiv]	ⓐ	accepted, assumed, alleged the **putative** father of the child 아이의 아빠로 추정되는	추정되는
26	**rapid*** [rǽpid]	ⓐ	speedy, swift, fast, fleet ↔ slow, sluggish, gradual **rapid** growth of South Korea 한국의 빠른 성장	빠른, 신속한

DAY 08

59

27	**ration** [rǽʃən]	n	① distribution	① 일정한 배급량, 정량
			be put on **rations** 징액 지급을 받다, 배급 받다	
		n	② apportionment	② 배급, 분배, 할당
28	**rejoice** [ridʒɔ́is]	v	delight	기쁘게 하다
			rejoice with the family 가족들과 즐거워하다	
29	**resident** [rézədnt]	a	inhabitant, citizen, local	거주하는
			a **resident** tutor 입주 가정 교사	
30	**resonance** [rézənəns]	n	echo	여운, 반향
			a **resonance** chamber 공명 상자	
31	**restore** [ristɔ́:r]	v	renew, renovate, repair, return, recover	회복하다, 되돌리다
			restore the tax on medicine 약품의 세금을 반환하다	
32	**reveal**** [rivíːl]	v	disclose, divulge, unveil	드러내다, 폭로하다
			reveal the answers 정답을 폭로하다	
33	**sage** [seidʒ]	n	wise man, philosopher, guru, master	현자, 철인
			Confucianism has holy men who are **sages** of intellectual and moral superiority. 유교는 지적이고 도덕적으로 우월한 현인들인 덕이 높은 사람들이 있었다.	
34	**shabby** [ʃǽbi]	a	ragged, beggarly, poor	허름한, 초라한
			shabby behavior 수치스러운 행동	
35	**stalk** [stɔːk]	n	stem	줄기
			cut the **stalk** to plant new tree 새나무를 심기 위해 줄기를 자르다	
		v	pursue, follow, hunt, shadow	몰래 접근하다
			stalk gane 사냥감에 살며시 다가가다	
36	**submarine** [sʌbməríːn]	a	underwater	해저의
			submarine boat 잠수함	
37	**summit***** [sʌmit]	n	peak, apex, pinnacle, acme, top, zenith	정상, 꼭대기
			NATO **summit** meeting 나토 정상 회의	
38	**trifling**** [tráifliŋ]	a	trivial, insignificant, unimportant, negligible, slight, petty	하찮은, 시시한
			appoint with **trifling** pay 하찮은 임금으로 임명되다	
			trifling talk 농담	
39	**vanish*** [vǽniʃ]	v	disappear, end, cease, fade	사라지다, 소실되다
			vanish from sight 시야에서 사라지다	
40	**venture*** [véntʃər]	n	jeopardy, hazard, danger, risk, peril	위험, 모험
		v	risk, peril, hazard	모험하다
			venture oneself 위험을 무릅쓰다, 과감히 나아가다	
			venture forth at night 밤에 과감히 나가다	

01. Obesity can increase the risk of various life-threatening ailments, such as heart disease.
   (A) sicknesses
   (B) young children
   (C) irritations
   (D) falls

02. Harsh conditions are routine for scientists who venture into Antarctica.
   (A) living
   (B) speculate
   (C) challenge
   (D) visit

03. The throat and cavities in the head provide the resonance necessary for singing.
   (A) tune
   (B) capability
   (C) echo
   (D) memory

04. Malnutrition results from eating poor, insufficient food.
   (A) inappropriate
   (B) inadequate
   (C) unstable
   (D) undiluted

05. Plants execute internal motions, such as the flow of sap.
   (A) outward
   (B) stationary
   (C) interior
   (D) breathing

06. Of the organisms that live in the ocean, however, only 250,000 species have been identified.
   (A) catchable
   (B) distinguished
   (C) isolated
   (D) extinguished

07. Mass movement is characterized by the slipping of large amounts of rock and soil, as it occurs in a landslide or mud slide.
   (A) earthquake
   (B) avalanche
   (C) hail
   (D) hurricane

08. The meeting was the first summit conference involving the heads of the Soviet Union and the United States.
   (A) summon
   (B) range
   (C) refuge
   (D) peak

09. Many Germans felt humiliated by their country's defeat in World War I and by the harsh treatment it received under the Treaty of Versailles
   (A) pleased
   (B) eulogized
   (C) encouraged
   (D) embarrassed

10. Virologists (scientists who study viruses) demonstrated in the early 1900's that viruses can cause cancer in animals.
   (A) questioned
   (B) proved
   (C) achieved
   (D) symbolized

11. Pilgrimages are journeys to the sites of holy objects or to places credited with miraculous healing powers.
    Ⓐ ultimate
    Ⓑ incredible
    Ⓒ happy
    Ⓓ always

12. Many photographers used the snap shot to take candid pictures of people who did not know they were being photographed.
    Ⓐ impartial
    Ⓑ unposed
    Ⓒ fantastic
    Ⓓ vague

13. When a neutrino collides with an atom in the ice, another subatomic particle, called a muon, is produced while emitting a flash of blue light.
    Ⓐ releasing
    Ⓑ minimizing
    Ⓒ attracting
    Ⓓ bringing

14. Over one hundred artificial languages have been framed by men in recent times, but the three are by far more widely known and used than any of the others.
    Ⓐ accepted
    Ⓑ destroyed
    Ⓒ eradicated
    Ⓓ constructed

15. Like detectives, astronomers gather indirect clues and carefully piece them together to reveal the story about the gases that exist between the galaxies.
    Ⓐ establish
    Ⓑ unveil
    Ⓒ compose
    Ⓓ cover

16. Solitary predators generally stalk their prey by slinking and hiding, while many of these hunters possess coats that blend in with their surroundings.
    Ⓐ observe   Ⓑ trace
    Ⓒ stem   Ⓓ hunt

17. As air travels down the opposite slopes of a mountain range, the temperature rises, the relative humidity decreases, and the clouds thin out or vanish.
    Ⓐ thicken
    Ⓑ emerge
    Ⓒ disappear
    Ⓓ change

18. One putative cause of the deformities, which was excess exposure to ultraviolet radiation, came under suspicion almost as soon as the malformations were discovered.
    Ⓐ supposed
    Ⓑ significant
    Ⓒ chief
    Ⓓ essential

19. Now that the human genome has been deciphered, much of the fanfare surrounding it has transferred to the proteome, the full complement of proteins made from the genetic "blue-prints" stored in our cells.
    Ⓐ deformed
    Ⓑ destroyed
    Ⓒ devised
    Ⓓ decoded

20. Egyptian mathematics had many practical applications, ranging from the surveying of fields after an annual flood, to making the intricate calculations necessary when building pyramids.
    Ⓐ complex   Ⓑ interest
    Ⓒ important   Ⓓ regular

01. procure the necessary funds
    Ⓐ acquire   Ⓑ continue
    Ⓒ rest   Ⓓ exhibit

02. the infamous massacre of Indians
    Ⓐ notorious   Ⓑ outdated
    Ⓒ vintage   Ⓓ unrivaled

03. a partial summary of the book
    Ⓐ uncompleted   Ⓑ rebelled
    Ⓒ disgraceful   Ⓓ retiring

04. contract oneself out of an obligation
    Ⓐ pertain   Ⓑ reminisce
    Ⓒ bargain   Ⓓ leave

05. diverse aspects of human life
    Ⓐ coax   Ⓑ various
    Ⓒ vertical   Ⓓ coarse

06. a matchless beauty
    Ⓐ harm   Ⓑ captivate
    Ⓒ despondent   Ⓓ unequalled

07. a contagious ward
    Ⓐ infectious   Ⓑ respective
    Ⓒ conscientious   Ⓓ unrivaled

08. an upright member of our organization
    Ⓐ biased   Ⓑ desperate
    Ⓒ manifold   Ⓓ honorable

09. organic life
    Ⓐ natural   Ⓑ unequaled
    Ⓒ modest   Ⓓ methodical

10. remain faithful
    Ⓐ suffer   Ⓑ stay
    Ⓒ encase   Ⓓ scale

11. suffered great mental anguish
    Ⓐ disturbance   Ⓑ agony
    Ⓒ hurt   Ⓓ anxiety

12. the timid new student
    Ⓐ righteous   Ⓑ shy
    Ⓒ incomparable   Ⓓ mean

13. enchant everyone in the room
    Ⓐ recall   Ⓑ demur
    Ⓒ fascinate   Ⓓ scream

14. supplement our diet with vitamins
    Ⓐ anxiety   Ⓑ interruption
    Ⓒ uprising   Ⓓ extension

15. Air will compress.
    Ⓐ squeeze   Ⓑ dissimilar
    Ⓒ ignite   Ⓓ outdated

16. kindle the sky
    Ⓐ combine   Ⓑ inflame
    Ⓒ charm   Ⓓ shout

17. a tumult of noise
    Ⓐ disturbance   Ⓑ plumage
    Ⓒ hurt   Ⓓ compact

18. embedded in hard sandstones
    Ⓐ encased   Ⓑ charmed
    Ⓒ acquired   Ⓓ coaxed

19. advocate of free market policies
    Ⓐ affiliate   Ⓑ trigger
    Ⓒ support   Ⓓ retract

20. revolt against her ballet training
    Ⓐ incomparable   Ⓑ mutiny
    Ⓒ harm   Ⓓ stay

표제어	품사	동의어와 예문	한글 뜻
1 advocate** [ǽdvəkèit]	v	proponent, support, argue for, speak for **advocate** peace of Iraq 이라크의 평화를 옹호하다	옹호하다
2 affable [ǽfəbl]	a	agreeable, very sociable, corteous Henry was clever, practical, **affable**, and scrupulous. 헨리는 영리하고 경험이 풍부하고 사교적이면서 양심적이다.	붙임성 있는, 정중한
3 anguish* [ǽŋgwiʃ]	n	suffering, agony, pain sensitive to the **anguish** of everyday experience 일상적인 경험의 고뇌에 민감한 mental **anguish** 정신적 고통	고통, 고뇌
4 associate** [əsóuʃièit]	v	connect, join, pertaining to, combine, affiliate **associate** with a particular symbols 특정 기호와 관련되다	관련하다, 가입하다
5 bargain* [bá:rgən]	v	contract, trade, sell, deal I **bargain** (that) he will be there on time. 나는 그가 제시간에 그곳에 꼭 올 거라는 것을 보증한다.	팔다, 계약하다, 보증하다
6 cajole [kədʒóul]	v	persuade; tempt, entice, beguile; entrap The mother tried to **cajole** her unwilling infant into eating. 그 엄마는 먹기 싫어하는 유아를 먹이려고 달래기를 시도하였다.	설득하다 / 부추기다 / 모함하다
7 compress* [kəmprés]	v	condense, squeeze **compress** one's lip 입을 굳게 다물다 The snow was **compressed** into ice. 눈이 얼음으로 응고되었다.	압축하다, 응고하다
8 contagious* [kəntéidʒəs]	a	communicable, infectious, transmissible a **contagious** laugh 전염되는 웃음	전염성의
9 contract* [kántrækt]	n	compact, bargain signed a new **contract** 새로운 계약에 서명하다	계약, 계약서
	v	negotiate, bargain; constrict, condense ↔ expand a **contracting** home market 위축되는 내수 시장	계약하다 / 수축 [응축] 하다
10 convince* [kənvíns]	v	persuade, influence, urge, coax **convince** the public of the same views 같은 견해로 대중을 설득하다	확신시키다, 설득하다
11 diverse* [divə́:rs]	a	various, divergent, diversified, dissimilar **diverse** aspects of human life 인생의 여러양상	다양한
12 emanate [émənèit]	v	emerge, spring, arise, derive, originate The light from the porch will **emanate** into the yard. 베란다로부터 그 빛이 뒷뜰로 퍼져나왔다.	발산하다, 퍼지다
13 embed* [imbéd]	v	encase, fix, fasten, root **embed** in hard sandstones 딱딱한 모래 암석에 새겨 넣다	끼워놓다, (마음에) 새기다, 고정시키다

14	**enchant** [intʃǽnt]	v	fascinate, captivate, charm The forest **enchanted** the people to do outdoor activities 그 숲은 사람들이 야외활동을 하도록 매혹시켰다 be **enchanted** with ~로 황홀해지다, ~에 매혹되다	매혹시키다
15	**infamous*** [ínfəməs]	a	notorious, disgraceful the **infamous** massacre of Indians 잔인한 인디언 학살	악명 높은
16	**kindle** [kíndl]	v	ignite, inflame, fire, trigger **kindle** a fire 불을 붙이다	시작하다, 유발시키다
17	**matchless***** [mǽtʃlis]	a	incomparable, unrivaled, unequaled, unparalleled **matchless** in experience 경험에서 비길 데 없는	무적의, 비길 데 없는
18	**mischief** [místʃif]	n	harm, injury, damage, hurt come to **mischief** 재난을 당하다, 손해를 입다	해악, 악독, 손해
19	**mount** [maunt]	v	ascend, climb, scale **mount** a hill 산에 오르다 **mount** in gold 금을 박아 넣다	올라가다, 장치하다
20	**organic** [ɔːrgǽnik]	a	natural, biological; systematic, methodical Soil consists chiefly of minerals mixed with **organic** matter. 토양은 주로 무기물과 유기물이 혼합되어 이루어져 있다.	유기체의 / 체계적인
21	**paralyze** [pǽrəlàiz]	v	benumb be **paralyzed** with fear 두려움 때문에 얼어붙다	무력하게 하다
22	**partial*** [pɑ́ːrʃəl]	a	biased, prejudiced, unfair, incomplete a **partial** eclipse of the sun 부분 일식	불공평한, 편파적인, 부분적인
23	**participate*** [pɑːrtísəpèit]	v	share, be involved in **participate** in a play 공연하다 Many political scientists **participate** in government programs as advisers. 많은 정치학자들이 고문으로 정부 프로그램에 참여한다.	함께하다, 참여하다
24	**plumage** [plúːmidʒ]	n	feathers, down, plumes The male and female of that bird have the different **plumage.** 암컷과 수컷 새가 서로 다른 깃털을 갖고 있다.	깃털
25	**procure***** [proukjúər]	v	acquire, gain, get, secure, win, obtain **procure** employment 직업을 얻다	획득하다
26	**recall** [rikɔ́ːl]	v	① remember, recollect, reminisce, muse ↔ forget I don't **recall** the exact number. 나는 그 숫자가 생각나지 않는다. ② revoke, withdraw, cancel, retract, rescind ↔ enact, affirm **recall** a promise 약속을 취소하다	① 상기하다 ② 철회하다
27	**remain***** [riméin]	v	① stay, wait, rest ↔ leave, depart **remain** at work 작업 중이다 ② last, continue, abide, prevail ↔ abandon **remain** a loyal friend 성실한 친구로 남다	① 남다 ② 잔존하다

28	**reverence**** [révərəns]	n	respect, worship, veneration, awe	경의
			show them the appropriate **reverence** and respect	
			그들에게 적절한 경의와 존경을 표하다	
			at the **reverence** of ~을 존경하여	
29	**revolt** [rivóult]	v	rebel, mutiny, resist	반항하다, 반역하다
			rise in **revolt** 반기를 들다, 반란을 일으키다	
30	**scream** [skri:m]	v	shriek, cry, shout	비명을 지르다
			scream with terror 공포로 소리지르다	
31	**spine** [spain]	n	backbone, vertebrate, spinal; barb, spur, needle	등뼈, 척추 / 가시
			live longer than any other animal with a **spine**	
			등뼈를 가진 다른 어떤 동물보다 오래살다	
32	**strata** [stréitə]	n	soil layer	지층, 층, 계급
			Sediment accumulates in layers known as **strata**.	
			충적물이 지층으로 알려진 층으로 축적된다.	
33	**suffocation** [sʌfəkéiʃən]	n	asphyxiation, putting to death	질식
			The fumes caused vomiting and **suffocation**.	
			매연은 구토와 질식의 원인이 된다.	
34	**supplement** [sʌpləmənt]	n	extension	보충
			a **supplement** to Time 「타임지」의 부록	
		v	add, augment	보충하다
			Broadcast today **supplemented** by images and text.	
			오늘 방송은 이미지와 텍스트로 보충하였다.	
35	**thereby** [ðɛərbái]	ad	thus	그러므로, 그것에 의하여
			Thereby hangs a tale.	
			거기에는 까닭이 있다.	
36	**timid** [tímid]	a	shy, fearful, modest, demure	겁 많은
			(as) **timid** as a rabbit 매우 겁이 많은	
37	**tumult*** [tjú:məlt]	n	commotion, disturbance, agitation, uprising	소란, 법석
			a **tumult** of noise 시끄러운 소리	
38	**upright*** [ʌpràit]	a	erect, vertical, perpendicular; conscientious, righteous	수직의 / 올바른, 똑바로 선
			an **upright** person 올바른 사람	
39	**vulgar*** [vʌlgər]	a	coarse, mean, rude	저속적인, 통속적인
			vulgar language 품위 없는 언사	
40	**wed** [wed]	v	marry; unite, combine	결혼하다 / 결합하다
			wed oneself to the cause of the poor	
			가난한 사람들의 복지를 위하여 헌신하다	

01. The League of Nations and the United Nations both advocated disarmament.
   (A) supported
   (B) remained
   (C) maintained
   (D) soothed

02. Wallace participated in decisions that lead to the development of the atomic bomb.
   (A) anticipated
   (B) experienced
   (C) took part
   (D) explained

03. Quark-gluon plasmas are produced when a collision compresses nuclei into a fraction of their normal volume.
   (A) separates
   (B) beats
   (C) condenses
   (D) bursts

04. Most patent laws follow the principle that a patent is a bargain between the inventor and society.
   (A) contract
   (B) order
   (C) joke
   (D) plan

05. Physical therapists help paralyzed stroke patients to move to prevent muscles from stiffening.
   (A) immobilized
   (B) painful
   (C) distressed
   (D) handicapped

06. Babies whimper when in distress and scream when frightened.
   (A) whisper
   (B) laugh
   (C) mutter
   (D) cry

07. Johnson objected to many comic sexual passages, which he considered vulgar.
   (A) intimate
   (B) impolite
   (C) personal
   (D) absurd

08. Gorillas occasionally made a tumult of noise.
   (A) weird
   (B) honest
   (C) agitation
   (D) tranquilness

09. Early in his administration, Roosevelt tried to convince the business world that he would not interfere in it's affairs.
   (A) assemble
   (B) persuade
   (C) enliven
   (D) success

10. Many of army officers revolted against the government.
   (A) remained
   (B) convinced
   (C) advocated
   (D) rebel

11. Faced with mounting debts, the decision to call it a day was inevitable.
    (A) hang
    (B) supporting
    (C) increasing
    (D) descending

12. A gentleman was someone who was truly reverent in worship and sincere in respecting his father and his ruler.
    (A) elucidated
    (B) blazed
    (C) solemn
    (D) respectful

13. In the Napoleonic War, the countries of Central and South America revolted against Spanish rule.
    (A) fought
    (B) rebelled
    (C) protested
    (D) violated

14. In 1603, the Scottish king, James VI, became James I of England, thereby uniting the English and Scottish crowns.
    (A) in return for
    (B) by the means of
    (C) by the way
    (D) in spite of

15. As a historian, a war reporter, and a biographer, Churchill showed a matchless command of the English language.
    (A) memorable
    (B) incomparable
    (C) faultless
    (D) impressive

16. Contagious diseases such as diphtheria and whooping cough spread rapidly from person to person.
    (A) Incomplete
    (B) Tangible
    (C) Infectious
    (D) Immunizing

17. Throughout history, sculpture has been closely associated with architecture, partly because similar materials and skills are used in both fields.
    (A) worshipped in
    (B) connected with
    (C) do away with
    (D) understood by

18. Smart cards have one or more embedded computer chips that store information about the user's bank balance and purchases.
    (A) calculated
    (B) added
    (C) inserted
    (D) precise

19. Many of the physical characteristics that distinguish human beings from other primates are related to the ability of people to stand upright and walk on two legs.
    (A) straight
    (B) proper
    (C) conscientious
    (D) precise

20. When the train broke down, some passengers managed to get home by bus, some by car, and those that remained spent the night on the train.
    (A) thrived
    (B) stayed
    (C) reappeared
    (D) published

01. qualify an opinion
  Ⓐ entitle   Ⓑ add
  Ⓒ quest   Ⓓ abate

02. The news astonished her.
  Ⓐ referred   Ⓑ surprised
  Ⓒ invigorated   Ⓓ twisted

03. It is my destiny.
  Ⓐ fate   Ⓑ belief
  Ⓒ quest   Ⓓ impairment

04. barren land
  Ⓐ reasonable   Ⓑ lifeless
  Ⓒ supported   Ⓓ desirous

05. explore the vast continent
  Ⓐ sterile   Ⓑ anxious
  Ⓒ large   Ⓓ agog

06. as stiff as a poker
  Ⓐ keen   Ⓑ devout
  Ⓒ reverent   Ⓓ rigid

07. adhere to a creed
  Ⓐ principle   Ⓑ consolation
  Ⓒ umpire   Ⓓ detriment

08. cite as an authority
  Ⓐ love   Ⓑ mention
  Ⓒ advocate   Ⓓ esteem

09. enliven one's spirits
  Ⓐ surprise   Ⓑ amaze
  Ⓒ collide   Ⓓ invigorate

10. the dialogue in a play
  Ⓐ communication   Ⓑ cherish
  Ⓒ occupation   Ⓓ force

11. scratch one's head
  Ⓐ claw   Ⓑ clash
  Ⓒ curtail   Ⓓ abridge

12. breach of trust
  Ⓐ confidence   Ⓑ colliding
  Ⓒ principles   Ⓓ communication

13. tried to reduce the noise
  Ⓐ animate   Ⓑ mock
  Ⓒ diminish   Ⓓ mark

14. I have an antipathy to snakes.
  Ⓐ fight   Ⓑ impairment
  Ⓒ judge   Ⓓ hatred

15. jeer at strangers
  Ⓐ ridicule   Ⓑ quest
  Ⓒ claw   Ⓓ astound

16. appeal to the referee
  Ⓐ judge   Ⓑ belief
  Ⓒ fate   Ⓓ faith

17. a perennial flower
  Ⓐ year-round   Ⓑ reverent
  Ⓒ ruthless   Ⓓ unbending

18. sanguinary language
  Ⓐ inflexible   Ⓑ lenient
  Ⓒ lifeless   Ⓓ ruthless

19. solace oneself with
  Ⓐ ridicule   Ⓑ comfort
  Ⓒ advocate   Ⓓ revere

20. Some programs conflicted with each other.
  Ⓐ trusted   Ⓑ repeated
  Ⓒ collided   Ⓓ jeered

표제어	품사	동의어와 예문	한글 뜻
1 **antipathy*** [æntípəθi]	n	dislike, disgust, hatred ↔ sympathy has an **antipathy** for computers 컴퓨터에 반감을 갖다	반감
2 **astonish** [əstániʃ]	v	amaze, surprise, astound, shock, startle, stun The news **astonished** her. 그 소식은 그녀를 깜짝 놀라게 했다.	놀라다
3 **avail*** [əvéil]	v n	make use benefit, advantage without **avail** 무익하게, 보람 없이	사용하다 이용
available* [əvéiləbl]	a	accessible, at hand made the office **available** 사무실을 이용 가능하게 만들다	이용 가능한
4 **barren*** [bǽrən]	a	sterile, lifeless, infertile, unproductive **Barren** deserts stretch across the southwest. 황량한 사막이 남서쪽을 가로질러 뻗어 있다.	황량한
5 **cite** [sait]	v	refer to, mention **cite** this article in your blog 당신의 블로그에 이 글을 인용하다	인용하다, 언급하다
6 **conflict** [kənflíkt]	v	collide, clash, contend, fight, combat a **conflict** of arms 무력 충돌, 교전	갈등하다, 충돌하다
7 **creed*** [kri:d]	n	belief, principles It is the only **creed** used in this religion. 이것이 이 종교에서 사용하는 유일한 신조이다. adhere to a **creed** 주의를 신봉하다	신조
8 **destiny*** [déstəni]	n	fate, doom the man of **destiny** 운명을 지배하는 사람	운명
9 **dialogue** [dáiəlɔ̀:g]	n	conversation, communication the **dialogue** in a play 연극에서의 대화	대화, 회화
10 **dilemma** [dilémə]	n	predicament, strait catch in a painful **dilemma** 고통스러운 궁지에 빠지다	곤경
11 **eager** [í:gər]	a	keen, anxious He is very **eager** in his studies. 그는 공부에 매우 열심이다.	열망하는
12 **enliven** [inláivən]	v	invigorate, animate, give life to **enliven** one's spirits 호연지기를 기르다	활기를 띠게 하다, 북돋우다
13 **fundamental*** [fʌndəméntl]	a	necessary, indispensable, vital the **fundamental** form 기본형 All chemists share certain **fundamental** ideas. 모든 화학자들은 어떤 중요한 아이디어를 공유한다.	필수적인, 중요한
14 **injury**** [índʒəri]	n	harm, damage, detriment, impairment Shock can occur with any serious illness or **injury**. 충격은 어떤 심각한 질병이나 부상으로 발생할 수 있다. serious knee **injury** 심각한 무릎 부상	해, 피해, 부상

15	jeer [dʒiər]	v	scoff, mock, ridicule	비웃다, 조소하다
			jeer at a person's idea ~의 생각을 우습게 여기다	
16	parallel [pǽrəlèl]	a	corresponding	평행의, 같은 방향의
			Parallel lines are defined as lines that never cross.	
			평행선은 절대 교차하지 않는 선으로 정의할 수 있다.	
17	perennial [pərénial]	a	year-round	다년생의, 지속하는
			Plants can be categorized as annuals, biennials, or **perennials**.	
			식물은 일년생, 이년생 또는 다년생으로 나눌 수 있다.	
			a **perennial** flower 사철 피는 꽃	
18	preside over [prizáid ouvər]	v	manage	관장하다
			A priest **presided** over the grove and the oak tree.	
			신부는 숲과 떡갈나무를 관장했다.	
19	qualify [kwáləfài]	v	fit, suit, entitle, equip	~에게 자격을 주다, 수정하다
			qualify as a plant doctor over 20 years ago	
			20년 전에 식물의사로서 자격을 갖추다	
			qualify an opinion 의견을 수정하다	
20	reduce** [ridjú:s]	v	diminish, decrease, abridge, curtail, abate, lessen	줄이다, 감소시키다
			reduce the risk of damage 상처 입을 위험을 줄이다	
21	referee [rèfərí:]	n	umpire, judge	심판원
			appeal to the **referee** 심판에게 항의하다	
22	regularly* [régjulərli]	ad	routinely	정기적으로
			Television networks **regularly** show dramas and comedies.	
			TV 방송망이 정기적으로 드라마와 코메디를 상영한다.	
			a **regular** customer 단골 손님	
23	religious* [rilídʒəs]	a	pious, devout, reverent; faithful, consistent	신앙심 깊은, 경건한 / 종교적인
			↔ impious	
			Much of the world's greatest music is **religious**.	
			세상의 많은 위대한 음악들이 종교적이다.	
			a **religious** service 예배	
24	salvage [sǽlvidʒ]	n	recovery, rescue, saving, salvation	해난 구조
			a **salvage** boat 구난선(구조선)	
25	sanguinary [sǽŋgwənèri]	a	bloody, bloodthirsty, cruel, ruthless	피비린내 나는, 잔인한, 지 독한
			a **sanguinary** fool 지독한 바보	
26.	scratch [skrætʃ]	v	mark, claw, cut, withdraw, cancel	긁다
			scratch one's head (난처해서) 머리를 긁다	
27	solace [sáləs]	n	comfort, consolation	위안, 위로
			find **solace** in music 음악으로 위안을 찾다	
28	stiff* [stif]	a	① rigid, solid, firm, unbending, inflexible	① 굳은, 단단한
			↔ pliant	
			a **stiff** piece of leather 딱딱한 가죽 조각	
			② strict, severe, stern, austere	② 엄격한
			↔ lenient	
			a **stiff** penalty for anti-drug 마약 방지의 엄한 벌	

29	**stress** [stres]	n	emphasis, accent, force, tension Shock can be caused by emotional **stress**. 충격은 감정적인 긴장으로 일어날 수도 있다.	강조, 압력, 긴장
		v	emphasize, dwell on Intellectuals reject war and **stress** peace education. 지식인들이 전쟁을 반대하고 평화 교육을 강조한다.	강조하다, 스트레스를 받다 [주다]
30	**synonymous** [sinánəməs]	a	equivalent, identical, similar, interchangeable Martha Graham is a name **synonymous** with modern dance. 마사 그레이엄은 현대 무용과 동일한 이름이다.	동의어인, 같은 뜻의
31	**terrain** [təréin]	n	ground, country, land, topography Most off-road races are long-distance events run on rough, desert **terrain**. 대부분의 오프로드 경주는 거친 사막 지형에서 실행하는 장거리를 가는 행사이다.	지역, 지형, 지세, 영역
32	**treasure** [tréʒər]	n	value, prize find a buried national **treasure** 묻혀 있던 국보를 찾다	보물, 보배
		v	cherish, esteem, love, revere **treasure** their advice 그들의 충고를 명심하다	소중히 하다, 존경하다
33	**trust** [trʌst]	n	confidence, belief, faith, credit Children need a feeling of **trust** and security. 어린이들은 신뢰와 안전의 감정이 필요하다.	신임, 의뢰
		v	believe, depend, rely, count on He was **trusted** his best friends. 그는 그의 가장 친한 친구를 믿었다.	믿다, 의존하다
34	**urge**** [əːrdʒ]	v	advocate, force, impel, press, instigate **urge** silence to everyone 모두에게 침묵을 강요하다	주장하다, 몰아대다
35	**valid*** [vǽlid]	a	just, sound, logical, cogent, legal conduct a **valid** conclusion 타당한 결론을 도출하다	근거가 확실한, 정당한
36	**vast**** [væst]	a	large, enormous, tremendous, immense, extensive traverse a **vast** expanse of desert 광막한 사막을 횡단하다	광대한, 거대한
37	**vocation** [voukéiʃən]	n	business, occupation, pursuit, profession Knowledge and skills need for success in many **vocations**. 지식과 기술은 많은 직업에서의 성공을 위해 필요하다.	천직, 직업, 사명감
38	**warp** [wɔːrp]	v	bend, deform, twist, contort Water will stain and **warp** a book. 물이 책을 물들게 하고 뒤틀리게 할 것이다. **warped** mind 삐뚤어진 마음	뒤틀다, 휘게 하다
39	**wildly** [wáildli]	ad	furiously Offender made **wildly** exaggerated claims. 위반자는 난폭하게 과장된 주장을 했다.	난폭하게, 미친듯이
40	**wrath** [ræθ]	n	anger, ire, rage, resentment, indignation, fury incur the **wrath** of human rights activist 인권 활동가의 분노를 초래하다 the **wrath** of God 신의 진노	분노, 노여움

01. The United States astonished the world
with its wartime output.
Ⓐ astute
Ⓑ astounded
Ⓒ archaic
Ⓓ articulated

02. Although beaten and scorned, Quixote still
believed in his heroic destiny.
Ⓐ accomplishment
Ⓑ life
Ⓒ fate
Ⓓ honor

03. Animal life evolved and flourished only
after plants became available as food.
Ⓐ obtainable
Ⓑ affordable
Ⓒ reasonable
Ⓓ disposable

04. The Himalaya consists of several parallel
mountain ranges.
Ⓐ vertical
Ⓑ horizontal
Ⓒ alongside
Ⓓ biased

05. Visit your doctor and dentist regularly.
So that doctors and dentists guard your
health.
Ⓐ recklessly
Ⓑ hesitantly
Ⓒ greatly
Ⓓ routinely

06. Oceangoing tugs take part in rescue and
salvage work.
Ⓐ protection
Ⓑ rescue
Ⓒ alignment
Ⓓ concealment

07. The moon's outer crust seems stiff and
strong, but much remains to be learned
about its interior.
Ⓐ sticky
Ⓑ rigid
Ⓒ dense
Ⓓ woven

08. From the very beginning, the Quakers
emphasized inward spiritual experiences
rather than specific creeds.
Ⓐ concepts
Ⓑ beliefs
Ⓒ movements
Ⓓ studies

09. A companion volume was devoted to
modern work and was enlivened by
interviews with sculptors.
Ⓐ embellished
Ⓑ invigorated
Ⓒ incarved
Ⓓ trimmed

10. Abolitionists and black leaders urged that
a war must be fought to end slavery, and
they demanded the use of black troops.
Ⓐ advocated
Ⓑ created
Ⓒ permitted
Ⓓ prepared

DAY 10

73

11. Furniture makers use plastic to produce cabinet doors and tabletops that look like wood but are easier to clean and do not warp.
    Ⓐ break
    Ⓑ contort
    Ⓒ saturate
    Ⓓ change

12. Vocational high school graduates must complete a year of special study before they enter college.
    Ⓐ Profession
    Ⓑ Society
    Ⓒ Philosophy
    Ⓓ Uniform

13. Metaphysics is the study of the fundamental nature of reality and existence and the essences of things.
    Ⓐ paramount
    Ⓑ great
    Ⓒ basic
    Ⓓ economical

14. Traditional Asian sculpture was developed primarily to communicate religious and political ideas, for ritual purposes, or to glorify a ruler.
    Ⓐ aristocratic
    Ⓑ devout
    Ⓒ commercial
    Ⓓ social

15. Students were eager to attend Professor Micheal Kim's lecture on Friday night and the discussion afterwards.
    Ⓐ wealthy
    Ⓑ knowledgeable
    Ⓒ regular
    Ⓓ enthusiastic

16. This amendment shall not be so construed as to affect the election or term of any senator chosen before it becomes a valid part of the Constitution.
    Ⓐ impractical
    Ⓑ authentic
    Ⓒ reliable
    Ⓓ honest

17. Even in a complex society like ours, with all of its conflicting traditions and theories, most ethical decisions do not present us with such a dilemma.
    Ⓐ predicament
    Ⓑ discussion
    Ⓒ agreement
    Ⓓ stage

18. With continued international cooperation and care for the Antarctic environment, the frozen continent will continue to serve as a vast treasure of information about the Earth's past, present, and future.
    Ⓐ indication
    Ⓑ record
    Ⓒ warehouse
    Ⓓ rare things

19. By stressing certain elements, a painter can make his pictures easier to understand and bring out some particular mood or theme.
    Ⓐ emphasizing
    Ⓑ adjusting
    Ⓒ controlling
    Ⓓ exhausting

20. The International Committee of the Red Cross, located in Geneva, serves as a neutral intermediary for the protection of war victims during conflicts between nations.
    Ⓐ unsuits   Ⓑ invalids
    Ⓒ unintelligent Ⓓ confrontations

01. an enlarged photograph
   Ⓐ perplexed   Ⓑ rumbled
   Ⓒ interrupted   Ⓓ augmented

02. probe the source of the funds
   Ⓐ complain   Ⓑ investigate
   Ⓒ laud   Ⓓ assert

03. Terror invaded our minds.
   Ⓐ abandoned   Ⓑ attacked
   Ⓒ evacuated   Ⓓ relinquished

04. an agile movement
   Ⓐ nimble   Ⓑ light
   Ⓒ wily   Ⓓ devout

05. Trust is the mother of deceit.
   Ⓐ drill   Ⓑ juncture
   Ⓒ chaos   Ⓓ fraud

06. seize a person by the hand
   Ⓐ grieve   Ⓑ forerun
   Ⓒ grasp   Ⓓ remonstrate

07. reveal the answers
   Ⓐ disclose   Ⓑ renovate
   Ⓒ arrange   Ⓓ vanish

08. keeps student interest at a maximum
   Ⓐ height   Ⓑ remonstration
   Ⓒ plot   Ⓓ confusion

09. a slight ailment
   Ⓐ break   Ⓑ crack
   Ⓒ disease   Ⓓ frame

10. The plot of this story is very intricate.
   Ⓐ soiled   Ⓑ smutty
   Ⓒ deficient   Ⓓ complicated

11. vanish from sight
   Ⓐ disappear   Ⓑ file
   Ⓒ solve   Ⓓ embarrass

12. bargain with individual clients
   Ⓐ trade   Ⓑ persuade
   Ⓒ encase   Ⓓ secure

13. be paralyzed with terror
   Ⓐ united   Ⓑ presented
   Ⓒ benumbed   Ⓓ rebelled

14. stress point in this case
   Ⓐ disgust   Ⓑ fate
   Ⓒ accent   Ⓓ indignation

15. made the office available
   Ⓐ animated   Ⓑ comforted
   Ⓒ deformed   Ⓓ usable

16. scream with terror
   Ⓐ mutiny   Ⓑ depart
   Ⓒ present   Ⓓ shout

17. vulgar language
   Ⓐ retiring   Ⓑ coarse
   Ⓒ infectious   Ⓓ manifold

18. salvage a few things from the fire
   Ⓐ impel   Ⓑ recover
   Ⓒ press   Ⓓ esteem

19. fall into a dilemma
   Ⓐ detriment   Ⓑ doom
   Ⓒ predicament   Ⓓ disgust

20. treasure the memory of my first home run
   Ⓐ withdraw   Ⓑ scoff
   Ⓒ reverse   Ⓓ esteem

01. Many Americans disregard traditional marriage patterns.
    - (A) ceremony
    - (B) custom
    - (C) engagement
    - (D) matrimony

02. A pilot can figure out the true air speed by checking the indicator and the outside air temperature.
    - (A) calculate
    - (B) express
    - (C) entangle
    - (D) consume

03. Many space vehicles include facilities for heating frozen and chilled food.
    - (A) cooled
    - (B) fuel
    - (C) tested
    - (D) lifted

04. Latin-American novel has been the unprecedented international attention.
    - (A) planned
    - (B) discovered
    - (C) unexample
    - (D) documented

05. Before the 1400's, the vast majority of people in Europe were illiterate.
    - (A) untamed
    - (B) geographical
    - (C) unbalanced
    - (D) enormous

06. Car accidents have become a major cause of death and injury throughout the world.
    - (A) fright
    - (B) hurt
    - (C) sorrow
    - (D) disease

07. Our knowledge about Socrates' ideas and methods comes mainly from the dialogues written by his pupil Plato.
    - (A) conversations
    - (B) descriptions
    - (C) fantasies
    - (D) witticisms

08. The hardest minerals can scratch glass.
    - (A) glitter
    - (B) revealed
    - (C) mark
    - (D) clasp

09. Your intellectual background and verbal memory change and grow with each reading experience.
    - (A) short
    - (B) technical
    - (C) spoken
    - (D) written

10. The names in the Smithsonian Museum are famous for the highlights in their collections.
    - (A) softness
    - (B) distortions
    - (C) extensions
    - (D) emphases

11. Much of cell biology is devoted to the study of structures and functions in specialized cells.
    (A) is dedicated to
    (B) is composed of
    (C) is main of
    (D) is part of

12. In 1982, Thatcher won praise for her decisive handling of a conflict with Argentina.
    (A) strength
    (B) applause
    (C) right
    (D) vote

13. Most road races are open to all runners, and many races award prize money to the winners.
    (A) deny
    (B) recommend
    (C) guarantee
    (D) grant

14. Both lice and scabies mites cause the skin to itch and are contagious.
    (A) resistant
    (B) bad
    (C) infectious
    (D) harmful

15. In a process called metastasis, malignant tumors can invade surrounding tissues and spread to distant parts of the body through the circulatory system.
    (A) transform
    (B) tear off
    (C) penetrate
    (D) disperse

16. Like regular radio newscasts, daily TV news programs provide only a brief account of a relatively few stories.
    (A) short
    (B) pleasant
    (C) bright
    (D) wet

17. If a person does not get enough riboflavin, cracks may develop on the skin at the corners of the mouth.
    (A) cysts
    (B) abscess
    (C) indigestions
    (D) fissures

18. Modern methods of communication are so rapid that a buyer can find out the price a seller is asking for, even though he is a thousand miles away.
    (A) quick
    (B) complete
    (C) careful
    (D) economical

19. Even if dealings are restricted to a particular location, dealers may still consist wholly or in part of agents acting on behalf of clients far away.
    (A) at a long distant
    (B) nearby
    (C) at home
    (D) abroad

20. Computer artists usually adjust many visual effects, such as camera focus and transparency, during the rendering phase.
    (A) forms
    (B) alter
    (C) concerns
    (D) depicts

01. Monochromatic color schemes use variations of a color, such as in several shades.
    - Ⓐ pictures
    - Ⓑ designs
    - Ⓒ frames
    - Ⓓ architectures

02. In circuits, the collision of material atoms hinders the flow of electrons which causes them to lose some energy through heat.
    - Ⓐ requires
    - Ⓑ loosens
    - Ⓒ measures
    - Ⓓ impedes

03. A small portion of the material remained to form a nebula that began to rotate and contract.
    - Ⓐ deflate
    - Ⓑ weaken
    - Ⓒ constrict
    - Ⓓ elongate

04. A lot of volunteers take part in rescue and salvage work.
    - Ⓐ recycling
    - Ⓑ recovering
    - Ⓒ significance
    - Ⓓ survivorship

05. Each color differs from all the others by degrees of hue, lightness, and chroma.
    - Ⓐ substance
    - Ⓑ color
    - Ⓒ secretion
    - Ⓓ element

06. Livestock owners may shoot, trap, or poison wild animals that they consider dangerous to their herds.
    - Ⓐ contaminate
    - Ⓑ capture
    - Ⓒ exterminate
    - Ⓓ irradicate

07. Many of the students felt that domestic work did not hinder their studies.
    - Ⓐ require
    - Ⓑ measure
    - Ⓒ loosen
    - Ⓓ impede

08. The universe of a cell is quite complex and diverse.
    - Ⓐ surrounding
    - Ⓑ various
    - Ⓒ small
    - Ⓓ particular

09. An infamous crime is one punishable by death or imprisonment.
    - Ⓐ notorious
    - Ⓑ dreaded
    - Ⓒ loathed
    - Ⓓ investigated

10. A person may qualify with a degree in any discipline, plus three years of work experience.
    - Ⓐ manipulate
    - Ⓑ certify
    - Ⓒ succeed
    - Ⓓ balance

11. Among black African and American Indian groups, traditional dances remain a vital part of religious ceremonies, as well as a form of entertainment.
Ⓐ helpful
Ⓑ clinical
Ⓒ acquired
Ⓓ important

12. Innovative pictures and witty texts create a humorous retelling of traditional tales.
Ⓐ Beautiful
Ⓑ Extraordinary
Ⓒ Revolutionary
Ⓓ Glamorous

13. Fainting occurs when there is an insufficient supply of blood to the brain for a short period of time.
Ⓐ inappropriate
Ⓑ undiluted
Ⓒ unstable
Ⓓ inadequate

14. After Napoleon's downfall in 1815, the monarchy was restored in Spain, and it seemed possible that the Holy Alliance might try to restore Spain's colonies as well.
Ⓐ disappeared
Ⓑ reconstructed
Ⓒ remained
Ⓓ retreated

15. Famine, plagues, and other natural calamities caused a radical decline in population.
Ⓐ placations
Ⓑ comforts
Ⓒ epidemic
Ⓓ swamps

16. If the same number is subtracted from each side of an equation, the new numbers remain equal.
Ⓐ qualified
Ⓑ deducted
Ⓒ added
Ⓓ asserted

17. Some chronic diseases, such as diabetes and kidney disease, are also linked to miscarriages.
Ⓐ permanent
Ⓑ long-term
Ⓒ epidemic
Ⓓ familiar

18. When an author is preparing a manuscript, he or she should double space and leave margins on the top, bottom, and the sides of every page.
Ⓐ centers
Ⓑ peripheries
Ⓒ covers
Ⓓ contents

19. The hero of Don Quixote is a Spanish landowner who enliven his monotonous life by reading fictional tales about knights of the past, which he believes to be true and accurate.
Ⓐ simple
Ⓑ unnatural
Ⓒ stationary
Ⓓ disgraceful

20. Most chemists of the early 1800's believed that organic compounds could be produced only with the aid of a vital force, the life force present in plants and animals.
Ⓐ artificial
Ⓑ corporate
Ⓒ systematic
Ⓓ biological

무분별한	- rash, reckless, heedless, indiscreet, imprudent
압도적인	- landslide, overwhelming, conclusive, avalanche
악명 높은	- infamous, notorious, disgraceful
피비린내 나는	- sanguinary, bloody, bloodthirsty, cruel, ruthless
굳은, 단단한	- stiff, rigid, solid, firm, unbending, inflexible
표면의	- superficial, shallow, external, outward
겸손한	- decent, right, proper, nice, pure, modest
민첩한	- agile, nimble, quick, light
교활한	- cunning, clever, skillful, wily, shrewd, tricky, sly
무적의	- matchless, incomparable, unrivaled, unequaled, unparalleled
황량한	- barren, sterile, lifeless, infertile, unproductive
확대하다	- enlarge, extend, augment, amplify, magnify, expand
피신시키다, 비우다	- evacuate, shelter, remove, leave, abandon, desert, relinquish
삼키다	- swallow, eat, gorge, engulf, devout, inhale, consume
전멸시키다	- exterminate, annihilate, destroy, eradicate, eliminate
해독하다	- decipher, decode, interpret, solve
노출하다, 밝히다	- disclose, reveal, divulge, unveil
긁다	- scratch, mark, claw, cut, withdraw, cancel
전염병	- plague, epidemic, outbreak
위생	- sanitation, hygiene, health, condition
독	- poison, venom, potion, toxin, pollutant
병	- ailment, disease, ill, sickness, disorder
고통	- anguish, suffering, agony, pain
소란, 법석	- tumult, commotion, disturbance, agitation, uprising
피해, 상처	- injury, harm, damage, detriment, impairment

THE BIG BANG THEORY

The Big Bang theory is the ❶ <u>prevailing</u> cosmological model for the early development of the universe, began with a big explosion some 15 billion years, which is considered the age of the universe. At this time, the universe was in an ❷ <u>extremely</u> hot and dense state and began expanding rapidly. ❸ <u>Radiation</u> and cosmic materials have been emitted outward ever since. After the initial expansion, the universe cooled sufficiently to allow energy and these materials to be ❹ <u>converted into</u> gas, and then huge clouds were denser than average.

These cores or gravitational centers, started pulling at the surrounding materials in a process called gravitational condensation. Though simple atomic nuclei formed rapidly after the Big Bang, thousands of years passed before the first electrically neutral atoms formed. The majority of atoms that were produced by the Big Bang are hydrogen, along with helium and traces of lithium. Giant clouds of these primordial elements later ❺ <u>coalesced</u> through gravity to form stars, planets, supernovae and galaxies.

In 1964, the observational confirmation supporting the Big Bang came with the discovery of cosmic microwave background radiation (CMBR), thought to be a ❻ <u>remnant</u> from the original explosion. The Big Bang offers a ❼ <u>comprehensive</u> explanation for a broad range of observed ❽ <u>phenomena</u>, including the abundance of ❾ <u>light</u> elements, the cosmic microwave background, and large scale structure. The core ideas of the Big Bang—the expansion, the early hot state, the formation of light elements, and the formation of galaxies—are derived from these and other observations. Since then, astrophysicists have ❿ <u>incorporated</u> observational and theoretical additions into the Big Bang model, and serves as the framework for current investigations of theoretical cosmology.

The word that closest meaning to

1. prevailing	Ⓐ depending	Ⓑ trifling	Ⓒ cunning	Ⓓ predominating
2. extremely	Ⓐ typically	Ⓑ enthusiastically	Ⓒ very	Ⓓ putatively
3. radiation	Ⓐ emission	Ⓑ junction	Ⓒ expansion	Ⓓ divergence
4. converted into	Ⓐ qualified as	Ⓑ transformed to	Ⓒ unchanged to	Ⓓ categorized into
5. coalesced	Ⓐ amend	Ⓑ united	Ⓒ clustered	Ⓓ aroused
6. remnant	Ⓐ random	Ⓑ accelerating	Ⓒ coarse	Ⓓ residual
7. comprehensive	Ⓐ popular	Ⓑ fixed	Ⓒ inclusive	Ⓓ placid
8. phenomena	Ⓐ happening	Ⓑ miracle	Ⓒ logics	Ⓓ tumult
9. light	Ⓐ brightness	Ⓑ dark	Ⓒ weak	Ⓓ not heavy
10. incorporated	Ⓐ integrated	Ⓑ demonstrated	Ⓒ convinced	Ⓓ enlarged

빅뱅이론

빅뱅이론The Big Bang theory은 우주의 나이라고 여겨지는 15억 년 전에 큰 폭발a big explosion로 시작된 우주의 초기 발달the early development of the universe에 관한 보편화된prevailing 우주론cosmological 모델이다. 이때부터 우주는 매우 뜨거웠고extremely hot 밀도가 짙어진 상태dense state가 되었고 급격하게 확장하기expanding rapidly 시작하였다. 복사에너지radiation와 우주물질cosmic materials이 그때부터 줄곧 바깥쪽으로 방사되어 왔다have been emitted outward. 초기의 팽창initial expansion 이후에 우주는 에너지를 줄 정도로to allow energy 충분히 냉각되었고, 그러한 물질들은 가스로 전환되었고to be converted into gas 그 다음에 커다란 구름이 보통 수준보다 더 밀도가 짙어졌다denser than average.

이러한 중심핵cores 또는 중력중심은 중력집중gravitational condensation이라고도 부르는 과정으로 주변의 물질들을 끌어당기기pulling at the surrounding materials 시작했다. 단순한 핵이 빅뱅 이후에 빠르게 형성되었음에도 최초의 전자적으로 중성인 원자electrically neutral atoms가 형성되기 전까지 수천 년이 지나야 했다. 빅뱅에 의해 생성된 대부분의 원자는 수소 이외에 헬륨과 미량의 리튬traces of lithium이었다. 이런 원시 원소의 엄청난 구름은 나중에 별과 행성planets과 초신성supernovae과 은하galaxies를 형성하도록 중력에 의하여 합쳐졌다coalesced through gravity.

1964년에 빅뱅이론을 지지하는 실측적인 확정observational confirmation이 최초의 폭발the original explosion로부터 남은 잔재물a remnant인 것으로 생각되는 우주(마이크로파)배경복사의 발견으로 따라왔다. 빅뱅이론은 가벼운 원소의 존재abundance of light elements와, 우주마이크로파배경과 거대구조를 포함하는 광범위한 관찰된 현상observed phenomena에 대한 포괄적인 설명a comprehensive explanation을 제공한다. 폭발, 초기의 뜨거운 상태, 가벼운 원소의 형성과 은하의 형성에 대한 빅뱅의 핵심적인 개념the core ideas은 이런 관찰과 다른 관찰로부터 비롯되었다. 그때부터 천체물리학자들astrophysicists은 빅뱅모델에 실측적 이론적 추가물theoretical additions을 통합하였고, 이론우주학theoretical cosmology의 현행 연구current investigations를 위한 뼈대the framework로서 역할을 하고 있다.

1. ⓓ   2. ⓒ   3. ⓐ   4. ⓑ   5. ⓑ
6. ⓓ   7. ⓒ   8. ⓐ   9. ⓓ   10. ⓐ

DAY 11 Daily Checkup

01. grant a degree
    - Ⓐ cleave
    - Ⓑ fascinate
    - Ⓒ bestow
    - Ⓓ deliver

02. commemorate the milestone in our history
    - Ⓐ fascinate
    - Ⓑ encourage
    - Ⓒ redeem
    - Ⓓ celebrate

03. Air is the vehicle of sound.
    - Ⓐ carrier
    - Ⓑ receptible
    - Ⓒ velocity
    - Ⓓ enthusiasm

04. feel awkward
    - Ⓐ discriminated
    - Ⓑ cumbersome
    - Ⓒ insolent
    - Ⓓ impudent

05. sever husband and wife
    - Ⓐ rescue
    - Ⓑ divide
    - Ⓒ gather
    - Ⓓ survive

06. be wary of explicit statements
    - Ⓐ hard
    - Ⓑ definite
    - Ⓒ insolent
    - Ⓓ licit

07. attentive audience
    - Ⓐ willing
    - Ⓑ rude
    - Ⓒ watchful
    - Ⓓ cumbersome

08. a spontaneous cure
    - Ⓐ disrespectful
    - Ⓑ dexterous
    - Ⓒ voluntary
    - Ⓓ unambiguous

09. outstrip (all) competitors
    - Ⓐ surpass
    - Ⓑ rend
    - Ⓒ sustain
    - Ⓓ upset

10. inflate the lung
    - Ⓐ crush
    - Ⓑ laud
    - Ⓒ expand
    - Ⓓ teeter

11. a subjective evaluation
    - Ⓐ brazen
    - Ⓑ rare
    - Ⓒ individual
    - Ⓓ unskilled

12. the fury of the elements
    - Ⓐ wrath
    - Ⓑ stranger
    - Ⓒ conspiracy
    - Ⓓ theme

13. masked treachery
    - Ⓐ information
    - Ⓑ cure-all
    - Ⓒ conveyance
    - Ⓓ treason

14. defer making a decision
    - Ⓐ survive
    - Ⓑ fascinate
    - Ⓒ capsize
    - Ⓓ yield

15. an absolutely inappropriate remark
    - Ⓐ unsuitable
    - Ⓑ instant
    - Ⓒ lawful
    - Ⓓ contradictory

16. stroll along the beach
    - Ⓐ teeter
    - Ⓑ redeem
    - Ⓒ branch out
    - Ⓓ ramble

17. an impertinent detail
    - Ⓐ definite
    - Ⓑ lawful
    - Ⓒ unsuitable
    - Ⓓ impudent

18. intrigued by her story
    - Ⓐ wandered
    - Ⓑ attracted
    - Ⓒ diverged
    - Ⓓ gathered

19. sever all relations with Japan
    - Ⓐ crush
    - Ⓑ entrust
    - Ⓒ swell
    - Ⓓ cut off

20. Her voice wobbled.
    - Ⓐ conferred
    - Ⓑ teetered
    - Ⓒ endured
    - Ⓓ greeted

표제어	품사	동의어와 예문	한글 뜻
1 **alchemy** [ǽlkəmi]	n	medieval chemistry At one time, **alchemy** was a major source of chemical knowledge. 한때 연금술은 화학지식의 주요 원천이었다.	연금술
2 **amass*** [əmǽs]	v	collect, gather, accumulate **amass** a competence 상당한 자산을 모으다	축적하다
3 **attentive** [əténtiv]	a	heedful, alert, watchful, careful very **attentive** to his colleague 그의 동료들에게 매우 친절한	주의깊은, 세심한, 친절한
4 **awkward**** [ɔ́:kwərd]	a	clumsy, unskillful, cumbersome, inept ↔ agile, dexterous **awkward** on the dance floor 공연장에서 어색한	어색한, 서투른
5 **clue**** [klu:]	n	solution, information, hint, suggestion, indication light on a **clue** 우연히 실마리를 발견하다 Fossils provide **clues** to changes on the earth. 화석은 지구에서의 변화에 대한 단서를 제공한다.	실마리, 단서
6 **commend** [kəménd]	v	entrust, laud, praise, exalt, applaud be highly **commanded** from the public for his role 그의 역할에 대해 대중으로부터 격찬 받다	칭찬하다
7 **commemorate** [kəmémərèit]	v	celebrate, remember, salute Many rituals **commemorate** events in the history of religions. 많은 종교의식이 종교 역사에서 주요 사건을 기념한다.	기념하다, 축하하다
8 **conjecture***** [kəndʒéktʃər]	n	speculation hazard a **conjecture** 어림짐작으로 말하다	사색, 추측, 억측
9 **defer*** [difə́:r]	v	postpone, yield **defer** payment 지불을 미루다	연기하다, 미루다
10 **distinguish**** [distíŋgwiʃ]	v	discriminate, differentiate, distinct **distinguish** colors 색깔을 식별하다	구별하다, 식별하다
11 **explicit*** [iksplísit]	a	clear, unambiguous, definite be wary of **explicit** statements 명확한 언급을 경계하다	명백한, 명확한, 애매하지 않은
12 **fury*** [fjúəri]	n	rage, anger, wrath fly into a **fury** 격노하다	분노, 격노
13 **hardly**** [háːrdli]	ad	scarcely, rarely, barely, seldom I can **hardly** believe it. 거의 믿어지지 않는다	거의 ~않다
14 **impertinent*** [impə́:rtənənt]	a	insolent, impudent, rude, brazen, disrespectful an **impertinent** detail 관계없는 세부사항	무례한, 건방진, 주제넘은
15 **inappropriate*** [ìnəpróupriət]	a	unsuitable **inappropriate** behavior as a top officials 고위 관리로서의 부적절한 행동	적당하지 않은

16	**inflate** [infléit]	v	swell, expand **inflate** the balloon for the children 아이들을 위해 풍선을 불다	부풀리다, 확장하다
17	**instantly** [ínstəntli]	ad	immediately, instantaneously die **instantly** 곧 죽다	즉각적으로, 곧
18	**intrigue*** [intrí:g]	v	plot, conspire; fascinate, attract **intrigued** particularly by your experience at school 학교에서 당신의 경력이 특히 흥미를 돋우다	음모를 꾸미다 / 흥미를 끌다
19	**legitimate**** [lidʒítəmət]	a	licit, legal, lawful a **legitimate** conclusion 논리적인 결론	합법적인, 정당한
20	**mania** [méiniə]	n	excitement, enthusiasm He has a **mania** for gambling. 그는 도박에 미쳐 있다.	열광, 열중의 대상
21	**mournful** [mɔ́:rnfəl]	a	plaintive, doleful, dismal, sad, unhappy, miserable A sad person may play a **mournful** tune on a guitar. 슬픈 사람은 기타나 피아노로 슬픈 노래를 연주할 것이다.	슬픔에 잠긴, 애처로운
22	**outsider** [àutsáidər]	n	stranger, incomer, visitor become a political **outsider** as a Korean in Congress 국회 개회 중에 한국인으로서 정치적인 문외한이 되다	낯선 사람, 문외한
23	**outstrip**** [autstrip]	v	surpass **outstrip** my rivals 경쟁자들을 이기다	따라잡다, 능가하다
24	**overwhelm**** [òuvərhwélm]	v	overpower, crush, capsize, upset, overturn **overwhelm** the enemy 적군을 전복시키다	압도하다, 전복시키다
25	**panacea** [pænəsí:ə]	n	cure-all, elixir **panacea** for all our problems 우리의 모든 문제들을 위한 만병통치약	만병통치약
26	**paradoxical*** [pærədáksikəl]	a	contradictory, inconsistent, dilemmatic sound **paradoxical** 역설적으로 들리다	역설의
27	**plot*** [plat]	n	① chart, scheme, intrigue, conspiracy **plot** for a person's assassination 누구의 암살 모의 ② patch, site a **plot** of land 경작 구역	① 음모, 계략 ② 구역
28	**radiate**** [réidièit]	v	spread out, emit, branch out, diverge **radiate** in all directions 사방팔방으로 퍼지다	펼치다
29	**reservoir** [rézərvwà:r]	n	receptacle a **reservoir** of knowledge 지식의 축적	저장소, 용기
30	**salute** [səlú:t]	v	greet **salute** one's superior officer with a hand 상관에게 거수경례를 하다	인사하다
31	**sever*** [sévər]	v	cut off, separate, divide, cut, cleave, rend **sever** all relations with Japan 일본과 모든 관계를 단절하다	절단하다
32	**spontaneous**** [spantéiniəs]	a	voluntary, willing, uncompelled the **spontaneous** reaction of a child 아이의 자발적인 반응	자발적인
33	**stroll** [stroul]	v	ramble, wander, roam, saunter **stroll** down the ramp 비탈길을 걸어 내려가다	배회하다

34	**subjective*** [səbdʒéktiv]	a	personal, individual	주관의, 개인적인
			a **subjective** evaluation 개인적 평가	
35	**texture** [tékstʃər]	n	grain, feel, surface; structure	직물, 질감 / 구조
			Texture refers to the surface appearance or feel of the items.	
			질감은 표면의 모양이나 항목의 느낌을 말한다.	
			the **texture** of a society 사회 구조	
36	**thus** [ðʌs]	prep	therefore	그러므로, 이와 같이
			Worked hard **thus**, the research will succeed.	
			열심히 일했으므로 연구는 성공할 것이다.	
			thus far 지금까지는 (= so far)	
37	**treachery** [trétʃəri]	n	betrayal, treason	배반, 배신
			masked treachery 감춰진 음모	
38	**unquenchable** [ʌnkwéntʃəbl]	a	quenchless, insatiate, unsatiable	막을 수 없는, 억제할 수 없는
			Children has **unquenchable** curiosity about every new things.	
			아이들은 모든 새로운 것들에 대한 막을 수 없는 호기심이 있다.	
39	**vehicle*** [víːikl]	n	a means of conveying, carrier, conveyance, transport	운송수단, 자동차
			a trackless **vehicle** 무한궤도차	
40	**wobble** [wábl]	v	teeter	흔들거리다
			Her voice **wobbled**.	
			그녀의 목소리가 떨렸다.	

Practice Test 11

01. The six-passenger vehicle was powered by batteries located under the seats.
   - (A) escape
   - (B) conveyance
   - (C) ends
   - (D) material

02. The Western Front hardly moved for 31/2 years in spite of the fierce combat.
   - (A) carefully
   - (B) probably
   - (C) scarcely
   - (D) slowly

03. In Philadelphia, Lincoln heard of a report on an assassination plot.
   - (A) conspiracy
   - (B) chart
   - (C) keeping
   - (D) preparation

04. An imperial power could amass riches by looting subjugated lands of valuable resources.
   - (A) harsh
   - (B) accumulate
   - (C) gear
   - (D) warm up

05. Reservoirs in the Catskills help supply New York City with water.
   - (A) Laboratories
   - (B) Reserves
   - (C) Reactors
   - (D) Showcases

06. Men and women not in uniform salute by placing their right hand over the heart.
   - (A) inform
   - (B) celebrate
   - (C) greet
   - (D) grant

07. It is legitimate to use force to secure the observance of international agreements.
   - (A) meaningless
   - (B) denied
   - (C) infamous
   - (D) legal

08. Every year a music festival is held to commemorate the anniversary of this event.
   - (A) remember
   - (B) learn
   - (C) replay
   - (D) cooperate

09. Until the 1600's, alchemy was the major source of chemical knowledge.
   - (A) chemistry
   - (B) medieval science
   - (C) physics
   - (D) biology

10. Inflation may be caused by wage increases that outstrip productivity.
   - (A) clumsy
   - (B) surpass
   - (C) sustain
   - (D) constitute

11. Digital cameras, which were introduced in the early 1990's, can produce an image almost instantly.
    (A) perfectly
    (B) clearly
    (C) directly
    (D) regularly

12. Flares can radiate much light into space, and astronomers can photograph them against the light background of the sun.
    (A) soak
    (B) expand
    (C) emit
    (D) shoot

13. Washington commended Knox publicly for his role in the campaign, and he was promoted to brigadier general.
    (A) praised
    (B) perceived
    (C) disputed
    (D) restrained

14. In *The Merchant of Venice*, Shakespeare combined comic intrigue with a vivid portrait of hatred and greed.
    (A) plot
    (B) aggravation
    (C) offended
    (D) terrified

15. The spontaneous interest in work under primitive conditions was reinforced by a number of social values attached to it.
    (A) simultaneous
    (B) constant
    (C) incredible
    (D) impromptu

16. Because different parts of the body grow at different rates during puberty, many adolescents temporarily look and feel awkward.
    (A) acquainted
    (B) dynamic
    (C) clumsy
    (D) weird

17. During the winters of 1835-1836, the people of Texas decided to sever their relations with Mexico because of their dissatisfaction towards the Mexican government.
    (A) connect   (B) terminate
    (C) create   (D) broaden

18. By analyzing the growth rings of living and dead trees, scientists can distinguish between years of relatively favorable weather from years of stressful weather.
    (A) inventive
    (B) classify
    (C) different
    (D) eminent

19. Some disabilities can make it difficult for a child to get along with others, and they may cause the child to behave inappropriately.
    (A) quaintly
    (B) unsuitably
    (C) indiscreetly
    (D) peculiarly

20. Eastern orthodox Christiandom was overwhelmed by and gave way to Western influences at the end of the seventeenth century.
    (A) choosen
    (B) popularized
    (C) overcomed
    (D) founded

DAY 12 Daily Checkup

01. man of ability
Ⓐ nuisance   Ⓑ antagonism
Ⓒ talent   Ⓓ abeyance

02. an idle carpenter
Ⓐ reliable   Ⓑ unoccupied
Ⓒ comic   Ⓓ compassionate

03. lack of logic
Ⓐ skill   Ⓑ group
Ⓒ enigma   Ⓓ reason

04. according to trustworthy information
Ⓐ inconstant   Ⓑ humorous
Ⓒ comic   Ⓓ reliable

05. His influence slowly decreased.
Ⓐ pointed   Ⓑ postponed
Ⓒ lessened   Ⓓ jumped

06. a different kind of leadership
Ⓐ sort   Ⓑ enmity
Ⓒ abeyance   Ⓓ problem

07. the decline in the power
Ⓐ reasons   Ⓑ deterioration
Ⓒ antagonisms   Ⓓ problems

08. an area with a sparse population
Ⓐ stanch   Ⓑ relentless
Ⓒ inexorable   Ⓓ scattered

09. rescued his plays from oblivion
Ⓐ problem   Ⓑ rudiment
Ⓒ abeyance   Ⓓ expedition

10. merciless treatment
Ⓐ ruthless   Ⓑ inappropriate
Ⓒ elevated   Ⓓ eminent

11. pacify the angry customers
Ⓐ ameliorate   Ⓑ tantalize
Ⓒ spoil   Ⓓ traverse

12. wanted to suspend the party
Ⓐ irritated   Ⓑ scrutinized
Ⓒ interrupted   Ⓓ refused

13. things animate and inanimate
Ⓐ dependable   Ⓑ precarious
Ⓒ lifeless   Ⓓ inconstant

14. traverse an office
Ⓐ cross   Ⓑ originate
Ⓒ furnish   Ⓓ amend

15. lofty mountains
Ⓐ vacant   Ⓑ high
Ⓒ unsuited   Ⓓ numerous

16. imminent danger
Ⓐ arrogant   Ⓑ impending
Ⓒ solitary   Ⓓ inexorable

17. agro-chemical residues
Ⓐ antagonisms   Ⓑ problems
Ⓒ expeditions   Ⓓ remainders

18. the innumerable stars in the sky
Ⓐ a little   Ⓑ sluggish
Ⓒ countless   Ⓓ inappropriate

19. be frustrated in one's ambition
Ⓐ subdued   Ⓑ gleamed
Ⓒ vaulted   Ⓓ disappointed

20. report the cessation of business
Ⓐ end   Ⓑ trouble
Ⓒ question   Ⓓ neglect

표제어	품사	동의어와 예문	한글 뜻
1 **ability**** [əbíləti]	n	① skill, talent, dexterity, knack, gift ↔ inability She had great athletic **ability**. 그녀는 대단한 운동 능력을 가졌다. ② power, capacity, means the **ability** to pay 지불할 능력	① 재능 ② 능력
2 **beam*** [bi:m]	v	shine, gleam, glitter, radiate, ray Spot-light **beamed** down on a small stage. 조명이 작은 무대 위를 비추었다.	빛나다, 반짝이다
	n	ray, flash, glint a **beam** of hope 희망의 빛	광선, (전자의) 빔
3 **bit**** [bit]	a	somewhat, a little That sounds was listened a **bit** technically. 그 소리들은 약간 기교적으로 들렸다. **bits** and pieces 잡동사니	소량의
4 **bother*** [báðər]	n v	trouble, nuisance, annoyance, worry annoy, worry, harass, disturb He **bothers** me to lend him money. 그는 내게 돈을 꾸어 달라고 조른다.	성가신 일 귀찮게 하다, 걱정하다
5 **cessation** [seséiʃən]	n	stop, halt, end report the **cessation** of business 폐업 신고를 내다	중지, 중단
6 **crush*** [krʌʃ]	v	① shatter, smash, crumble compress, pulverize **crush** (out) the juice from grapes 포도에서 과즙을 짜내다 ② overpower, conquer, subdue, stifle **crush** a rebellion 반란군을 진압하다	① 부수다, 깨다 ② 진압하다
7 **decay*** [dikéi]	v	deteriorate, decline, decompose, rot, spoil **decay** in a muddy swamp 진흙 늪에서 썩게 하다	부패하다, 타락하다
8 **decline*** [dikláin]	v	① refuse, reject ② decrease, degenerate, diminish, dwindle ↔ increase For a time, oil consumption **declined**. 한동안 오일 소비가 감소했다.	① 거절하다 ② 약하게 하다, 쇠퇴하다
	n	dwindling, decay, deterioration a **decline** in the power of Europe 유럽 세력의 쇠퇴	감소, 쇠퇴
9 **desiccate** [désikèit]	v	dry out, dehydrate **desiccate** the slice of apple 사과 절편을 건조시키다	건조시키다, 생기를 잃게 하다
10 **frustrate*** [frʌstreit]	v	① disappoint, irritate, baffle, discourage, tantalize **frustrate** a plan to assassinate the general 장군을 암살할 계획을 좌절시키다 ② block, foil, thwart, annul, nullify The new law **frustrated** his plans. 새로운 법은 그의 계획을 쓸모없게 하였다.	① 좌절하다 ② 무효가 되다

11	**hostility** [hastílǝti]	n	enmity, antagonism stir **hostility** against Japanese people in the United States 미국에 있는 일본사람에 대하여 적대감이 일다 suspend **hostilities** 전투 행위를 중지하다	적대, 적대 [전투] 행위
12	**idle*** [áidl]	a	① lazy, sluggish, indolent, slothful ↔ industrious, diligent an **idle** person 게으른 사람 ② unoccupied, vacant, empty ↔ busy an idle carpenter 한가한 목수 ③ foolish, vain, unnecessary, unproductive, ineffective It is **idle** to say that ~라고 말하는 것은 무의미하다	① 게으른 ② 비어 있는, 한가한 ③ 무의미한
13	**imminent*** [ímǝnǝnt]	a	impending, be about to, take place **imminent** danger in wartime 전시의 절박한 위험	임박한
14	**inanimate** [inǽnǝmǝt]	a	lifeless stones and other **inanimate** objects 돌과 다른 무생물들	죽은, 생기 없는
15	**inapt** [inǽpt]	a	unsuited, unsuitable, inappropriate, unfit **inapt** handling of dangerous organic solvents 위험한 유기용매의 부적절한 취급	적절치 못한
16	**ineffective** [iniféktiv]	a	empty, devoid, destitute an **ineffective** manager 무능한 관리자	효과적이지 못한
17	**innumerable*** [injú:mǝrǝbl]	a	countless, numberless, numerous the **innumerable** stars in the sky 하늘의 무수한 별들	셀 수 없이 많은, 무수한
18	**issue*** [íʃu:]	n	subject, point, problem, question, flow today's **issue** of a paper 오늘자 발행 신문의 화제	문제, 화제, 발행, 유출
19	**kind*** [kaind]	a	benign, humane, compassionate ↔ mean, hostile a **kind** comment 친절한 설명	친절한, 인간적인, 애정 있는
		n	group, sort, type, class, species make up another **kind** of social group 또다른 종류의 사회그룹을 만들다	종류, 일종
20	**lofty*** [lɔ́:fti]	a	① towering, high, elevated, sublime ↔ low, sunken a **lofty** mountain 높은 산 ② grand, distinguished, noted, eminent a **lofty** career 뛰어난 경력 ③ proud, haughty, arrogant, vain ↔ modest **lofty** ideals 고상한 이상	① 매우 높은 ② 구별되는, 뛰어난 ③ 오만한, 고상한
21	**logic** [ládʒik]	n	reason, good sense Mathematics is based upon **logic**. 수학은 논리에 기초를 두고 있다. lack **logic** 어불성설이다	논리학, 논리
22	**lonely** [lóunli]	a	abandoned, lone, solitary, apart He was **lonely** and unhappy during his school years. 그는 학창 시절 동안 외롭고 불행했었다. a **lone** traveler 고독한 여행자	고립된, 외로운

23	**merciless***** [mə́:rsilis]	ⓐ	ruthless, pitiless, relentless, inexorable **merciless** treatment 사정없는 취급	무자비한, 무정한
24	**oblivion** [əblíviən]	ⓝ	neglect, abeyance **oblivious** of country life 염두에 없는 시골 생활	망각
25	**pacify*** [pǽsəfài]	ⓥ	calm, tranquilize, assuage, ameliorate **pacify** an angry man 화난 사람을 달래다	평화롭게 하다, 진정되다
26	**repair**** [ripέər]	ⓥ	mend, remodel, amend, fix, renew ↔ impair **repair** a motor 모터를 수리하다	수선하다
27	**research*** [risə́:rtʃ]	ⓥ	investigate, study, examine, scrutinize **research** cancer 암을 연구하다	연구하다, 조사하다
28	**residue** [rézədjù:]	ⓝ	remainder, remnant Researcher detected the pesticides **residue** on plants and soils. 연구원이 식물과 토양에서 살충제 잔류를 검출하였다.	잔여, 나머지, 잔류물
29	**revenue*** [révənjù:]	ⓝ	income, gain, proceeds the public **revenue** 국고 세입	세입, 수익금
30	**riddle** [rídl]	ⓝ	enigma, conundrum, puzzle set a **riddle** 수수께끼를 내다	수수께끼
31	**rudiment*** [rú:dəmənt]	ⓝ	basic master the **rudiments** of grammar 문법의 기초를 끝내다	기본
32	**ruthless***** [rú:θlis]	ⓐ	pitiless, unrelenting, relentless, inexorable, cruel, harsh was a strong and **ruthless** leader 강하고 무자비한 리더였다 punish **ruthlessly** 가차없이 벌을 주다	무자비한, 무정한
33	**sparse*** [spa:rs]	ⓐ	scattered, meager ↔ dense live a **sparse** population in a vast area 광대한 지역에 희박한 인구가 살다	성긴, 희박한
34	**spring** [spriŋ]	ⓥ	leap, jump, bound, hop, vault; emerge, originate **spring** up 뛰어오르다 **spring** over a rock 바위 위로 뛰어 오르다	도약하다 / 발생하다
35	**suspend***** [səspénd]	ⓥ	① hang, defer, postpone, delay **suspend** one's judgment 판결을 보류하다 ② stop, cease, interrupt, arrest He has the power to **suspend** the law if necessary. 그는 만약 필요하다면 법을 중지시킬 힘을 가지고 있다.	① 연기하다 ② 중지하다, 보류하다
36	**traverse** [trǽvə:rs]	ⓥ	cross, pass over, go across **traverse** a plain across a railway 철로를 따라 평원을 가로지르다	가로지르다
37	**trustworthy** [trʌstwə́:rði]	ⓐ	reliable, true, stanch, dependable, credible Gould was a **trustworthy** person. 굴드는 미더운 사람이었다.	신뢰할 수 있는, 믿을 수 있는
38	**unstable***** [ʌnstéibl]	ⓐ	variable, unsteady, precarious, inconstant, unsettled Family life in medieval Europe was **unstable**. 중세유럽의 가족생활은 불안정했다.	불안정한, 변하기 쉬운
39	**voyage*** [vɔ́iidʒ]	ⓝ	journey, trip, cruise, sailing, expedition go for a **voyage** round the world 세계를 일주하는 항해를 가다	항해, 여행
40	**witty** [wíti]	ⓐ	amusing, clever, comic, humorous have a smooth and **witty** tongue 넉살을 부리다	재치 있는, 익살맞은

01. Cities grow, and factories spring up.
    A increase
    B close
    C appear
    D diffuse

02. The electron microscope is a device that uses a beam of electrons to magnify an object's image.
    A ray
    B measure
    C spot
    D speed

03. Some owners and operators used their power fairly, but others acted as ruthless dictators.
    A merciless
    B clear
    C artful
    D gradual

04. A set theory is a way of solving problems in mathematics and logic.
    A reasoning
    B writing
    C calculus
    D operation

05. People born under the star sign of Gemini are supposedly talkative and witty.
    A intriguing
    B lengthy
    C practical
    D humorous

06. Ulysses was trustworthy, so his father often sent him on business trips.
    A revered
    B industrious
    C reliable
    D generous

07. *Gulliver's Travels* (1726) written by Jonathan Swift of England combines a tale of a fantastic voyage with social criticism.
    A lover
    B journey
    C view
    D cliff

08. Private companies maintain several hundred laboratories in California for conducting research and testing new products.
    A advertising
    B trading
    C analysis
    D learning

09. In Gabon, logging is the country's second largest source of revenue, employing more than a quarter of it's workforce.
    A income
    B revenge
    C cause
    D patent

10. Slavery had become a much greater issue 23 years later, when Lincoln was nominated for President.
    A training
    B rebounds
    C subjects
    D benefits

11. Soviet efforts to reach the moon were also frustrated by the continued failure of the giant N-1 booster.
    - (A) thwarted
    - (B) canceled
    - (C) discouraged
    - (D) accomplished

12. Crushed granite is produced in the north-central and northeastern parts of the state.
    - (A) Bright
    - (B) Grainy
    - (C) Compressed
    - (D) Magnificent

13. As more species are becoming endangered, ecosystems are becoming unstable and may eventually collapse.
    - (A) deficient
    - (B) steadfast
    - (C) insecure
    - (D) unreliable

14. The earliest vertebrates most likely fed on small bits of dead animals or tiny creatures on the sea floor or in the water.
    - (A) often
    - (B) little pieces
    - (C) supposed
    - (D) appreciable

15. By the mid-1800's, traditional Asian systems began to prove ineffective against the increasing social problems.
    - (A) worthy
    - (B) adequate
    - (C) routine
    - (D) inefficient

16. At birth, elephants are often covered with sparse brown, black, or reddish-brown hair that gradually wears off as they get older.
    - (A) even
    - (B) sporadic
    - (C) diverse
    - (D) recent

17. In *Roscoe's Leap* (1987) by Gillian Cross, a 12-year-old boy confronts mysterious secrets in a decaying family mansion.
    - (A) decomposing
    - (B) compacting
    - (C) deteriorating
    - (D) liquefied

18. Before the end of the twentieth century, many languages in Africa, Asia, and America may pass into complete oblivion unless some competent linguists find the time to record them.
    - (A) power
    - (B) unawareness
    - (C) promise
    - (D) elaboration

19. In *The Sound and the Fury* (1929) and in his other novels, Faulkner dealt with the decline of Southern aristocratic families and the breakdown of traditional standards in behavior.
    - (A) prosperity
    - (B) allegiance
    - (C) falling
    - (D) tragedy

20. Many plants go through a regular sequence of growth rates, with an initial period of rapid growth followed by a period of little if any increase in volume, and eventually death after the complete cessation of growth and breakdown of tissues.
    - (A) reopening
    - (B) stopping
    - (C) destruction
    - (D) succession

DAY 13 Daily Checkup

01. the horrors of war
ⓐ traces　　ⓑ symbols
ⓒ particle　　ⓓ fears

02. It is a long lane that has no turning.
ⓐ path　　ⓑ alarm
ⓒ region　　ⓓ ceremony

03. an aromatic perfume
ⓐ pant　　ⓑ flavorful
ⓒ vaporizing　　ⓓ manipulate

04. suitable apparel for the occasion
ⓐ celebration　　ⓑ hinterland
ⓒ clothes　　ⓓ alarm

05. excavate a tunnel
ⓐ categorize　　ⓑ classify
ⓒ manipulate　　ⓓ dig out

06. undertake social and political reforms
ⓐ attempt　　ⓑ keep
ⓒ wield　　ⓓ ignore

07. retaliate on one's enemy
ⓐ dedicate　　ⓑ revenge
ⓒ rent　　ⓓ fissure

08. an unqualified liar
ⓐ complete　　ⓑ proportional
ⓒ mutual　　ⓓ uninterrupted

09. calculate the sale price
ⓐ confine　　ⓑ convoy
ⓒ excuse　　ⓓ reckon

10. answer unequivocally
ⓐ symmetrically　　ⓑ healthfully
ⓒ unendingly　　ⓓ definitely

11. wholesome environment
ⓐ guard　　ⓑ healthy
ⓒ guide　　ⓓ persistent

12. Charlie had to overlook a large number of students.
ⓐ guide　　ⓑ arrange
ⓒ look after　　ⓓ survive

13. tear open an envelope
ⓐ endorse　　ⓑ scratch
ⓒ handle　　ⓓ vaporize

14. a solitarily speck of cloud
ⓐ spot　　ⓑ dread
ⓒ route　　ⓓ suggestion

15. Test takers were detained by an accident.
ⓐ manipulated　　ⓑ conducted
ⓒ retarded　　ⓓ disregard

16. devote one's heart and soul (to)
ⓐ disregard　　ⓑ dedicate
ⓒ excuse　　ⓓ smear

17. I escort him to the door.
ⓐ avenge　　ⓑ guard
ⓒ wake　　ⓓ arranged

18. concentration of power
ⓐ accumulation　　ⓑ arrangement
ⓒ ceremony　　ⓓ indication

19. symmetrical windows
ⓐ proportionally balanced　　ⓑ common
ⓒ unstable　　ⓓ fragrant

20. exonerate a person from payment
ⓐ release　　ⓑ inscribe
ⓒ request　　ⓓ determine

표제어	품사	동의어와 예문	한글 뜻
1 **apparel*** [əpǽrəl]	n	clothes, dress, garb, attire, costume put on an intimate **apparel** 실내복 [잠옷]을 입다	의상
2 **aromatic*** [ærəmǽtik]	a	flavorful, fragrant an **aromatic** perfume 향기로운 향수	향기로운
3 **botany** [bátəni]	n	plant life, relate to plant the **botany** of Korea 한국의 식물	식물학, 식물
4 **by-product** [báipràdʌkt]	n	derivative (of) Oxygen is released as a **by-product** of photosynthesis. 산소가 광합성의 부산물로서 방출되었다.	부산물
5 **calculate*** [kǽlkjulèit]	v	determine, count, figure, reckon, compute **calculate** a solar eclipse 일식일을 계산해 내다 **calculate** the sale price 판매가격을 계산하다	계산하다, 추산하다
6 **categorize** *** [kǽtəgəràiz]	v	classify, arrange, sort Animals can be **categorized** by whether the mouth develops. 동물은 입이 (어디로부터) 발달했는지에 따라 분류될 수 있다.	분류하다
7 **climb** [klaim]	v	mount, ascend, scale, rise ↔ descend **climb** a tree using the claws 발톱을 이용하여 나무를 오르다 **climb** in a jeep 지프차에 타다	(산을) 오르다
8 **concentration*** [kànsəntréiʃən]	n	accumulation; density Many people still worried about the **concentration** of financial power. 많은 사람들은 여전히 금융권력의 집중에 대해 걱정한다.	집중 / 농도
9 **detain** [ditéin]	v	confine, arrest, keep **detain** (a person) for protection 보호 검속하다	구류하다, 보호를 목적으로 구류(유치)하다
10 **devote*** [divóut]	v	dedicate, reserve (for), devout, loyal, ardent ↔ unfaithful, disloyal **devote** himself to writing 글쓰는 데 (그 자신이) 충실하다(전념하다)	충실하다, 헌신하다
	a	loving, affectionate, attentive be **devoted** to nursing of parent 부모를 간호하는 데 헌신적이다	애정 어린, 다정한, 헌신적인
11 **escort** [éskɔ:rt]	v	convoy, guard, guide Guides **escort** visitors through the buildings. 가이드가 건물을 통해 방문자들을 호위하다. under the **escort** of ~의 호위 하에	호송하다
12 **evaporate** [ivǽpərèit]	v	vaporize My money seemed to have **evaporated**. 돈이 흐지부지 없어졌다.	증발하다, 사라지다

13	**excavate**** [ékskəvèit]	**v**	dig out **excavate** a tunnel 터널을 뚫다	파다, 뚫다
14	**exonerate** [igzánərèit]	**v**	acquit, excuse, discharge, vindicate, exculpate Ray discovered the book to **exonerate** her from the accusation. 레이는 결백을 입증할 책을 발견했다.	해방시키다, 무죄가 되게 하다
15	**feast*** [fi:st]	**n**	celebration, anniversary, ceremony After the job was finished, everyone celebrated with a lively **feast**. 일을 끝마친 후에 모두가 활기찬 축제로 축하했다. a **feast** for eyes 눈요깃거리	축하, 기념일, 의식
16	**gasp** [gæsp]	**v**	pant breathe with **gasps** 숨을 헐떡이다	숨을 헐떡거리다
17	**granular** [grǽnjulər]	**a**	fine particle, grains have a **granular** or crystalline core that to be dense 밀도가 높은 과립상 또는 결정형 핵을 가지다	낟알의, 과립 모양의
18	**groom** [gru:m]	**n**	husband, stableman, hostler newly married bride and **groom** 새로 결혼한 신랑과 신부	신랑, 마부
		v	train **groom** a horse 말을 돌보다(솔질하다)	돌보다
19	**hinterland*** [híntərlænd]	**n**	region, back country was a **hinterland** of rough tribal warfare 거친 부족 전쟁의 배후지였다	지역, 지방, 배후지
20	**horror** [hɔ́:rər]	**n**	fear, dread, panic, dread, alarm, awe announce the **horrors** of war 전쟁의 참사를 알리다	공포
21	**incessant*** [insésnt]	**a**	uninterrupted, ceaseless, unending, persistent the **incessant** crying of the sick baby 아픈 아기의 끊임없는 울음 chatter **incessantly** 쉴 새 없이 수다를 떨다	끊임없는
22	**lane** [lein]	**n**	path, way, passage, alley, route a **lane** leading to a farmhouse 농장으로 가는 길	좁은 길, 골목길
23	**manage**** [mǽnidʒ]	**v**	① handle, manipulate, wield I'll **manage** it somehow. 내가 어떻게든 해보겠다 ② conduct, control, direct, administer **manage** the team 팀을 이끌다	① 다루다, 처리하다 ② 이끌다, 감독하다
24	**necrotic** [nekrátik]	**a**	unstable, abnormal, compulsive Some leaves was diseased with the **necrotic** symptom. 일부 잎들이 괴사성 증상으로 병들었다.	괴사성의
25	**obese** [oubí:s]	**a**	excessively, overweight He is **obese**. 그는 지나치게 뚱뚱하다.	뚱뚱한
26	**overlook*** [ouvərluk]	**v**	disregard, neglect, ignore; excuse, forgive **overlook** the danger 위험을 못 보고 지나치다	간과하다 / 용서하다
27	**reciprocal** [risíprəkəl]	**a**	mutual a **reciprocal** treaty 호혜 조약	상호의, 공동의
28	**recommend*** [rèkəménd]	**v**	commend, approve, endorse, commend, sanction **recommend** one's own person 자신의 사람을 추천하다	추천하다

29	**retaliate** [ritǽlièit]	v	avenge, revenge, requite **retaliate** on one's enemy 적에게 복수하다	보복하다, 앙갚음을 하다
30	**sign*** [sain]	n	indication, trace, hint, suggestion, token, mark, symbol a **sign** of freedom 자유의 표시	신호, 암시, 표시
		v	endorse, initial, inscribe, autograph **sign** in the paper and seal 서류에 서명하고 봉하다	서명하다, 표시하다
31	**speck** [spek]	n	spot, particle a **speck** of oil 기름 얼룩	작은 얼룩, 흠
32	**spouse** [spaus]	n	husband or wife, partner, mate put an advertisement for a **spouse** 구혼 광고를 내다	배우자
33	**symmetrical** [simétrikəl]	a	proportionally balanced, equilibrium A circle has **symmetrical** about a diameter. 원형은 직경에 대해서 대칭이다.	대칭의
34	**tear** [tiər]	v	split, rend, rupture **tear** open an envelop 봉투를 찢어 열다	찢다, 자르다
35	**unanimous** [ju:nǽnəməs]	a	agreed, common with **unanimous** applause 만장일치로	합의하는, 동의하는, 만장일 치인
36	**unequivocally**** [ʌnikwívəkəli]	ad	definitely, absolutely, clearly, explicitly answered to that problem **unequivocally** 그 문제에 대하여 명쾌하게 대답하다	명백하게, 명확하게
37	**undertake**** [ʌndərtéik]	v	attempt, set about, contract, engage, pledge **undertake** an experiment 실험에 착수하다	떠맡다, 착수하다
38	**unqualified*** [ʌnkwάləfàid]	a	complete; ill-equipped an **unqualified** liar 지독한 거짓말	순전한 / 철저한, 자격이 없는
39	**wake** [weik]	v	arouse, provoke, stimulate, activate, motivate The flowers **wake** in spring. 꽃은 봄에 소생한다.	깨우다, 소생하다
40	**wholesome** [hóulsəm]	a	healthful, healthy, salutary the most **wholesome** and necessary for the public good 가장 건전하고 공익에 필요한	건전한, 유익한

01. Many registered dietitians manage food services in schools, nursing homes, and restaurants.
   A handle
   B examine
   C project
   D provide

02. The Carter Presidential Center stands on a hill that overlooks downtown Atlanta.
   A close by
   B related to
   C behind
   D tower above

03. The smallest speck that can be seen under an ordinary microscope contains more than 10 billion atoms.
   A swirl
   B mound
   C particle
   D clump

04. In primitive societies, when a feast is given, the people who produce the food keep the best portions for themselves.
   A celebration
   B service
   C document
   D tradition

05. In certain cultures, marriage involves a gift from the groom or bride's family to the other family.
   A father-in-law
   B mother-in-law
   C bridegroom
   D grandfather

06. Most slaves married and lived with the same spouse until death.
   A owner
   B buyer
   C wife
   D baby

07. Everyone has the right not to be arbitrarily detained or imprisoned.
   A confined
   B embarrassed
   C disdained
   D deplored

08. Seaweed helps provide sea animals with oxygen, which is released as a by-product of photosynthesis.
   A material
   B outcome
   C chemicals
   D ingredient

09. Most of the economic efforts in primitive society are devoted to the production of food.
   A are absorbed to
   B are operated by
   C are dedicated to
   D are connected with

10. At the end of the opera, Marguerite dies and a chorus of angels escorts her to heaven.
   A captures
   B picks
   C misleads
   D guides

11. In the United States, recent studies show that about one-fourth of U.S. adults are obese.
    Ⓐ gainfully employed
    Ⓑ upwardly mobile
    Ⓒ excessively overweight
    Ⓓ privately educated

12. In 1950, Chuck Cooper signed up with the Boston Celtics, becoming the first black player in the history of the NBA.
    Ⓐ traded
    Ⓑ dealt
    Ⓒ worked
    Ⓓ contracted

13. In places where water is chronically insufficient, plants may grow poorly, leaves may be small and abnormally colored, and marginally necrotic.
    Ⓐ rotten
    Ⓑ wilted
    Ⓒ mutated
    Ⓓ faded away

14. No one knows how high temperatures may climb, but the temperature inside the hottest star is millions of degrees.
    Ⓐ descend
    Ⓑ be caused
    Ⓒ ascend
    Ⓓ change

15. Many agents work only with writers who have been recommended by editors or professional authors.
    Ⓐ studied
    Ⓑ discommended
    Ⓒ grown
    Ⓓ advised

16. The Senate usually decides on a bill through a simple motion or by unanimous consent – that is, without anyone's objection.
    Ⓐ accepted
    Ⓑ agreed
    Ⓒ suitable
    Ⓓ uniform

17. After 1910, many photographers believed that un-retouched photographs had the beauty and elegance unmatched by other works of art.
    Ⓐ exaggerated
    Ⓑ underestimated
    Ⓒ unparalled
    Ⓓ compared

18. When the drug is withdrawn, the segregation phenomenon is reversed, and the fibrillar and granular components become interspersed.
    Ⓐ like flagella
    Ⓑ fine particle
    Ⓒ spiral
    Ⓓ sticky

19. The music played by such bands as the Jimi Hendrix Experience and Clapton's Cream were sometimes categorized as progressive rock.
    Ⓐ clarified
    Ⓑ strengthened
    Ⓒ classified
    Ⓓ exposed

20. Global warming which results from the greenhouse effect, dries up the planet by evaporating moisture from oceans, soil and plants.
    Ⓐ creating
    Ⓑ dehydrating
    Ⓒ raining
    Ⓓ dampening

DAY 14 Daily Checkup

01. generate electricity
    - (A) peep
    - (B) produce
    - (C) infiltrate
    - (D) expand

02. be in a state of disorder
    - (A) bait
    - (B) chaos
    - (C) immobility
    - (D) independence

03. Mercury expands with heat.
    - (A) strives
    - (B) represents
    - (C) accelerates
    - (D) enlarges

04. studied the principles of multiplication
    - (A) baits
    - (B) distress
    - (C) anguish
    - (D) laws

05. received an unexpected reward
    - (A) paramount
    - (B) award
    - (C) bonus
    - (D) anguish

06. appropriate the money to payment
    - (A) dilate
    - (B) entrust
    - (C) replenish
    - (D) recompense

07. the fragrance of roses
    - (A) scent
    - (B) gift
    - (C) bait
    - (D) defame

08. weave cloth out of thread
    - (A) infiltrate
    - (B) represent
    - (C) intertwine
    - (D) improve

09. deposit money in a bank
    - (A) entend
    - (B) distend
    - (C) improve
    - (D) entrust

10. classify the types of insects
    - (A) peer
    - (B) categorize
    - (C) interwind
    - (D) propound

11. sovereign authority
    - (A) woe
    - (B) mess
    - (C) dilemma
    - (D) supreme

12. emphasize my remarks
    - (A) curl
    - (B) bounty
    - (C) underline
    - (D) swell

13. manifold reasons of my opinion
    - (A) suitable
    - (B) multiple
    - (C) infinite
    - (D) elated

14. nature and nurture
    - (A) nurse
    - (B) emphasis
    - (C) scent
    - (D) defame

15. a cumbersome baggage
    - (A) grand
    - (B) jubilant
    - (C) burdensome
    - (D) saturated

16. a tranquil heart
    - (A) fragrant
    - (B) creed
    - (C) serene
    - (D) religious

17. boost the economy
    - (A) compensate
    - (B) raise
    - (C) create
    - (D) categorize

18. snared the animal
    - (A) produced
    - (B) stored
    - (C) improved
    - (D) trapped

19. permeate though the system
    - (A) meander
    - (B) infiltrate
    - (C) award
    - (D) qualified

20. sorrow of everyday living
    - (A) mess
    - (B) emphasis
    - (C) predicament
    - (D) sadness

표제어	품사	동의어와 예문	한글 뜻
1 **appropriate**** [əpróupriət]	a	suitable, proper, fitting, relevant bring **appropriate** clothing 알맞은 옷을 가지고 오다	적절한
	v	assign, apportion, allocate **appropriate** for peoples who are living in different parts of the world 세상의 다른 지역에 살고 있는 사람들에게 할당하다	할당하다
2 **boost** [buːst]	v	raise, increase, develop, encourage, promote **boost** our confidence 우리의 신뢰를 높이다	밀어 올리다, 응원하다
3 **classify*** [klǽsəfài]	v	categorize, rank, systematize **classify** the species of insects 곤충의 종을 분류하다 **classify** the grade 등수를 정하다	분류하다, 등급을 나누다
4 **cumbersome*** [kʌmbərsəm]	a	burdensome, awkward, clumsy, inconvenient, bulky a **cumbersome** package 번거로운 짐	부담스런, 귀찮은
5 **deposit** [dipázit]	v	lay, save, store, entrust **deposit** money in a bank 은행에 돈을 예금하다	저장하다, 맡기다
6 **disorder** [disɔ́ːrdər]	n	mess, confusion, chaos hope to avoid a war by crushing the **disorder** in Boston 보스톤의 소요사태를 진압해서 전쟁이 나는 것을 피하기를 희망하다 **disorder** in the classroom 난장판 교실	무질서, 혼란, 소요
7 **eligible*** [élidʒəbl]	a	qualified, acceptable, entitled, suitable **eligible** as a member 회원으로 자격이 있는	적임의
8 **emphasize**** [émfəsàiz]	v	stress, highlight, underline **emphasize** the point 중점을 역설하다	강조하다, 두드러지게 하다
9 **endlessly*** [éndlisli]	ad	infinitely, boundless, limitless, continuous ↔ limited, finite work **endlessly** 끊임없이 일하다	끝없이
10 **expand**** [ikspǽnd]	v	① stretch, enlarge, swell, dilate, distend ↔ contract **expand** the size of the vegetable garden 정원의 크기를 확장하다 ② develop, increase, strengthen, accelerate ↔ reduce **expand** the business 사업을 확장하다 **expand** its wings 날개를 펼치다	① 부풀게 하다 ② 전개하다
11 **faith*** [feiθ]	n	① belief, confidence, trust The letters discuss problems of **faith** and conduct. 그 편지들은 믿음과 행실의 문제들을 논의했다. ② creed, religion, belief, doctrine, persuasion free to worship in one's **faith** 신념에 따른 숭배의 자유	① 믿음 ② 신조, 신념
12 **fragrance*** [fréigrəns]	n	scent, perfume, aroma, odor smell the **fragrance** of roses 장미 향기를 맡다	향기, 향수

13	**from time to time*** [frəm taim tu taim]	ad	now and then, occasionally, once in a while We has a regular meeting **from time to time**. 우리는 때때로 정기적인 모임을 갖는다.	때때로, 가끔
14	**generate*** * [dʒénərèit]	v	produce, give rise to, breed, cause, create Almost all water power is used to **generate** electricity. 거의 모든 수력발전소는 전기를 발생시키는 데 사용된다.	발생시키다
15	**highest point** [háiist pɔint]	n	emphasis, zenith At its **highest** points, the icecap rises as high as 4,100 meters above sea level. 빙원은 가장 높은 지점에서는 해수면 4,100미터까지 높이 상승한다.	최고의 시기, 중대한 시점
16	**irregular*** [irégjulər]	a	uneven, variable, random, occasional Quartz break into pieces with **irregular** surfaces. 석영은 불규칙한 표면을 가진 조각들로 깨진다.	불규칙한
17	**joyful** [dʒɔifəl]	a	glad, delighted, buoyant, elated, jubilant several of the **joyful** ceremonies of the marriage sacrament 결혼 성사의 몇몇의 즐거운 행사	기쁜, 즐거운
18	**lubricate** [lú:brəkèit]	v	oil, grease, smear **lubricate** the machinery regularly 기계류를 정기적으로 기름칠하다	기름을 치다, 매끄럽게 하다
19	**majestic*** * [mədʒéstik]	a	imposing, splendid, magnificent stately, grand, august He made his **majestic** appearance. 그가 늠름한 자태를 나타냈다.	웅장한, 장엄한
20	**manifold*** [mǽnəfòuld]	a	various, numerous Our education system faces **manifold** problems. 우리 교육체계는 다양한 문제점에 직면하고 있다.	다양한, 다수의
21	**nurture*** * [nə́:rtʃər]	v	improve, nurse **nurture** a talent 인재를 양성하다	양육하다, 육성하다
22	**out of the blue** [aut əv ðə blu:]	prep	unexpected event, unexpectedly, suddenly evaluation that came **out of the blue** 갑자기 온 평가	느닷없이, 돌연, 갑자기
23	**permeate*** * [pə́:rmièit]	v	pass through, penetrate, infiltrate, saturate The water **permeates** through the soil. 물이 땅속으로 스며든다.	스며들다, ~에 퍼지다
24	**plane** [plein]	n	① aircraft, aeroplane, jet, airliner This was the world's largest military **plane**. 이것은 세계에서 가장 큰 군용비행기였다.	① 비행기
			② level, position, stage, condition, degree live on a higher moral **plane** of existence 존재의 더 높은 도덕 수준에서 살다	② 수준, 정도, 평평한
		a	flat, even, horizontal a **plane** surface 평면	평평한
25	**plight** [plait]	n	predicament, dilemma The organization publicizes the **plight** of endangered species. 그 단체는 멸종 위기 종의 상태를 공표한다.	곤경, 궁지, (어려운) 상태
		v	pledge **plight** one's troth 서약하다, 약혼하다.	맹세하다
26	**pose*** [pouz]	v	① state, assert; present, effect, represent **pose** a question to the challengers 도전자들에게 문제를 내다	① 주장하다 / 제출하다, 내포하다
			② posture, model; pretend, feign **pose** for a picture 사진을 위해 포즈를 취하다	② 자세를 취하다 / ~인 체하다

27	**premium** [prí:miəm]	n	bonus, gift, reward at a **premium** 프리미엄이 붙어, 액면 이상으로	상금, 상품
28	**principle***** [prínsəpl]	n	main, law Newton's first law is known as the **principle** of inertia. 뉴턴의 제1법칙은 관성의 법칙으로 알려져 있다. in **principle** 원칙적으로, 대체로	원리, 원칙
29	**reasonable***** [rí:zənəbl]	a	rational, logical, sensible, judicious **reasonable** terms 온당한 조건	분별있는, 사리 있는
30	**reward** [riwɔ́:rd]	v	recompense, prize, bounty, favor, award ↔ punishment, penalty in **reward** for ~에 대한 상으로서	보답하다, 보상하다
31	**slander*** [slǽndər]	n	libel, blame, defame The various libels and **slanders** on internet may led to anybody's death. 인터넷상의 다양한 비방과 중상이 누군가의 죽음을 이끌어 낼 것이다.	중상, 비방
32	**snare** [snɛər]	n	trap, lure, bait set a **snare** 덫을 놓다	함정, 덫
33	**sorrow*** [sárou]	n	distress, anguish, grief, sadness, woe His **sorrow** gave rise to a belief that he had planned to study abroad. 그의 슬픔은 그가 유학을 계획했었다는 믿음을 상승시켰다.	슬픔, 비탄
34	**sovereign***** [sávərin]	n	supreme, chief, paramount, independent recognize as a **sovereign** authority 주권자로서 인정하다	주권자, 군주
35	**stationery*** [stéiʃənèri]	n	letter, paper, writing materials a **stationery** store 문방구점	문구, 문방구
		a	unmoving, fixed, immobile Plants are **stationary** and generally respond to environmental stimuli. 식물은 움직이지 않고 일반적으로 환경적인 자극에 반응한다.	정지된, 움직이지 않는
36	**toil** [tɔil]	v	work, labor, strive **toil** at a task 부지런히 일하다	힘써 일하다, 수고하다
37	**tranquil**** [trǽŋkwil]	a	serene, placid, quiet, calm a **tranquil** heart 편안한 마음	조용한, 편안한
38	**unevenly*** [ʌní:vənli]	a	unequally The rain is distributed **unevenly**. 비는 고르지 않게 분포한다.	한결같지 않은
39	**vital*** [váitl]	a	essential, indispensable, important, critical **vital** power 생명력	극히 중요한, 치명적인
40	**interweave*** [ìntə:rwí:v]	v	intertwine, twist, curl, meander, twine, spiral, coil Many of the causes are so closely **interwoven**. 많은 원인들이 너무 밀접하게 엮여 있다.	엮다, 관련지우다

01. The earth has an abundant supply of water, but the water is unevenly distributed.
    A sparsely
    B normally
    C unequally
    D sometimes

02. The highest point on earth is the peak at Mount Everest − 8,848 meters above sea level.
    A range
    B sea
    C summit
    D volcano

03. Heat changes the orderly pattern of snowflakes into a disorderly pattern.
    A rain
    B water
    C confusing
    D salt

04. NBA players became eligible to play in the Olympic Games in 1992.
    A encouraged
    B qualified
    C expected
    D dispatched

05. This symbolic process permeates human life at its most primitive as well as at its most civilized levels.
    A penetrates
    B transmits
    C suspends
    D breaks up

06. Portrait photographers must know how to make their subjects pose as well as how to create pleasing effects.
    A picture
    B arrange
    C stand
    D order

07. A basso profundo has an especially low voice and usually sings majestic, serious roles.
    A responsible
    B free
    C devoted
    D noble

08. If a student answers a test question incorrectly, the disc automatically responds with the appropriate information.
    A guide
    B proper
    C power
    D fund

09. A slippery fluid between the epicardium and the pericardium lubricates the heart and enables it to contract smoothly.
    A oils
    B relieves
    C abrasives
    D improves

10. In primitive societies, the principle that a man should get a reward for his labor is not recognized.
    A payment
    B land
    C position
    D house

11. After the Spaniards introduced sheep to the Southwest, the Pueblo began to weave woolen cloth for clothing.
    - (A) buy
    - (B) sell
    - (C) knit
    - (D) exchange

12. Certain channels, such as the premium movie channel, charge an extra fee that a customer pays in addition to the monthly fee for basic cable service.
    - (A) award
    - (B) worst
    - (C) payment
    - (D) educational

13. Catholics believe that people achieve salvation through faith in God's grace and also by their own merit-that is, by doing good deeds.
    - (A) diligence
    - (B) innocence
    - (C) belief
    - (D) loyalty

14. Lakes may appear when rivers deposit silt while the natural outlet to the sea is closed, and the water backs up.
    - (A) saves
    - (B) accumulate
    - (C) position
    - (D) warm

15. To overcome problems in describing and matching colors, color experts have developed various systems in classifying colors.
    - (A) categorizing
    - (B) photographing
    - (C) embellishing
    - (D) drawing

16. Researchers typically analyze the fragrance of coffee beans roasting through gas chromatography coupled with olfactometry.
    - (A) design
    - (B) texture
    - (C) scent
    - (D) freshness

17. The government grants subsidies because it believes that a merchant fleets are vital to a country's foreign trade and national defense.
    - (A) crucial
    - (B) inattentive
    - (C) acquired
    - (D) helpful

18. Mandelbrot coined the term "fractal" from the Latin word fractus, to highlight the fragmented and irregular nature of this graphic.
    - (A) unattractive
    - (B) uneven
    - (C) impractical
    - (D) inadequate

19. Most booklists of bibliographies for recommended children's books are published monthly or annually in pamphlet form, but a few are published in book form and may be revised from time to time.
    - (A) quickly
    - (B) regularly
    - (C) occasionally
    - (D) simply

20. Melted water from mountain glaciers may have boosted the ocean by as much as five centimeters in the past 100 years, and this continuing influx will most likely elevate sea levels even more quickly in the future.
    - (A) ensured
    - (B) arranged
    - (C) glided
    - (D) raised

DAY 15 Daily Checkup

01. turn back abruptly
- Ⓐ strenuously
- Ⓑ impressively
- Ⓒ arduously
- Ⓓ suddenly

02. a solemn face
- Ⓐ lacking
- Ⓑ serious
- Ⓒ habitual
- Ⓓ confirmed

03. damp air
- Ⓐ unbending
- Ⓑ submissive
- Ⓒ naughty
- Ⓓ humid

04. spend a pleasant evening
- Ⓐ majestic
- Ⓑ soaked
- Ⓒ acute
- Ⓓ satisfying

05. conserve our natural resources
- Ⓐ suspend
- Ⓑ invalidate
- Ⓒ maintain
- Ⓓ remainder

06. a sparsely populated outskirt
- Ⓐ surrounding region
- Ⓑ process
- Ⓒ pouch
- Ⓓ ferocity

07. an enraged crowd
- Ⓐ resolute
- Ⓑ submissive
- Ⓒ agitated
- Ⓓ docile

08. strenuous opposition
- Ⓐ arduous
- Ⓑ unmoving
- Ⓒ stuttered
- Ⓓ sober

09. cleave the shield with one stroke
- Ⓐ assume
- Ⓑ split
- Ⓒ acquaint
- Ⓓ invalidate

10. an obedient horse
- Ⓐ minute
- Ⓑ drenched
- Ⓒ humorous
- Ⓓ docile

11. legal procedure
- Ⓐ frenzy
- Ⓑ course
- Ⓒ remainder
- Ⓓ pouch

12. troublesome work
- Ⓐ immobile
- Ⓑ enjoyable
- Ⓒ laborious
- Ⓓ ingenuous

13. inflexible rules
- Ⓐ fixed
- Ⓑ naughty
- Ⓒ subservient
- Ⓓ impressive

14. amused by the naive freshmen
- Ⓐ imposing
- Ⓑ candid
- Ⓒ exchanged
- Ⓓ faltering

15. He stammered over a few words.
- Ⓐ stuttered
- Ⓑ aggravated
- Ⓒ maintained
- Ⓓ intermitted

16. send an emissary
- Ⓐ surplus
- Ⓑ version
- Ⓒ messenger
- Ⓓ counterpart

17. a minuscule amount of time
- Ⓐ unmoving
- Ⓑ tiny
- Ⓒ compliant
- Ⓓ habitual

18. the pacesetter for political change
- Ⓐ leader
- Ⓑ advance
- Ⓒ outskirt
- Ⓓ fury

19. There's no substitute for parents.
- Ⓐ hinder
- Ⓑ assume
- Ⓒ replacement
- Ⓓ hesitate

20. Malnutrition obviously weakens the patient.
- Ⓐ Pouch
- Ⓑ Surplus
- Ⓒ Procedure
- Ⓓ Not good in nutrition

표제어	품사	동의어와 예문	한글 뜻
1 **abruptly**** [əbrʌ́ptli]	ad	suddenly, forthwith cease work **abruptly** 갑자기 하던 일을 멈추다	갑자기, 불쑥
2 **chronic*** [kránik]	a	habitual, confirmed ↔ acute help the people with **chronic** disease 만성병을 가진 사람들을 돕다	상습적인, 만성적인
3 **cleave*** [kli:v]	v	split, break, divide, separate, burst **cleave** it open 그것을 베어 가르다	쪼개다
4 **comic** [kámik]	a	funny, humorous **Comic** dramas from many lands deals with foolish people. 많은 나라들의 희극 드라마들이 어리석은 사람들을 다루고 있다.	희극적인, 우수꽝스러운
5 **commercial** [kəmə́:rʃəl]	a	business, mercantile a **commercial** artist 상업 미술가 By 1988, all nations had halted **commercial** whaling. 1988년에 모든 국가들이 상업적 포경을 중단했다.	상업상의
6 **conserve**** [kənsə́:rv]	v	retain, preserve, keep, sustain, maintain ↔ squander, waste The **conservation** of forests helps conserve biodiversity, water, and soil. 산림보호는 생물의 다양성, 물과 토양을 보존하는 데 도움이 된다.	보존하다
7 **counterparts** [káuntərpà:rts]	n	version, opposite be the exact **counterpart** of ~와 꼭 닮다 Korean teenagers tend to behave like their American **counterparts**. 한국 청소년들이 미국의 청소년(상대방)들과 같이 행동하고 싶어한다.	대응물, 상대방
8 **damp**** [dæmp]	a	moist, humid, wet, drenched, dank, soaked ↔ dry The interior of a cave is a dark, **damp** place where sunlight never enters. 동굴의 내부는 어둡고 축축한 곳으로 햇볕이 전혀 들어오지 않는다.	축축한, 습기찬, 의기소침한
9 **development**** [divéləpmənt]	n	growth, advance Gold rushes played an important role in the **development** of the West. 골드러시는 서부의 발달에 중요한 역할을 하였다.	발달
10 **driven** [drívən]	a	forced Some airplane are propeller **driven**, but most have jet engines. 일부 비행기는 프로펠러 구동이지만, 대부분은 제트 엔진이다.	강제된, (기계를) 구동하는
11 **emissary** [éməsèri]	n	messenger, carrier, courier, envoy send an **emissary** 밀사를 보내다	사절, 밀사
12 **enrage** [inréidʒ]	v	anger, aggravate, infuriate, inflame, vex The president **enraged** the people. 대통령이 국민을 분노케 하였다.	분노케 하다, 악화시키다

| 13 | **foliage**
[fóuliidʒ] | **n** | leaves, leaflet
beautiful fall **foliage** of that ginkgo tree 그 은행나무의 아름다운 단풍 | 나뭇잎 |

| 14 | **however**
[hauévər] | **ad** | but
Operagoers today, **however**, still prefer older, traditional works.
그러나 오늘날의 오페라 애호가들은 오래되고 전통적인 작품들을 선호한다. | 그러나 |

| 15 | **implement***
[ímpləmənt] | **n** | tool, utensil
Farmers prefer to use modern agricultural **implements**.
농부들은 현대적인 농기구들의 사용을 선호한다. | 도구, 기구 |
| | | **v** | carry out, perform, fulfil
implement a policy 정책을 실행하다 | 실행하다 |

| 16 | **inflexible****
[infléksəbl] | **a** | rigid, stern, resolute, steadfast, unbending
inflexible rules 변경할 수 없는 규칙 | 유연성이 없는, 딱딱한 |

| 17 | **interrupt****
[ìntərʌ́pt] | **v** | suspend, intermit, stop, hinder
interrupt an electric current 전류를 차단하다 | 방해하다, 간섭하다 |

| 18 | **lash**
[læʃ] | **v** | hang, fasten, join, tie; whip, blow, hit, strike
be **lashed** 매맛을 보다
Workers **lashed** down freights and boxes with ropes before the typoon.
작업자들이 태풍이 오기 전에 밧줄로 짐과 박스들을 묶었다. | 묶다 / 채찍질하다 |

| 19 | **malnutrition**
[mælnju:tríʃən] | **n** | not good in nutrition
Many died of disease resulting from **malnutrition**.
많은 사람들이 영양실조에서 비롯된 병으로 죽었다.
suffer from **malnutrition** 영양실조로 고통받다 | 영양실조 |

| 20 | **minuscule***
[mínəskjù:l] | **a** | tiny, minute
The collective productivity of the **minuscule** chloroplasts is prodigious.
작은 엽록체들의 집단 생산성은 경이적이다. | 미세한, 상세한, 작은 |

| 21 | **naive****
[na:í:v] | **a** | ingenuous, candid
He is **naive** and gullible.
그는 고지식해서 남의 말을 곧이 듣는다. | 순진한 |

| 22 | **notify***
[nóutəfài] | **v** | inform, acquaint
Witness **notified** the police of the accident.
목격자가 그 사고를 경찰에 신고했다. | 통지하다, 알리다 |

| 23 | **nullify***
[nʌ́ləfài] | **v** | cancel, annul, invalidate
nullify a contract by the law 법에 따라 계약을 취소하다 | 취소하다 |

| 24 | **obedient****
[oubí:diənt] | **a** | submissive, docile, compliant, subservient
↔ naughty
obedient to his parents 부모님께 순종하는 | 순종하는, 유순한 |

| 25 | **outskirt**
[áutskə:rt] | **n** | at the edge, surrounding region, border, fringe
Enemy attacked one of the forts on the **outskirts** of the city.
적이 도시 외곽에 있는 요새 중 하나를 공격했다. | 변두리, 교외, 외곽 |

| 26 | **pacesetter**
[péissètər] | **n** | leader, pacemaker
The new rule will be a **pacesetter** in our community relations.
새로운 규칙이 우리 동호회 관계에 있어 모범이 될 것이다. | 선도적인 사람 [일], 지도자 |

| 27 | **perspective**
[pərspéktiv] | **n** | point of view
the story of the American Civil War from a financial **perspective**
재정적 관점으로부터의 미국독립전쟁 이야기
a **perspective** plan 투시도(透視圖) | 시각, 관점, 견해, 원근법 |

DAY 15

28	**pleasant** [plézənt]	ⓐ	agreeable, enjoyable, satisfying, comfortable, congenial Some color combinations can create **pleasant** effects to the eye. 어떤 색들의 조합은 보기에 즐거운 효과를 만들어낸다.	즐거운, 유쾌한
29	**procedure** [prəsíːdʒər]	ⓝ	process, proceeding, course legal **procedure** 소송 절차 An employee became the president under the new **procedure**. 한 직원이 새로운 절차에 따라 사장이 되었다.	절차, 순서
30	**rage** [reidʒ]	ⓝ	anger, fury, wrath, frenzy, fury, ferocity fly into a **rage** 벌컥 화내다 Facial expressing, cover many emotions, including excitement, fear, and **rage**. 얼굴 표정은 많은 감정, 흥분, 공포와 분노를 포함한다.	분노, 격노
31	**sac** [sæk]	ⓝ	pouch Our lung consists of numbers of tiny air **sacs**. 우리의 폐는 수많은 작은 공기 주머니들로 구성되어 있다. pollen **sac** 꽃가루 주머니	주머니
32	**seem** [siːm]	ⓥ	appear, assume, look It would **seem** that the weather is improving. 날씨가 좋아질 것 같다.	~인 듯하다
33	**solemn**** [sáləm]	ⓐ	grave, sober, serious, impressive, imposing, majestic a **solemn** apology in a solemn event 엄숙한 행사에서 진지한 사과	엄숙한, 침통한
34	**stammer** [stǽmər]	ⓥ	stutter, hesitate, falter **stammer** out an excuse 더듬거리며 변명하다	말을 더듬다
35	**streamlined** [stríːmlaind]	ⓐ	smoothly shaped drive a **streamlined** racing car 유선형의 경주 차를 운전하다	유선형의
36	**strenuous**** [strénjuəs]	ⓐ	vigorous, arduous, energetic, active, eager, zealous After **strenuous** work or exercise, a person may need a period of rest. 격렬한 일이나 운동을 한 사람은 휴식기간을 필요로 할 것이다. **strenuous** opposition 맹렬한 반대	격렬한, 고생스러운
37	**substitute**** [sʌbstətjùːt]	ⓥ	exchange, replace, change, switch **substitute** for the manager 지배인의 대리 근무를 하다 Cheap barbed wire **substituted** for wood fences. 값싼 가시 철조망이 나무 울타리를 대신하였다.	대신하다
38	**surplus** [sə́ːrplʌs]	ⓝ	remainder, extra Children and pregnant women need a **surplus** of calories for growth. 아이들과 임산부는 성장을 위한 여분의 칼로리를 필요로 한다. a **surplus** population 과잉 인구	나머지, 잔여, 여분의 양
39	**tier** [tiər]	ⓥ	row, layer, line, rank The auditorium had **tiered** galleries with some private boxes. 강당은 개인용 칸막이 좌석이 있는 층으로 된 관람석이 있다.	층층으로 쌓다
40	**troublesome** [trʌ́blsəm]	ⓐ	annoying, laborious, difficult, arduous, burdensome **troublesome** chores 귀찮은 집안일 British troops treated **troublesome** colonists as rebels. 영국군은 성가신 식민지인들을 반군으로 취급하였다.	까다로운, 귀찮은

01. Papyrus was a vegetable substance that decayed rapidly in damp climates.
    - Ⓐ damage
    - Ⓑ stretch
    - Ⓒ moist
    - Ⓓ examine

02. Many countries have implemented literacy programs that rely on volunteer teachers.
    - Ⓐ appraised
    - Ⓑ increased
    - Ⓒ carried out
    - Ⓓ abolished

03. Most big airports are located on the outskirts of central cities.
    - Ⓐ surrounding regions
    - Ⓑ stock yards
    - Ⓒ back streets
    - Ⓓ manufacturing district

04. Malnutrition is another problem in world health.
    - Ⓐ Obesity
    - Ⓑ Cancer
    - Ⓒ Famine
    - Ⓓ Diabetes

05. Homemade or commercially prepared formulas can be substituted for mother's milk.
    - Ⓐ enhanced
    - Ⓑ replaced
    - Ⓒ catalyzed
    - Ⓓ provided

06. A surplus in crops pushes prices down because there is more food than people need.
    - Ⓐ tax
    - Ⓑ financial
    - Ⓒ extra
    - Ⓓ precious

07. Radio and TV stations can interrupt their regular programming at any time to broadcast a news bulletin.
    - Ⓐ change
    - Ⓑ supplement
    - Ⓒ erase
    - Ⓓ suspend

08. The whole subject of happiness has, in my opinion, been treated too solemnly.
    - Ⓐ slowly
    - Ⓑ weakly
    - Ⓒ somberly
    - Ⓓ carefully

09. The British tax on tea enraged Adams and most of his fellow colonists.
    - Ⓐ eased
    - Ⓑ hurt
    - Ⓒ infuriated
    - Ⓓ surprised

10. The art of carving is a strenuous and time-consuming process, which ties up the sculptor's money with expensive materials.
    - Ⓐ various
    - Ⓑ arduous
    - Ⓒ outdoor
    - Ⓓ competitive

11. The rodent has about 30,000 genes, 99 percent of which have counterparts in human DNA.
   Ⓐ complements
   Ⓑ components
   Ⓒ chromosomes
   Ⓓ matches

12. Hurricanes occasionally lash at the Massachusetts coastline.
   Ⓐ strike
   Ⓑ expand
   Ⓒ cause
   Ⓓ destroy

13. For example, a sponge circulates water laden with food particles throughout its otherwise stationary body.
   Ⓐ secure
   Ⓑ flexible
   Ⓒ immobile
   Ⓓ hung

14. After the bombing of Pearl Harbor, some Americans directed their rage at people of Japanese ancestry.
   Ⓐ focus
   Ⓑ respect
   Ⓒ jealousy
   Ⓓ fury

15. Real lines help to define space and create perspective, the illusion of depth and distance.
   Ⓐ scenary
   Ⓑ interval
   Ⓒ far and near
   Ⓓ dream

16. If you think positive, reasonable, and healthy thoughts, you can help make your life more pleasant and successful.
   Ⓐ popular
   Ⓑ valuable
   Ⓒ delightful
   Ⓓ attractive

17. Food was not as plentiful as it once had been, because the Europeans had driven the Indians into poorer land.
   Ⓐ followed
   Ⓑ forced
   Ⓒ rerouted
   Ⓓ resettled

18. Calhoun claimed that a state could nullify any law passed by Congress which it believed had violated the Constitution.
   Ⓐ declare
   Ⓑ denounce
   Ⓒ negate
   Ⓓ pass through

19. Diabetes, known for decades in many countries as the "silent killer," has rapidly become a major chronic disease for the Chinese people.
   Ⓐ disagreeable
   Ⓑ unseasonable
   Ⓒ long-term
   Ⓓ momentous

20. Because air is one of the most common causes of friction, automobiles and airplanes are streamlined to make them move more easily through the air.
   Ⓐ tough
   Ⓑ brightly spotted
   Ⓒ striped
   Ⓓ smoothly shaped

DAY 11-15 Exercise

01. Martin saluted stately.
    - (A) fascinated
    - (B) sauntered
    - (C) saved
    - (D) greeted

02. a legitimate government
    - (A) lawful
    - (B) foreign
    - (C) new
    - (D) tyrannical

03. radiate in all directions
    - (A) saunter
    - (B) brazen
    - (C) applaud
    - (D) spread out

04. commend her for her excellent grades
    - (A) award
    - (B) laud
    - (C) fascinate
    - (D) crush

05. punish ruthlessly
    - (A) precariously
    - (B) relentlessly
    - (C) diligently
    - (D) meagerly

06. an unstable government
    - (A) precarious
    - (B) clever
    - (C) devoid
    - (D) impending

07. an ineffective manager
    - (A) sluggish
    - (B) devoid
    - (C) destitute
    - (D) impending

08. advertising revenue
    - (A) subject
    - (B) enmity
    - (C) income
    - (D) enigma

09. with unanimous applause
    - (A) fragrant
    - (B) particle
    - (C) agreed
    - (D) dread

10. the by-product of modern-day living
    - (A) alley
    - (B) hinterland
    - (C) derivative
    - (D) anniversary

11. irregular heartbeats
    - (A) various
    - (B) unevenly
    - (C) suitable
    - (D) sensible

12. You are eligible to membership.
    - (A) buoyant
    - (B) elated
    - (C) qualified
    - (D) jubilant

13. lubricate the machinery regularly
    - (A) smooth
    - (B) saturate
    - (C) spiral
    - (D) meander

14. unevenly distributed
    - (A) equivocally
    - (B) unequally
    - (C) increasingly
    - (D) inevitably

15. a matter of vital importance
    - (A) essential
    - (B) unequal
    - (C) serene
    - (D) judicious

16. interrupt an electric current
    - (A) hinder
    - (B) falter
    - (C) cancel
    - (D) replace

17. nullify a contract
    - (A) invalidate
    - (B) separate
    - (C) assemble
    - (D) sustain

18. surplus material
    - (A) needed
    - (B) extra
    - (C) flimsy
    - (D) expensive

19. counterparts in Western Europe
    - (A) pacemakers
    - (B) opposites
    - (C) borders
    - (D) extras

20. a cause of chronic stress
    - (A) ingenuous
    - (B) minute
    - (C) habitual
    - (D) vigorous

01. Wool can be made into an extremely strong fabric with either a rough or smooth texture.
    A apparel
    B jacket
    C fabric
    D blouse

02. Commodity prices and real-estate values became inflated.
    A pivotal
    B swollen
    C depressed
    D insignificant

03. In a word-recognition strategy called structural analysis, a reader uses clues within the word itself to guess what the word means.
    A meanings
    B prefixes
    C summaries
    D indications

04. Free nations grant the press the right to report news and opinions without government interference.
    A share
    B teach
    C send
    D give

05. The body uses food to build new tissues and to repair those that have worn out.
    A establish
    B heal
    C amass
    D reshape

06. Excessive use of some chemical fertilizers may decrease the ability of bacteria to decay humus and produce nutrients naturally.
    A diminish
    B remove
    C limit
    D vary

07. Competition among journalists often creates sensational news reports calculated to attract a large audience.
    A informed
    B aimed
    C given
    D suggested

08. As more and more plastic packaging is used by consumers, more plastic waste is generated.
    A requested
    B estimated
    C caused
    D produced

09. The plants would certainly desiccate in the absence of rain for weeks.
    A seek
    B oppose
    C dehydrate
    D forage

10. Agricultural science and it's education expanded after 1900 in response to the need for more technical knowledge and skills.
    A relaxed
    B structured
    C increased
    D unused

11. The golden rule is the principle states that people should treat others as they would like to be treated themselves.
    Ⓐ law
    Ⓑ movement
    Ⓒ study
    Ⓓ product

12. Automobile companies, and especially Hyundai, built cars that offered comfort, style, and speed at a reasonable price.
    Ⓐ perfect
    Ⓑ speedy
    Ⓒ economical
    Ⓓ simple

13. Scientists have discovered that the speed and direction of seismic waves change abruptly at certain depths.
    Ⓐ creatively
    Ⓑ suddenly
    Ⓒ dramatically
    Ⓓ gracefully

14. John R. Parkes and his colleagues at the University of Bristol, have found somewhat higher concentrations of microorganisms living in sediments beneath the ocean floor.
    Ⓐ actions
    Ⓑ populations
    Ⓒ convergence
    Ⓓ temperatures

15. The English had governed Ireland for centuries, but the Irish hated English rule.
    Ⓐ considered
    Ⓑ abhorred
    Ⓒ differentiated
    Ⓓ acquiesced

16. By studying fossils, paleontologists learn what kind of life existed during various periods of the earth history.
    Ⓐ used
    Ⓑ provided
    Ⓒ obliterated
    Ⓓ lived

17. By using language, human beings have developed the ability to reason and to solve problems on a far higher level than any other animal.
    Ⓐ demand
    Ⓑ capability
    Ⓒ velocity
    Ⓓ approach

18. Many of neoclassical critics were bothered by Shakespeare's failure to follow rules that Aristotle had established certain rules for writing drama.
    Ⓐ checked
    Ⓑ intrigued
    Ⓒ annoyed
    Ⓓ argued

19. Enzyme therapy is expensive, and must be delivered intravenously, because enzymes are proteins that can break down if they are digested orally.
    Ⓐ contracted
    Ⓑ vaporized
    Ⓒ fused
    Ⓓ separated

20. In the United States, factories and steam-producing power plants draw about 600 billion liters of water every day from wells, rivers, or lakes.
    Ⓐ derive
    Ⓑ console
    Ⓒ entertain
    Ⓓ fascinate

01. Wilderness campers must notify the superintendent or a park ranger of their plans.
    (A) condoned   (B) deformed
    (C) emulated   (D) informed

02. Many scientists hoped that certain chemicals might be found on the moon to give clues as to how life began on the earth.
    (A) knowledge
    (B) hints
    (C) obstacles
    (D) process

03. The television industry would rate programs on their explicitly violent or sexual content.
    (A) prematurely
    (B) economically
    (C) specifically
    (D) proudly

04. Mozart's compositions are undoubtedly amongst the world's greatest.
    (A) deductively
    (B) irrevocably
    (C) inconclusively
    (D) unquestionably

05. The basic themes in science fiction include time travel, space travel, marvelous inventions or discoveries, life in other worlds, and the invasion of Earth by alien beings.
    (A) extraterrestrial organisms
    (B) unidentified flying objects
    (C) magician
    (D) superman

06. In general, children's books emphasize illustrations much more than do books for adult readers.
    (A) define
    (B) respect
    (C) imitate
    (D) stress

07. Life was finally inscrutable, and its joy was to be found in studying its paradoxes.
    (A) contradictories
    (B) poignant
    (C) mystics
    (D) paramount

08. Heat and pressure change some of the rocks into metamorphic rocks, such as marble and slate.
    (A) hardened
    (B) transformable
    (C) transmutable
    (D) abnormal

09. An imperial power could amass riches by looting subjugated lands of valuable resources.
    (A) manage
    (B) dismiss
    (C) procure
    (D) elevate

10. Until other sources of energy are further developed, nations must conserve fossil fuels to make the supply last as long as possible.
    (A) reactionary
    (B) cautious
    (C) save
    (D) traditional

11. In some cultures, the ancestors are considered as evil spirits, and rituals are used to pacify them.
    (A) engage
    (B) divide
    (C) soothe
    (D) worship

12. When the water evaporates from rivers, lakes, and oceans, it is suspended in the atmosphere, clouds appear.
    (A) excited
    (B) coagulated
    (C) hung
    (D) postponed

13. When building houses, construction workers first begin by excavating holes or trenches for the footing, the lowest part of the foundation.
    (A) planning
    (B) exploration
    (C) digging
    (D) preparation

14. Children learn obedience toward their parents, and both children and adults are expected to show respect for their elders.
    (A) conservation
    (B) skill
    (C) safe
    (D) acquiescence

15. In 1895, during a depression that made conditions worse, a revolution broke out again and threatened to go on endlessly.
    (A) incessantly
    (B) finally
    (C) dominantly
    (D) hardly

16. After harvesting a crop, farmers leave the residues from the crop on the field as a covering for the soil, instead of plowing them under.
    (A) foliages   (B) remains
    (C) wastes   (D) branches

17. After the Declaration of Independence in 1776, each former British colony called itself a state to indicate its sovereign position.
    (A) constitutional
    (B) powerful
    (C) legitimate
    (D) independent

18. Industrial-grade diamonds include stones that are imperfectly formed, contain many inclusions or other flaws, or have poor color.
    (A) incompletely
    (B) unnoticeably
    (C) incredibly
    (D) rapidly

19. Microtubules are unbranched, thin, hollow, tubelike structures composed of protein; they are of varying length and tend to be between 15 and 25 nanometers in diameter.
    (A) column
    (B) dense
    (C) empty
    (D) sparse

20. Health experts suggest that certain people should avoid alcohol altogether, those including children and adolescents; pregnant women; people who are about to drive; anyone who is taking medicine; and individuals who are unable to limit their drinking.
    (A) as a whole
    (B) realistically
    (C) individually
    (D) understandably

합법적인	- legitimate, licit, legal, lawful
재미있는	- witty, amusing, clever, comic, humorous
임박한	- imminent, impending, be about to, take place
귀찮은	- cumbersome, burdensome, awkward, bulky, clumsy, inconvenient
적임의	- eligible, qualified, acceptable, entitled, suitable

순진한	- naïve, ingenuous, candid
극히 중요한	- vital, essential, indispensible, important, critical
딱딱한, 유연성이 없는	- inflexible, rigid, stern, resolute, steadfast, unbending
배회하다	- stroll, ramble, wander, roam, saunter
부패하다	- decay, deteriorate, decline, decompose, rot, spoil

보복하다	- retaliate, avenge, revenge
연구하다	- research, investigate, study, examine, scrutinize
깨우다, 소생하다	- wake, arouse, provoke, stimulate, activate, motivate
말을 더듬다	- stammer, stutter, hesitate, falter, murmur
중상, 비방하다	- slander, libel, blame, defame, scandalize, vilify

적대	- hostility, enmity, antagonism
수입, 세금	- revenue, income, gain, proceeds
수수께끼	- riddle, enigma, conundrum, puzzle, quiz
얼룩	- speck, spot, particle, dot, splotch
대칭	- symmetry, balance, equilibrium

만병통치약	- panacea, cure-all, elixir
곤경, 궁지	- plight, predicament, dilemma
슬픔, 비탄	- sorrow, distress, anguish, grief, sadness, woe
주권자	- sovereign, supreme, chief, paramount, independent
변두리	- outskirt, at the edge, surrounding region, border, fringe, rural

SOLAR OPTIONS FOR ECO-FARMING (EFFECTS OF LEDS ON LEAF LETTUCE)

Researchers at the Chungbuk Province Agricultural Research and Extension Services are onto a ❶ bright idea, as they are using solar energy to grow vegetables ❷ indoors. Scientists ❸ shed some light on the advantages and ❹ challenges of LEDs and fluorescent lights in vegetables such as cabbage and lettuce cultivation in a tightly controlled environment.

In the life cycle of plants, most developmental processes are dependent on light. ❺ Significant biological processes such as germination, shade avoidance, circadian rhythms, and flower induction are all affected by light. Recent advancements in the use of LED lighting in plant and vegetable production systems has researchers looking for ❻ insights into the effects of these ❼ artificial lights on the growth and yield of crops.

The increased use of LEDs in environmentally controlled closed-type plant production systems allows crop production throughout the year, regardless of ❽ external weather conditions. LEDs have some advantages over traditional lighting sources in plant cultivation, In addition, LEDs are available in a variety of narrow wavebands; hence, it is possible to optimize light quality to improve both crop yield and quality.

Many experiments confirmed that both blue and red LEDs have a positive effect on the accumulation of antioxidant phenolic compounds and lettuce growth, respectively. Red light irradiation in the absence of blue light was effective at stimulating the biomass accumulation of lettuce plants; however, this lighting alone induced ❾ abnormal leaf shape and had a negative effect on polyphenolics and antioxidant levels. Therefore, mixture of blue and red lights recommended to ❿ enhance plant growth, quality, and yield because chlorophyll a and b efficiently absorb wavelengths in the blue and red ranges. This budding agricultural technique will help farmers to produce vegetables all year long without the use of pesticides.

The word that closest meaning to

1. bright   Ⓐ very smart   Ⓑ vital   Ⓒ bleach   Ⓓ witty
2. indoors   Ⓐ outdoor   Ⓑ workplace   Ⓒ within a house   Ⓓ exterior
3. shed light on   Ⓐ indicate   Ⓑ clarify   Ⓒ search   Ⓓ receive
4. challenges   Ⓐ invite   Ⓑ utterance   Ⓒ hostility   Ⓓ confront
5. significant   Ⓐ irregular   Ⓑ typical   Ⓒ important   Ⓓ meaningless

6. insights   Ⓐ understanding   Ⓑ splotch   Ⓒ center   Ⓓ scrutiny
7. artificial   Ⓐ authentic   Ⓑ archaic   Ⓒ alarm   Ⓓ man-made
8. external   Ⓐ endemic   Ⓑ outer   Ⓒ foreign   Ⓓ domestic
9. abnormal   Ⓐ diffident   Ⓑ normal   Ⓒ similar   Ⓓ unusual
10. enhance   Ⓐ reduce   Ⓑ expand   Ⓒ improve   Ⓓ stretch

친환경농업을 위한 태양광의 선택 (상추잎에 LED의 효과)

충청북도 농업기술원에 근무하는 연구사researchers가 태양에너지를 이용하여 실내에서 채소를 재배하는to grow vegetables indoors 좋은 아이디어a bright idea를 갖고 있다. 과학자들scientists은 엄격하게 조절되는 환경a tightly controlled environment에서 양배추와 상추와 같은 채소 재배 시in vegetables such as cabbage and lettuce cultivation LED와 형광등의 어떤 장점과 어려움some the advantages and challenges을 명확하게 밝혔다shed light on.

식물의 생활사life cycle에서 대부분의 발육과정은 빛에 의존한다. 발아germination, 음지회피shade avoidance, 활동일주기circadian rhythms와 개화유도flower induction와 같은 중요한 생물적 과정significant biological processes들은 모두 빛의 영향을 받는다are all affected by light. 식물과 채소 생산체계에 LED조명을 사용하는 최근의 진흥recent advancements은 과학자들로 하여금 작물의 생장과 생산량에 이러한 인공조명artificial lights의 효과를 통찰하기 위해 들여다보게 하였다looking for insights into.

환경적으로 조절되는environmentally controlled 밀폐형 식물 생산체계에서 증가하는 LED의 사용은 외부 기상조건과 상관없이regardless of external weather conditions 연중으로throughout the year 작물생산을 가능하게 하였다. LED는 식물재배에서 전통적인 광원traditional lighting sources을 뛰어넘는 여러 장점들을 가지고 있다. 게다가, LED는 다양한 좁은 범위의 파장대로 이용이 가능하기 때문에 작물생산과 품질 모두를 개선하는 데 빛의 질을 최적화하는 것이to optimize light quality 가능하다.

파랑과 빨강 LED가 각각 항산화적 페놀 화합물antioxidant phenolic compounds의 축적과 상추 생장에 긍정적인 효과positive effect를 갖고 있다는 것이 많은 실험들로 확인되었다. 파랑 빛이 없을 때 빨강 빛의 조사red light irradiation는 상추의 생물량 축적biomass accumulation을 자극하는 데 효과적이었지만, 이 빛은 비정상적인 잎의 모양을 유도induced abnormal leaf shape하였고 폴리페놀과 항산화물질의 수준에 부정적인 효과a negative effect를 가져왔다. 따라서 파랑 빛과 빨강 빛의 혼합이 클로로필 a와 b가 파랑과 빨강 범위에서 파장을 효과적으로 흡수하기efficiently absorb wavelength 때문에 식물의 생장, 품질과 생산량을 증진시키는 데 추천되고 있다. 이 개발단계에 있는 농업기술this budding agricultural technique은 농약의 사용 없이without the use of pesticides 오랫동안 농부가 채소를 연중 생산할 수 있도록 도와줄 것이다.

1. Ⓐ   2. Ⓒ   3. Ⓑ   4. Ⓓ   5. Ⓒ
6. Ⓐ   7. Ⓓ   8. Ⓑ   9. Ⓓ   10. Ⓒ

01. **assume** the chair
    - (A) impair
    - (B) take on
    - (C) stretch
    - (D) satisfy

02. a **brutal** person
    - (A) announced
    - (B) delicate
    - (C) cruel
    - (D) abnormal

03. **subdue** the light
    - (A) defeat
    - (B) amaze
    - (C) dissect
    - (D) suppress

04. at full **strain**
    - (A) tension
    - (B) staple
    - (C) sac
    - (D) virtue

05. **spoiled** by mosquitoes
    - (A) marred
    - (B) retract
    - (C) tension
    - (D) censure

06. **pronounce** a word correctly
    - (A) articulate
    - (B) repeat
    - (C) recede
    - (D) scrutinize

07. **condemn** the actions
    - (A) glorify
    - (B) ascribe
    - (C) inform
    - (D) judge

08. We need to **preserve** the forest.
    - (A) involve
    - (B) keep
    - (C) procure
    - (D) barter

09. a **torrential** rain
    - (A) menacing
    - (B) violent
    - (C) viscous
    - (D) broad

10. seek **refuge** with a person
    - (A) uprightness
    - (B) disciple
    - (C) affinity
    - (D) haven

11. **exalt** a person to a high office
    - (A) frighten
    - (B) praise
    - (C) involve
    - (D) recede

12. This invention is **ascribed** to Mrs. Dr. Choi.
    - (A) astonished
    - (B) involved
    - (C) attributed
    - (D) divulged

13. **purchase** of land
    - (A) declare
    - (B) damage
    - (C) buy
    - (D) conquer

14. on one's own **merits**
    - (A) sufferings
    - (B) values
    - (C) distress
    - (D) affinities

15. A long thread is easily **entangled**.
    - (A) divulged
    - (B) involved
    - (C) acclaimed
    - (D) tamed

16. an **insecure** hiding place
    - (A) unsafe
    - (B) unreliable
    - (C) lenient
    - (D) diffident

17. **scrutinize** (a person) through one's spectacles
    - (A) subjugate
    - (B) corrupt
    - (C) affirm
    - (D) examine

18. I **esteem** your advice.
    - (A) respect
    - (B) merit
    - (C) recede
    - (D) adherent

19. His illness **incapacitated** him for work.
    - (A) scared
    - (B) marred
    - (C) disabled
    - (D) astounded

20. **interchangeable** parts
    - (A) unsafe
    - (B) timid
    - (C) viscous
    - (D) equivalent

표제어	품사	동의어와 예문	한글 뜻
1 **acquainted*** [əkwéintid]	a	familiar with, informed about be **acquainted** with law 법률에 정통하다	정통한
2 **ascribe**** [əskráib]	v	assume to, be true of, attribute, impute, refer The alphabet is usually **ascribed** to the Pheonicians. 알파벳은 통상적으로 페니키아 사람이 발명한 것으로 여겨진다.	~에 돌리다, ~가 발명한 것으로 여기다
3 **brutal*** [brú:tl]	a	savage, cruel, inhuman, ruthless, barbarous People convicted of crimes were given **brutal** public punishment. 유죄판결을 받은 사람들이 잔인한 공개 처벌을 받았다.	잔인한, 비인간적인
4 **cognizant** [kágnəzənt]	a	aware, knowledgeable, familiar He was **cognizant** and aware of the difficulty. 그는 어려움을 인식하고 깨닫고 있다.	인식한, 깨달은
5 **comprehensive*** [kàmprihénsiv]	a	exhaustive, inclusive, broad, extensive, sweeping receive a **comprehensive** mind 넓은 마음으로 받아들이다	포괄적인
6 **condemn*** [kəndém]	v	① blame, censure, disapprove, denounce ↔ applaud, praise **condemn** war as evil 전쟁을 악이라고 비난하다 ② sentence, judge, convict, damn, doom ↔ forgive, pardon **condemn** the criminal to life imprisonment 피고에게 종신형을 선고하다	① 비난하다 ② 유죄 판결을 하다, 선고하다
7 **culminate** [kʌ́lmənèit]	v	close, finish, conclude, come to a climax The festivities will **culminate** with a fireworks display. 그 축제들이 불꽃놀이로 최고조가 될 것이다.	최고조에 달하다, 완결시키다
8 **domesticate*** [dəméstikèit]	v	tame, docile We **domesticated** a wild animal in Jeju island. 우리는 제주도에서 야생동물을 길들였다	길들이다
9 **entangle** [intǽŋgl]	v	complicate, involve A long thread is easily **entangled**. 긴 실은 얽히기 쉽다.	관련시키다, 뒤얽히게 하다
10 **esteem*** [istí:m]	v	prize, value, respect I **esteem** your advice highly. 당신의 충고를 매우 존중합니다.	존경하다
11 **exalt*** [igzɔ́:lt]	v	glorify, extol, acclaim, praise **exalt** the national prestige with folk song 민요로 국위를 선양하다	높이다, 칭찬하다
12 **exceptionally**** [iksépʃənli]	ad	specially, abnormally Strict standards for safety requirement have made ships **exceptionally** safe. 엄격한 안전요구기준이 배들을 특별히 안전하게 만들었다.	예외적으로, 특별히

13	**exchange**** [ikstʃéindʒ]	ⓥ barter, interchange, swap	교환하다, 바꾸다
		exchange goods with foreign countries 외국과 교역하다	
14	**gelatinous** [dʒəlǽtənəs]	ⓐ viscous, gelatin-like	점성의
		The fertilized eggs of amphibians have only a **gelatinous** coat. 양서류의 수정된 알은 점성의 외막만을 가지고 있다.	
15	**incapacitate** [ìnkəpǽsətèit]	ⓐ disable	무능력한
		His diseases **incapacitated** him for work. 그의 병은 그를 일할 수 없게 하였다.(병 때문에 그는 일을 할 수 없었다.)	
16	**insecure**** [ìnsikjúər]	ⓐ ① unsafe, untrustworthy, unreliable, precarious ↔ safe	① 안정되지 못한, 불안전한
		an **insecure** hiding place 불안전한 은신처	
		② timid, shy, hesitant, diffident, nervous ↔ confident, certain	② 불안한, 걱정스러운
		an **insecure** feeling about the future 미래에 대한 불안감	
17	**interchangeable*** [intə:rtʃéindʒəbl]	ⓐ equivalent	교환할 수 있는, 호환성이 있는
		Single-lens reflex cameras can utilize a variety of **interchangeable** lenses. 단일렌즈 반사형 카메라는 다양한 호환 가능한 렌즈를 활용할 수 있다.	
18	**merit*** [mérit]	ⓝ worth, virtue, excellence, value	장점, 가치, 공적
		achieve on one's own **merits** 자기 실력으로 달성하다	
19	**misery** [mízəri]	ⓝ wretchedness, distress, suffering, torture	고통, 비참
		Moral rules protect us from **misery** and chaos. 도덕적인 규범은 우리를 불행과 혼란으로부터 보호한다.	
		miseries of mankind 인류의 불행	
20	**mock** [mak]	ⓥ ridicule, sneer	조롱하다, 흉내내며 놀리다
		Comic scenes **mock** the vanity of the legal system. 코믹한 장면이 법체계의 허황함을 조롱한다.	
21	**partisan** [pá:rtizən]	ⓝ adherent, supporter, follower, disciple	도당, 일당
		partisan feeling 당파적 감정	
22	**pouch** [pautʃ]	ⓝ sac, pocket	낭, 주머니
		The nipples of most female marsupials are in a **pouch**. 대부분의 암컷 유대류의 유두는 주머니 안에 있다.	
23	**preserve** [prizə́:rv]	ⓥ save, maintain, keep, conserve, shelter, protect	보존하다, 유지하다
		Laws protect the endangered species and **preserve** their habitat. 법은 멸종위기 종을 보호하고 그들의 서식처를 보존한다.	
		preserve a person from harm ~을 위해로부터 보호하다	
24	**pronounce** [prənáuns]	ⓥ declare, affirm, announce	발음하다
		Accent marks and symbols tell how to **pronounce** the word. 강세부호와 기호들은 단어를 어떻게 발음하는지 알려준다.	
25	**purchase** [pə́:rtʃəs]	ⓥ buy, procure	구입하다, 사다
		purchase a new car 새 차를 구입하다	
26	**refuge** [réfju:dʒ]	ⓝ sanctuary, haven	피난, 도피, 위안물
		a **refuge** from the war-torn city 전쟁으로 폐허가 된 도시로부터 도피	
27	**retire** [ritáiər]	ⓥ withdraw, retreat, recede, retract	물러가다, 퇴직하다
		retire into a country 낙향하다, 시골에 칩거하다	

28	**retreat** [ritríːt]	Ⓥ	withdraw (from) The troops had **retreated** into its own territory. 부대는 자신들의 영토로 퇴각했다.	퇴각하다
29	**scrutinize*** [skrúːtənàiz]	Ⓥ	examine, investigate, study, dissect **scrutinize** the documents 그 문서를 세밀히 조사하다	정밀하게 조사하다
30	**sheath** [ʃiːθ]	Ⓝ	covering, casing, case, cover The base of the leaf of grasses forms a **sheath** that envelops the stem. 초본류의 잎의 기부에는 줄기를 둘러싸는 잎집을 형성한다.	집, 덮개, 씌우개
31	**spoil**** [spɔil]	Ⓥ	damage, go bad, impair, ruin, mar, harm, corrupt This summer is **spoiled** by mosquitoes. 이번 여름은 모기로 망쳤다.	망쳐놓다, 손상하다
32	**staple** [stéipl]	Ⓝ	basic element, basic part **staple** commodities 필수 상품	주요 산물, 원료
33	**strain** [strein]	Ⓥ	stretch, tighten, tension The Revolutionary War severely **strained** the United Kingdom's economy. 독립전쟁은 영국 경제에 심각한 타격을 입혔다. on the **strain** 긴장하여	잡아당기다, 큰 타격을 주다
34	**subdue**** [səbdjúː]	Ⓥ	conquer, defeat, suppress, subjugate, subject **subdue** one's voice 목소리를 낮추다	정복하다, 억제하다
35	**tender*** [téndər]	Ⓐ	① soft, delicate, fragile An elephant has surprisingly **tender** skin. 코끼리는 놀라울 정도로 부드러운 피부를 가지고 있다.	① 부드러운, 연한
			② compassionate, lenient, kind, gentle, loving ⋯ harsh, mean **tender** loving care 상냥하고 사랑스런 보살핌	② 상냥한
			③ sensitive, painful a **tender** wound 만지면 아픈 상처	③ 만지면 아픈
36	**threateningly** [θrétniŋli]	Ⓐⱽ	menacingly **threateningly** clouds 한바탕 비를 뿌릴 것 같은 구름	위협적인
37	**torrential** [tɔːrénʃəl]	Ⓐ	wild, violent Thunderstorms produce hail, **torrential** rains, or strong winds. 천둥번개는 우박, 호우 또는 강풍을 동반한다.	맹렬한, 격한
38	**virtue*** [və́ːrtʃuː]	Ⓝ	goodness, uprightness, morality, justice a woman of **virtue** 정숙한 여인	미덕, 장점
39	**woe** [wou]	Ⓝ	distress, affliction, sorrow, grief, anguish, agony blame all their country's economic **woes** 모든 국가들의 경제적 재난을 비난하다	고통, 슬픔, 재난
40	**zenith** [zíːniθ]	Ⓝ	pinnacle, apex, peak, top ⋯ bottom, nadir The empire reached its **zenith** of wealth and power. 그 제국은 부와 힘의 절정에 도달했다.	정점, 절정

01. Only domesticated animals are usually regarded as livestock.
    (A) uncontrolled
    (B) tamed
    (C) implanted
    (D) hunted

02. Many violent crimes are committed by people who are acquainted with their victims.
    (A) compensated
    (B) worried about
    (C) informed about
    (D) concerned over

03. Dickinson dressed everyday in white, as if to mock the traditions of marriage.
    (A) observe
    (B) describe
    (C) accept
    (D) ridicule

04. The ancient world permitted a variety of family practices that most people would condemn today.
    (A) hostile
    (B) sad
    (C) denounce
    (D) pity

05. The humpback whale's most outstanding feature is its exceptionally long flippers, which may be as long as one 1/3 of its body.
    (A) especially
    (B) normally
    (C) extremely
    (D) uncomparably

06. Yugoslavia had the most effective resistance movement of all the partisans.
    (A) underground fighters
    (B) politicians
    (C) soldiers
    (D) civilians

07. Many food crops tend to spoil quickly, so farmers ship these crops to the market as soon as possible after harvesting.
    (A) melt
    (B) get used up
    (C) go bad
    (D) liquefy

08. Certain red algae are the source of agar, a gelatin-like substance used in laboratories to grow bacteria.
    (A) granular
    (B) crusted
    (C) viscous
    (D) motionless

09. The nipples of most female marsupials are situated in a pouch, called the marsupium, which lies on the stomach.
    (A) organ
    (B) sac
    (C) wound
    (D) artery

10. The South tried to adjust to meet wartime needs, but its economy became strained almost to the breaking point.
    (A) destitute
    (B) strived
    (C) resented
    (D) tensioned

11. Some thunderstorms could become severe and produce hail, torrential rains, or strong winds.
    (A) instant
    (B) long-term
    (C) hard
    (D) beneficial

12. The troops retreated hastily back to Canada, when the destruction of their British fleet threatened their supply lines.
    (A) attacked
    (B) pursued
    (C) withdrew
    (D) intercepted

13. It was language that preserved the memories, common experience and the historical records of the nation.
    (A) transported
    (B) disappeared
    (C) appreciated
    (D) conserved

14. During the late 1850's and early 1860's, the Indians supplied some wagon trains with vegetables and buffalo meat in exchange for tobacco, whiskey, and pieces of iron.
    (A) replace
    (B) sell
    (C) buy
    (D) barter

15. A saint is a holy person who becomes a religious hero by exemplifying a virtues or virtues of his or her religion.
    (A) rituals
    (B) custom
    (C) righteousness
    (D) doctrines

16. The state library houses a comprehensive collection on New York history, including the records of the early Dutch colonists.
    (A) incredible
    (B) thorough
    (C) varied
    (D) rare

17. The luminosity serves a variety of purposes: to identify and recognize species, to lure potential prey, to startle a predator and to warn mates of danger.
    (A) initiate
    (B) correspond
    (C) estimate
    (D) surprise

18. Many Germans blamed all of their country's economic woes on the hated Treaty of Versailles, which forced Germany to give up territory and resources and pay large reparations.
    (A) failure
    (B) inflation
    (C) depression
    (D) distress

19. Millions of seabirds, turtles, fish, and marine mammals die each year by becoming entangled in or consuming the plastic components of litter.
    (A) distinct
    (B) starving
    (C) trapped
    (D) sick

20. The empire reached its zenith of wealth and power under Sultan Suleiman I, known to the Western world as Suleiman the Magnificent.
    (A) completion
    (B) pinnacle
    (C) outset
    (D) decline

01. invent a new device
   Ⓐ create   Ⓑ shock
   Ⓒ render   Ⓓ abuse

02. gaze into a person's face
   Ⓐ regard   Ⓑ contribute
   Ⓒ reprimand   Ⓓ sleep

03. a precarious assumption
   Ⓐ block   Ⓑ explosion
   Ⓒ supposition   Ⓓ concern

04. cooperate with both
   Ⓐ strike   Ⓑ irritate
   Ⓒ devastate   Ⓓ collaborate

05. He involves me in everything.
   Ⓐ afford   Ⓑ shift
   Ⓒ reprimand   Ⓓ concerns

06. knowledge of the facts
   Ⓐ blockade   Ⓑ concern
   Ⓒ learning   Ⓓ vex

07. slash governmental spending
   Ⓐ disconcert   Ⓑ cut
   Ⓒ droop   Ⓓ shatter

08. put a person to trouble
   Ⓐ difficulty   Ⓑ inconvenience
   Ⓒ outcome   Ⓓ supplier

09. a rupture between friends
   Ⓐ statement   Ⓑ destruction
   Ⓒ breach   Ⓓ heritage

10. a soaring ambition
   Ⓐ slumbering   Ⓑ bothering
   Ⓒ staring   Ⓓ rising

11. a rich legacy of knowledge
   Ⓐ tradition   Ⓑ commodity
   Ⓒ demolition   Ⓓ instruction

12. order the police to disperse the crowd
   Ⓐ scold   Ⓑ scatter
   Ⓒ assign   Ⓓ comprise

13. the pensive look in her eye
   Ⓐ raucous   Ⓑ perpetual
   Ⓒ reflective   Ⓓ meditative

14. things indispensable to life
   Ⓐ steadfast   Ⓑ thoughtful
   Ⓒ disturbed   Ⓓ necessary

15. reproach a person
   Ⓐ annoy   Ⓑ include
   Ⓒ blame   Ⓓ beat

16. stable relationship
   Ⓐ annoy   Ⓑ enduring
   Ⓒ concern   Ⓓ surge

17. commodity trades
   Ⓐ legacy   Ⓑ mechanism
   Ⓒ item   Ⓓ breach

18. vexed issue of political union
   Ⓐ bewildered   Ⓑ annoyed
   Ⓒ wilted   Ⓓ destroyed

19. wilted leaves
   Ⓐ generated   Ⓑ cut
   Ⓒ withered   Ⓓ wrecked

20. produce testimony to
   Ⓐ supposition   Ⓑ statement
   Ⓒ justice   Ⓓ effort

표제어	품사	동의어와 예문	한글 뜻
1 **assumption*** [əsʌ́mpʃən]	n	supposition, presumption, premise, postulation He was suspicious of relying on a precarious **assumption**. 그는 근거 없는 추측에 의존하여 의심했다.	가정, 추정
2 **block** [blak]	n	inhibition, obstacle, blocking, blockade It's two **blocks** away. 두 블록 떨어져 있다. a traffic **block** 교통 마비	덩어리, 블록, 장애물, 방해
3 **brittle*** [brítl]	a	breakable, fragile a **brittle** marriage 덧없는 결혼 생활 Airplane windows made of plastics are lighter and less **brittle** than glass. 플라스틱으로 만든 비행기 창문은 유리보다 가볍고 덜 깨진다.	부서지기 쉬운
4 **commodity** [kəmádəti]	n	article of trade, item Salt has been a precious **commodity** since ancient times. 소금은 고대 이래로 가치 있는 상품이었다.	상품, 물품
5 **cooperate*** [kouápərèit]	v	generate, collaborate, unite ↔ oppose hormone **cooperate** the part of body 호르몬은 몸의 일부분으로 작용한다	협력하다, 서로 작용하여 ~ 하다
6 **demolition*** [dèməlíʃən]	n	destruction, destroy, ruin the total **demolition** of the old bridge 오래된 다리의 완전한 붕괴	파괴, 폭파
7 **disconcert** [dìskənsə́:rt]	v	disturb, bewilder, perplex, embarrass He was **disconcerted** by careless response of mine. 그는 나의 부주의한 반응에 의해 당황했다.	당황하다, 방해하다
8 **disperse*** [dispə́:rs]	v	scattered, dissipate, diffuse **disperse** a demonstration 시위를 해산시키다	흩뿌리다, 해산시키다
9 **euphonious** [ju:fóuniəs]	a	having a pleasant sound; harmonious In the midst of the mediocre performance one man's **euphonious** voice stood out. 평범한 연극 중간에 한 남자의 듣기 좋은 목소리가 튀어나왔다.	음조가 좋은, 듣기 좋은
10 **forecast**** [fɔ́:rkæst]	v	predict, foretell, foresee This model **forecasts** the state of the atmosphere for another 1-day period. 이 모델은 다른 1일 기간 동안의 대기의 상태를 예측한다.	예측하다, 예보하다
11 **gaze** [geiz]	v	look, stare, gape, regard **gaze** into a person's face 누구의 얼굴을 응시하다	응시하다
12 **indispensable**** [ìndispénsəbl]	a	necessary, requisite, essential Staple commodity is **indispensible** things to life. 생필품은 살아가는 데 없어서는 안 될 물건들이다. an **indispensible** member of the staff 필요한 스태프 인원	필수불가결한, 필요한
13 **innate*** [inéit]	a	inborn, natural an **innate** instinct 타고난 본능	타고난, 선천적인

14	**invaluable**** [invǽljuəbl]	Ⓐ	priceless, precious Illustrations are **invaluable** to the process of learning and informing. 삽화는 교육 및 정보 제공 과정에서 매우 귀중하다. an **invaluable** article 천금을 주고도 사지 못할 물건	매우 귀중한
15	**invent*** [invént]	Ⓥ	create, originate, conceive, devise Toolmakers **invented** a new device to serve specialized purpose. 연장을 만드는 사람이 특수 목적에 맞추어 새 장치를 발명했다.	창조하다, 발명하다
16	**involve*** [inválv]	Ⓥ	include, embrace, contain, comprise, entail It will **involve** a heavy outlay. 많은 경비가 소요될 것이다.	관련되다, 포함하다
17	**jolt** [dʒoult]	Ⓝ	shock, surprise, startle startle by a loud noise or sudden **jolt** 시끄러운 소음이나 갑작스러운 충격에 깜짝 놀라다	심한 동요, 정신적 충격, 놀람
18	**knowledge** [nálidʒ]	Ⓝ	learning, education Books are a living record of human history and **knowledge**. 책은 인류 역사와 지식의 살아있는 기록이다. gain more **knowledge** 더 많은 지식을 얻다	지식
19	**legacy** [légəsi]	Ⓝ	tradition, culture, heritage, inheritance leave the **legacy** of the thousands of workers 수천의 노동자의 유산을 남기다	유산, 물려받은 것
20	**outburst*** [autbə:rst]	Ⓝ	explosion, outcome, surge an **outburst** of rage 분노가 치밀어 오름 spontaneous **outburst** 자연스러운 폭발	폭발, 분출
21	**pensive** [pénsiv]	Ⓐ	thoughtful, meditative, reflective a **pensive** gaze 생각에 잠긴 응시	생각에 잠긴
22	**permanent**** [pə́:rmənənt]	Ⓐ	lasting, constant, perpetual, everlasting **permanent** ink 바래지 않는 잉크 America indians built **permanent** houses and settled in small villages. 아메리카 인디언들은 영구주택을 짓고 작은 마을에 정착했다.	영구의, 불변하는
23	**preoccupation*** [pri:àkjupéiʃən]	Ⓝ	concern turn sharply away from the **preoccupations** of their predecessors 그들의 전임자의 편견으로부터 급격하게 외면하다	선점, 편견, 염려
24	**purveyor** [pərvéiər]	Ⓝ	supplier the **purveyor** of gourmet foods to the White House 청와대 지정 미식가 수준의 음식 조달업자	공급자, 조달업자
25	**raucous** [rɔ́:kəs]	Ⓐ	loud a **raucous** party 소란한 파티	귀에 거슬리는, 시끌벅적한
26	**render*** [réndər]	Ⓥ	provide, contribute, afford, present, assign **render** a verdict 판결을 내리다	주다, 해주다
27	**reproach*** [ripróutʃ]	Ⓥ	abuse, reprimand, condemn, rebuke, scold, blame **reproach** a person for being idle 누구의 나태함을 꾸짖다	비난하다, 꾸짖다
28	**rupture*** [rʌptʃər]	Ⓝ	bursting, breach a **rupture** between friends 친구 간의 불화	파멸, 불화
		Ⓥ	break, burst, sever	터뜨리다, 찢어지다

29	**self-evident**** [self-évədənt]	**a**	evident, obvious, clear, axiomatic	자명한

It is **self-evident** that my country do not have enough resources.
우리나라가 충분한 자원이 없다는 것은 자명한 일이다.
a **self-evident** axiom 자명한 원리

30	**slash** [slæʃ]	**v**	cut, curtail	베다

The blade **slashed** Jason's hand. 칼날이 제이슨의 손을 베었다.

31	**slumber** [slʌmbər]	**v**	sleep, nap, doze, rest	꾸벅꾸벅 졸다, 하는 일 없이 보내다

slumber away one's life 인생을 헛되이 보내다

32	**soar*** [sɔːr]	**n**	tower, rise, ascend, mount	솟아오름, 높이 솟다

soar up to the sky 하늘로 날아오르다

33	**stable***** [stéibl]	**a**	① fixed, invariable, steadfast, unchangeable	① 안정된, 변화없는

↔ flimsy
a **stable** fence 안전한 울타리
② enduring, lasting, steady, staunch, resolute ② 일정한, 견디는
↔ temporary
a **stable** government tentative 일정한 정부의 시안(시도)
③ sane, rational ③ 제정신의
↔ irrational, crazy
a **stable** personality 성실한 인물

34	**stroke** [strouk]	**n**	strike, blow, beat	타격, 때리기

at a **stroke** 단박에

35	**surge**** [səːrdʒ]	**v**	increase, shift	급격히 오르다

Prices are **surging** up. 물가가 급등하고 있다.
surging in interest 관심의 증가

36	**testimony*** [téstəmòuni]	**n**	evidence, statement	증언, 증거

bear **testimony** 증언(입증)하다
allows the **testimony** of unknown witnesses to be used as evidence
알 수 없는 증인의 증언을 증거로서 사용되도록 허용하다

37	**trouble*** [trʌbl]	**v**	① disconcert, annoy, irritate	① 괴롭히다

be **troubled** with a groundless rumor
근거 없는 소문으로 괴로움을 당하다
② effort, struggle, be concerned with, make an effort, take pains ② 수고하다

n ① difficulty, hardship, inconvenience, suffering, adversity ① 어려움, 고생
car **trouble** 차 고장
② bother, disturb, annoy, vex ② 불편, 성가심, 폐
identify the allergens causing the **trouble**
문제를 일으키는 알레르기 항원을 식별하다

38	**vex*** [veks]	**v**	annoy, bother	성가시게 하다

vex oneself 안달하다, 화내다

39	**wilt*** [wilt]	**v**	wither, fade, wane, droop	시들게 하다, 약해지다

This bacterial disease **will** wilt the leaves of the plants.
이 세균성 병은 식물의 잎을 시들게 할 것이다.

40	**wreck*** [rek]	**v**	destroy, devastate, ruin, shatter	파괴하다, 붕괴시키다

the **wreck** of one's life 인생의 파멸

01. Some animals disperse the seeds of some flower plants.
    (A) dig
    (B) disclose
    (C) scatter
    (D) germinate

02. Locke argued that there are no innate ideas, that is, people are not born with ideas.
    (A) creative
    (B) invaluable
    (C) congenital
    (D) competent

03. Airplane windows made of acrylic plastics are lighter and less brittle than glass.
    (A) petrified
    (B) dense
    (C) easily broken
    (D) sparkled

04. Concentration of pollutants also renders beaches unsafe for people.
    (A) obtains
    (B) masters
    (C) makes
    (D) finances

05. From the glacial to interglacial periods, for example, methane surged by about 50 and 75 percent, respectively.
    (A) decreased
    (B) increased
    (C) emerged
    (D) confined

06. The blade slashed Andrew's hand to the bone and cut him badly on the head.
    (A) shifted
    (B) cut
    (C) examined
    (D) presented

07. For many people, religion is an organized system of beliefs, ceremonies, practices, and worship that center on one supreme God, or Deity.
    (A) bought
    (B) transported
    (C) engrave
    (D) reverence

08. A stroke may result when a blood vessel ruptures and bleeds into the brain or the fluid surrounding it.
    (A) diminishs
    (B) floats
    (C) breaks
    (D) vanishes

09. Bombs wrecked houses, factories, and transportation and communication systems.
    (A) shaked
    (B) altered
    (C) pressed
    (D) destroyed

10. Illustrations are invaluable to the process of learning and giving information.
    (A) precious
    (B) supportive
    (C) useless
    (D) supplementary

DAY 17

131

11. During the ritual of courtship, whales may stroke each other with their flippers.
    (A) clean
    (B) hit
    (C) kill
    (D) help

12. The popularity of the radio soared for about 20 years, until the popularity of television began to boom after World War II (1939-1945).
    (A) lasted
    (B) developed
    (C) escalated
    (D) excelled

13. One of the results of the invention of printing was to make the spelling of fifteenth-century words permanent.
    (A) recordable
    (B) original
    (C) safe
    (D) lasting

14. The – NH2 and the – COOH groups in a protein's amino acid building block, bond together to form a chain.
    (A) pieces
    (B) lapse
    (C) casts
    (D) reproaches

15. Some cells are boxlike with six walls, but others assume a wide variety of shapes, depending upon their location and function.
    (A) regulate
    (B) take on
    (C) contract
    (D) confuse

16. In August 1965, 34 people died and almost 900 were injured in an outburst in the black ghetto of Watts, Los Angeles.
    (A) surge
    (B) round
    (C) explosion
    (D) performance

17. If startled by a loud noise or sudden jolt, they jerk their arms and legs in a reflex action called the startle reflex.
    (A) ride
    (B) delay
    (C) jump
    (D) bounce

18. The Army grants extra pay to various specialists, and to soldiers who serve in combat or perform hazardous duty, such as demolition work.
    (A) destruction
    (B) sale
    (C) renovation
    (D) demarcation

19. To reduce the pollutants in an automobile's exhaust fumes, oil companies cooperated with car manufacturers to produce unleaded gasoline.
    (A) traded with
    (B) learned with
    (C) purchased with
    (D) collaborated with

20. The declaration, which used the Declaration of Independence as a model, states that, "We hold these truths to be self-evident that all men and women are created equal."
    (A) enduring
    (B) obvious
    (C) important
    (D) necessary

01. The Grand Canyon has a lot of deep chasm.
   Ⓐ rift   Ⓑ pond
   Ⓒ layer   Ⓓ pattern

02. disappear in the crowd
   Ⓐ vanish   Ⓑ invade
   Ⓒ obstruct   Ⓓ hustle

03. capable of proof
   Ⓐ savor   Ⓑ apparatus
   Ⓒ evident   Ⓓ element

04. exert one's best efforts
   Ⓐ infringe   Ⓑ disperse
   Ⓒ wield   Ⓓ catalogue

05. reckless driving
   Ⓐ contestant   Ⓑ hyperbole
   Ⓒ imposing   Ⓓ heedless

06. have a heap of work to do
   Ⓐ root   Ⓑ element
   Ⓒ accumulation   Ⓓ devotion

07. spread a rope taut
   Ⓐ animated   Ⓑ dignified
   Ⓒ tedious   Ⓓ tightly stretched

08. No trespassing.
   Ⓐ obstructing   Ⓑ tasting
   Ⓒ intruding   Ⓓ flowing

09. painted in vivid colors
   Ⓐ energetic   Ⓑ accelerated
   Ⓒ antagonist   Ⓓ foe

10. with keen relish
   Ⓐ flavor   Ⓑ hyperbole
   Ⓒ testimony   Ⓓ recovery

11. The proud inheritors of
   Ⓐ dismal   Ⓑ senseless
   Ⓒ haughty   Ⓓ heedless

12. We deem that she is honest.
   Ⓐ enroll   Ⓑ narrate
   Ⓒ regard as   Ⓓ subjugate

13. rehabilitation of national culture
   Ⓐ flavor   Ⓑ imprisonment
   Ⓒ confinement   Ⓓ recovery

14. painted it a dreary color
   Ⓐ cheerless   Ⓑ dismal
   Ⓒ equivalent   Ⓓ dignified

15. an act of wanton cruelty
   Ⓐ lofty   Ⓑ contestant
   Ⓒ alike   Ⓓ senseless

16. dissent from the majority view
   Ⓐ verify   Ⓑ uphold
   Ⓒ disagree   Ⓓ vanquish

17. snap one's finger
   Ⓐ obstruct   Ⓑ accelerate
   Ⓒ click   Ⓓ overcome

18. hasten one's departure
   Ⓐ verify   Ⓑ cause
   Ⓒ hurry   Ⓓ percolate

19. confirm an agreement
   Ⓐ ratify   Ⓑ cause
   Ⓒ scheme   Ⓓ overwhelm

20. A prism decomposes sunlight into its various colors.
   Ⓐ expedites   Ⓑ fall apart
   Ⓒ invades   Ⓓ analyzes

표제어	품사	동의어와 예문	한글 뜻
1 **cavalier** [kævəlíər]	n	chivalrous man, knight, a gentleman The **cavalier** mounted his horse and took off for the mountains. 그 기사가 그의 말에 올랐고 산을 향해 떠났다.	기사
2 **chasm** [kǽzm]	n	rift, hiatus, division, split, breach, gap a great **chasm** between two schools 두 학교 간에 큰 의견차	갈라진 틈, 작은 협곡, 깊은 수렁
3 **comparable*** [kámpərəbl]	a	similar, equivalent, analogous, like, uniform, alike shops **comparable** to those on Fifth Avenue (뉴욕) 5번가의 가게들에 비해서 손색이 없는 가게들 It is often very hard to **compare** all-male and all-female jobs. 모든 남성과 모든 여성의 직업을 비교하기는 어렵다.	비슷한, 유사한
4 **confirm*** [kənfə́:rm]	v	① assure, verify, establish, authenticate, validate It is impossible to **confirm** the miraculous events described in the Bible. 성경에 기술된 기적의 사건들을 확인하기는 불가능하다. ② uphold, strengthen, fortify, support, reinforce **confirm** an argument 논쟁을 지지하다	① 확인하다 ② 지지하다
5 **custody** [kʌstədi]	n	imprisonment, confinement have the **custody** of ~을 보관하다	보관, 수감, 보호
6 **decompose** [dì:kəmpóuz]	v	break up, break down, decay A prism **decomposes** sunlight into its various colors. 프리즘은 태양광선을 여러가지 색으로 분해한다.	분해하다
7 **deem*** [di:m]	v	regard as We **deem** her (to be) honest. 우리는 그녀가 정직하다고 생각한다.	~로 간주하다, 생각하다
8 **disappear*** [dìsəpíər]	v	vanish, fade, evaporate **disappear** in the crowd 군중 속으로 사라지다	사라지다, 희미해지다
9 **dissent** [disént]	v	differ, disagree **dissent** from the opinion 그 의견에 반대하다	반대하다, 의견을 달리하다
10 **dreary*** [dríəri]	a	gloomy, dismal, cheerless; boring, dull, tedious, tiresome a **dreary** time 지루한 시간 a **dreary** sight 적막한 광경	황량한, 울적한 / 지루한
11 **efface** [iféis]	v	hide, erase, conceal She was shy and quick to **efface** any attention. 그녀는 어떠한 주목도 감추기 위해 빠르게 피하였다.	감추다, 지우다
12 **exert*** [igzə́:rt]	v	cause, exercise, wield, apply **exert** intelligence to fight 싸우는 데 지력을 쓰다	(권력 등을) 발휘하다
13 **feature*** [fí:tʃər]	n	elements, characteristic Illustrations are a notable **feature** of children's literature. 삽화는 아동문학에서 현저한 특징이 있다.	특징, 특색

14	**fidelity** [fidéləti]	n	loyalty, faithfulness, devotion promise the **fidelity** to the Queen 여왕에게 충성을 약속하다	충실함, 헌신
15	**flamboyant** [flæmbɔ́iənt]	a	brilliant, showy **flamboyant** speeches 미사여구를 구사한 연설	현란한
16	**hasten** [héisn]	v	accelerate, expedite, hurry, hustle, rush, urge **hasten** one's departure 출발을 서두르다	서두르다, 촉진하다
17	**heap*** [hi:p]	n	mass, pile, stack, accumulation a **heap** of stone 돌산	더미, 축적
18	**impulsive** [impʌ́lsiv]	a	emotional an **impulsive** action 충동적인 행동	충동적인
19	**noble*** [nóubl]	a	lofty, honorable, dignified, imposing, stately man of **noble** character 고매한 사람 known for their **noble** deeds 훌륭한 업적으로 알려지다	숭고한
20	**occult*** [əkʌ́lt]	a	supernatural, mythical, mysterious, secret, mystical Some people have been attracted to the **occult** sciences such as astrology. 어떤 사람들은 점성술과 같은 신비스런 과학에 관심을 가져왔다. the **occult** arts 마술	신비스러운, 초자연적인
21	**on the verge of** [ən ðə vəːrdʒ əv]	prep	at the margin of, edge, periphery, perimeter endanger **on the verge of** extinction 멸종 직전에 처하다	~하려고 하여, ~의 직전에
22	**ooze** [uːz]	v	seep, flow, percolate The secret **oozed** out. 비밀이 누설되었다.	흘러나오다, 스며 나오다
23	**opponent*** [əpóunənt]	a	adversary, antagonist, contestant, enemy, foe a most famous political **opponent** 가장 유명한 정적 an ardent **opponent** of Vietnam War 월남전의 열렬한 반대자	적대의, 반대의
24	**overpower*** [ouvərpáuər]	v	overcome, overwhelm, vanquish, subjugate, subdue, conquer be **overpowered** by the argument 말에 눌리다	이기다, 압도하다
25	**overstatement*** [ouvərstéitmənt]	n	exaggeration, hyperbole, overestimate, magnification It is not an **overstatement** to say it changed the world. 이것이 세상을 바꾸었다고 말하는 것은 과장이 아니다.	과장, 허풍
26	**proof** [pru:f]	n	evidence, testimony, confirmation Free blacks could be enslaved if caught without **proof** that they were free. 자유인이 된 흑인이 자유라는 증거 없이 잡힌다면 다시 노예가 될 수도 있었다. capable of **proof** 사실임을 입증할 수 있는	증거
27	**proud** [praud]	a	arrogant, haughty, overbearing, self-important be extremely **proud** of their ethnic heritage 그들의 인종적 유산을 매우 자랑스럽게 생각하다 the **proud** father (좋은 아들 등을 가져) 득의 양양한 아버지	뽐내는, 자랑하는
28	**reckless** [réklis]	a	irresponsible, heedless, careless, rash, imprudent **Reckless** driving is so risk taking behavior. 무모한 운전은 너무 위험한 행동이다.	앞뒤를 가리지 않는, 무모한

DAY 18

29	**recount** [rikáunt]	**v**	narrate, tell, recite	자세히 말하다, 이야기하다
			recount one's experience 경험담을 말하다	

30	**register** [rédʒistər]	**v**	enroll, list, record, catalogue	기재하다, 등록하다
			the electoral **register** 선거인 명부 An electronic thermometer **registers** the highest and lowest temperature of the day. 전자온도계는 하루 중 최고 및 최저 온도를 기록한다.	

31	**rehabilitation*** [rì:həbìlətéiʃən]	**n**	recovery	회복, 부흥, 재건
			The Red Cross spent much money for disaster relief and **rehabilitation**. 적십자가 재난 구호 및 재활을 위한 많은 돈을 보냈다. **rehabilitation** of national culture 민족 문화의 중흥	

32	**relish** [réliʃ]	**n**	taste, flavor, savor	맛, 풍미
			give **relish** to ~에 풍미를 더하다 Charlie ate quietly but ate with **relish**. 찰리는 조용히 그러나 맛있게 먹었다.	

33	**snap** [snæp]	**v**	break, seperate, bite, nip	탁 부서지다, 덥석 물다
			The wood **snapped** as it burned. 나무가 타면서 부러졌다.	

34	**sprinkle** [spríŋkl]	**v**	scatter, strew, disperse	끼었다, 뿌리다
			sprinkled cheese over his food 그의 음식 위에 치즈를 뿌리다	

35	**stem**** [stem]	**n**	base, root	줄기
			Papyrus was manufactured from the **stem** of the plant. 파피루스는 식물의 줄기로부터 만든다.	
		v	① stop, check, dam, obstruct, hinder	① 막다
			stem a wound 상처의 출혈을 막다	
			② come (from), derive, proceed, originate	② 유래하다
			All my problems **stem** from drinks. 나의 모든 문제는 술에서 비롯된다.	

36	**swirl** [swə:rl]	**v**	whirl, spin, twist	소용돌이치다, 빙빙 돌다
			protoplanetary disk **swirl** around the sun 원시 행성계 원반은 태양 주위를 돈다.	

37	**taut** [tɔ:t]	**a**	tightly stretched, rigid, tight, stiff, tense	긴장하는, 팽팽한
			Keep the string **taut** while you tie the tent. 천막을 묶는 동안 줄을 팽팽하게 유지해야 한다. The ropes was **tautened**. 줄이 팽팽했었다.	

38	**trespass*** [tréspəs]	**v**	encroach, infringe, intrude, invade	침입하다, 침해하다
			Some climbers **trespassed** on the farmer's apple orchard. 일부 등산가들이 그 농부의 사과밭에 무단 침입했다.	

39	**vivid** [vívid]	**a**	bright, animated, spirited, vivacious, vigorous, energetic	발랄한, 밝은, 생생한
			Color produces many effect of **vivid** picture. 색상은 생생한 모습의 많은 효과를 만들어준다.	

40	**wanton** [wɑ́ntən]	**a**	senseless, willful, needless, unjustified	제멋대로의, 이유가 없는
			wantonly murder 동기가 없는 살인 **wanton** destruction of our environment by wanton boys 제멋대로인 소년들의 우리 환경의 제멋대로의 파괴	

01. Inflamed skin may become crusty, and fluid may ooze from it.
    (A) appear
    (B) spread
    (C) erupt
    (D) seep

02. Solar salt works require a hot, dry climate to hasten evaporation.
    (A) permit
    (B) determine
    (C) accelerate
    (D) accompany

03. Because of over hunting, several species of whales are on the verge of extinction.
    (A) on the threshold of
    (B) on the brink of
    (C) on the top of
    (D) on the middle of

04. When sugar is heated, it decomposes into carbon and water.
    (A) dissolves
    (B) melts
    (C) breaks up
    (D) permeates

05. The prefrontal cortex can exert an inhibitory control over actions.
    (A) alleviate
    (B) concern
    (C) exhale
    (D) force

06. On the great decisions of his public career, history has proved him right and his opponents wrong.
    (A) competitors
    (B) administrators
    (C) fellows
    (D) professors

07. In August 1792, the people of Paris took custody of Louis XVI and his family and imprisoned them.
    (A) subsidies
    (B) respect
    (C) protection
    (D) revenue

08. In Islam, Muhammad is considered the final messenger of God, sent to confirm the authentic teachings of the previous prophets.
    (A) verified
    (B) suggested
    (C) proclaimed
    (D) resolved

09. The Italians used machine guns, tanks, and airplanes to overpower Ethiopia's poorly equipped army.
    (A) aid
    (B) encourge
    (C) overwhelm
    (D) depress

10. Many local governments and public enterprises recklessly spent funding on huge public construction programs.
    (A) cautiously
    (B) informatively
    (C) patiently
    (D) irresponsibly

11. Bluegrass features complex vocal and instrumental solos and elaborate harmony in singing.
    A groups
    B plays
    C spotlights
    D employs

12. The Red Cross spent nearly $146 million during the 1960's for disaster relief and rehabilitation.
    A operation
    B recovery
    C casting
    D relaxation

13. Impulsive generals sometimes issued proclamations to free slaves, but Lincoln overruled them.
    A Obedient
    B Impetuous
    C Stubborn
    D Liberal

14. Casimir Pulaski was a Polish noblemen who fought on the side of the American colonials in the Revolutionary War.
    A knight
    B aristocrat
    C lord
    D king

15. Axioms, also called postulates, are statements that are assumed to be true and are therefore accepted without proof.
    A financing
    B publications
    C evidence
    D recognition

16. Vigorous and flamboyant stage performances of Richard Penniman, provided a model for performers to follow.
    A devious
    B humorous
    C singular
    D showy

17. Many people have been attracted to the occult forms of supernatural teachings, such as astrology and spiritualism.
    A theoretical
    B anthropological
    C fundamental
    D supernatural

18. A taut story of flight and danger is set in the future United Kingdom, where technology is avoided and superstition abounds.
    A lightly tinted
    B somewhat opaque
    C tightly stretched
    D delicately made

19. Congress and the Supreme Court may prevent or end any presidential action that exceeds the limits of the president's powers and trespasses on their authority.
    A worsens
    B declines
    C encroaches
    D damages

20. Authors began writing biographies that used descriptive details and dialogues to create a vivid feeling of the subjects and the times in which they lived.
    A odd
    B pale
    C bright
    D simple

01. launch out into
    Ⓐ embark
    Ⓑ handle
    Ⓒ finance
    Ⓓ obey

02. surrender to the enemy
    Ⓐ empower
    Ⓑ abate
    Ⓒ yield
    Ⓓ prevail

03. learning new skills
    Ⓐ talents
    Ⓑ categories
    Ⓒ census
    Ⓓ apprehensions

04. refresh his memory
    Ⓐ stimulate
    Ⓑ conceal
    Ⓒ wide
    Ⓓ gullible

05. a latent, unexpressed hostility
    Ⓐ courageous
    Ⓑ gallant
    Ⓒ potential
    Ⓓ inflexible

06. a slightly lenient view
    Ⓐ hidden
    Ⓑ demanding
    Ⓒ merciful
    Ⓓ brave

07. be entertained with refreshments.
    Ⓐ renounced
    Ⓑ accounted
    Ⓒ pleased
    Ⓓ undertaken

08. obstruct a road
    Ⓐ wield
    Ⓑ block
    Ⓒ relinquish
    Ⓓ select

09. reign over the fashion
    Ⓐ block
    Ⓑ use
    Ⓒ govern
    Ⓓ choose

10. He is entitled to a pension.
    Ⓐ yielded
    Ⓑ qualified
    Ⓒ alarmed
    Ⓓ abated

11. hold a person in high regard
    Ⓐ adroitness
    Ⓑ account
    Ⓒ gadget
    Ⓓ population

12. without prejudice
    Ⓐ criteria
    Ⓑ flavor
    Ⓒ partiality
    Ⓓ base

13. a credulous person
    Ⓐ gullible
    Ⓑ complimentary
    Ⓒ mild
    Ⓓ headstrong

14. ascertain what the cost will be
    Ⓐ insult
    Ⓑ embark
    Ⓒ settle
    Ⓓ dwindle

15. obstinate resistance to
    Ⓐ cajole
    Ⓑ clement
    Ⓒ extensive
    Ⓓ stubborn

16. heroic ambition
    Ⓐ wholesale
    Ⓑ headstrong
    Ⓒ courageous
    Ⓓ potential

17. people drift towards the cities
    Ⓐ block
    Ⓑ determine
    Ⓒ move
    Ⓓ divert

18. The boat disintegrated.
    Ⓐ hidden
    Ⓑ abated
    Ⓒ leaved
    Ⓓ shattered

19. fear about one's future
    Ⓐ aptitude
    Ⓑ living
    Ⓒ fright
    Ⓓ mirth

20. hibernate in wintertime
    Ⓐ reanimate
    Ⓑ inactive
    Ⓒ drift
    Ⓓ perish

표제어	품사	동의어와 예문	한글 뜻
1 **affront** [əfrʌnt]	v	offend, insult, abuse She was **affronted** by his bad behavior. 그녀는 그의 나쁜 행동으로 모욕감을 느꼈다.	모욕을 주다, 상처를 주다
	n	insult, indignity, brickbat bear an extreme **affront** 곤욕을 참다	모욕, 수모
2 **ascertain*** [æsərtéin]	v	determine, settle, discover be **ascertain** the reality by law 법으로 진부를 확인하다	확인하다, 해결하다
3 **census** [sénsəs]	n	population count **census** returns 국세 조사 보고 Most countries in the world have taken at least one **census** in the past. 전세계의 대부분 국가들은 적어도 과거에 한 번의 인구 조사를 했다.	인구 조사
4 **credulous** [krédʒuləs]	a	gullible ↔ incredulous Children are generally more **credulous** than adults. 아이들이 성인들보다 일반적으로 잘 속는다.	속기 쉬운, 잘 믿는
5 **depart*** [dipáːrt]	v	① start, leave, quit, go part ↔ arrive **depart** from the battlefield 전쟁터를 떠나다 ② die, pass, perish, expire **depart** from this life 유명을 달리하다	① 출발하다, 그만두다 ② 사라지다
6 **devaluate*** [diːvǽljuèit]	v	underestimate Some scientists **devaluated** the effects of electron irradiation technique to kill insect. 일부 과학자는 곤충을 죽이는 전자빔 조사기술의 효과를 평가절하했다.	평가절하하다
7 **disintegrate*** [disíntəgrèit]	v	break into pieces, shatter, separate If meteorites are too small, they will **disintegrate** in the atmosphere. 만일 유성이 너무 작다면, 대기 중에서 분해될 것이다.	분해하다, 산산조각나다
8 **drift*** [drift]	v	move, move aimlessly People **drift** towards the cities. 사람들이 도시로 이동한다. left behind by the **drifters** 표류자들에 의해 뒤에 남겨지다	표류하다, 이동하다
9 **embellish** [imbéliʃ]	v	beautify, adorn, decorate To avoid prosecution, the criminal had to **embellish** the truth. 기소를 피하기 위해 범인은 진실을 미화해야만 했었다.	미화하다, 장식하다
10 **endorse** [indɔ́ːrs]	v	approve of **endorse** a policy or program 정책이나 프로그램에 찬성하다	시인하다, 찬성하다
11 **entertain*** [èntərtéin]	v	divert, amuse, please Biography of a great man **entertain** their readers to have a high aspiration. 위인의 전기는 독자들로 하여금 큰 포부를 갖도록 한다.	즐겁게 하다, (희망 등을) 마음속에 품다

12	**entitle** [intáitl]	v	empower, qualify; name He is **entitled** to a pension. 그는 연금 수혜 대상자가 되었다.	권한을 주다 / 제목을 붙이다
13	**fear** [fiər]	n	apprehension, dread, terror, fright, horror, panic in **fear** and trembling 무서워 떨면서	두려움, 우려
14	**flattering** [flǽtəriŋ]	a	complimentary, cajole, laud, extol ↔ criticize always a **flattering** remark to my supervisor 상사에게 비위 맞추는 말을 하다	비위 맞추는, 아첨하는
15	**gaiety** [géiəti]	n	mirth, glee, cheerfulness, joviality have the **gaiety** of nation 대중의 즐거움, 명랑한 풍조를 갖다	활발함, 기분 좋음
16	**heroic** [hiróuik]	a	brave, courageous, dauntless, gallant Most early medieval poems were epics about **heroic** figures. 대부분의 초기 중세의 시들은 영웅적인 인물에 대한 서사시였다. a **heroic** explorer 대담한 탐험가	영웅적인, 용감한
17	**hibernate*** [háibərnèit]	v	dormant, inactive, inert, asleep Some kinds of mammals **hibernate** to avoid winter food shortages. 어떤 종류의 동물들은 겨울의 먹이 부족을 피하기 위하여 동면한다.	동면하다
18	**imposing**** [impóuziŋ]	a	substantial, demanding, impressive **imposing** appearance 멋들어진 풍채 an **imposing** Gothic Cathedral 으리으리한 고딕식 대사원	인상적인, 눈길을 끄는
19	**latent**** [léitnt]	a	hidden, concealed, potential The high **latent** heat of water is related to water's heat capacity. 물의 높은 잠재열은 물의 열 용량과 관련되어 있다. **latent** ability 잠재(능)력	숨어 있는, 보이지 않는 (잠복기의)
20	**launch**** [lɔ:ntʃ]	v	set afloat, send off, begin, embark, undertake Shipbuilders **launch** a canoe to the valley. 배 만드는 사람이 카누를 물에 띄우다.	물에 띄우다, 시작하다
21	**lenient*** [lí:niənt]	a	mild, merciful, clement be **lenient** toward another's errors 타인의 실수를 너그러이 대하다	너그러운, 관대한
22	**lessen** [lésn]	v	diminish, decrease, abate, dwindle **lessen** the length of ~의 길이를 줄이다	적게 하다, 줄이다
23	**livelihood** [láivlihùd]	n	living; vitality, energy write for a **livelihood** 생계로 글을 쓰다, 글을 써서 생활하다	생계, 살림 / 원기, 향기
24	**obstinate*** [ábstənət]	a	unyielding, stubborn, inflexible, headstrong, dogged **obstinate** resistance to ~에 대한 완강한 저항	완고한, 고집 센
25	**obstruct** [əbstrʌkt]	v	block, bar Protestants **obstruct** the administration of justice 항의자들이 법의 집행을 방해한다.	차단하다, 방해하다
26	**pedestal** [pédəstl]	n	base, stand, support Statues rest on their **pedestals**. 각기 받침대에 얹혀 있다.	받침대, 근거
27	**prejudice**** [prédʒudis]	n	bias, partiality Racial **prejudice** has Issued in American History. 인종적 편견은 미국 역사에서 논쟁이 되어 왔다. cast away all **prejudice** 모든 편견을 버리다	편견, 선입관

DAY 19

28	**ratify**** [rǽtəfài]	**v** confirm, sanction, validate, endorse The article was **ratified** by a majority vote. 그 조항은 과반수 찬성으로 승인되었다. **ratify** a treaty 조약을 비준하다	확인하다, 승인하다
29	**refresh**** [rifréʃ]	**v** freshen, enliven, reanimate **refresh** one's memory 기억을 되살리다	새롭게 하다
30	**regard*** [rigá:rd]	**v** consider, account, deem, hold, suppose The matter does not **regard** you at all. 그 일은 너와는 전혀 관계가 없다.	간주하다, 여기다
31	**reign** [rein]	**v** rule, govern, prevail, predominate ↔ obey She **reigned** for 63 years, the longest reign in British history. 그녀는 영국 역사에서 가장 긴 통치인 63년 동안 통치했다.	군림하다, 통치하다
32	**savor** [séivər]	**n** taste, flavor I don't have the time to **savor** this win. 나는 이번 승리에 취할 시간이 없다.	맛, 풍미
33	**scare**** [skɛər]	**v** terrify, alarm, startle, frighten, shock, intimidate An elephant may **scare** an enemy away by sticking its ears. 코끼리는 귀를 찰싹대어 적을 깜짝 놀라게 할 수 있다.	깜짝 놀라게 하다, 위협하다
34	**select**** [silékt]	**v** choose, take, opt for Statisticians **selected** a sample from a larger population. 통계학자는 더 큰 인구로부터 표본을 선택했다. **select** the books 책을 고르다	고르다, 선택하다
35	**skill**** [skil]	**n** ability, talent, knack, aptitude, expertise, adroitness learn behaviors and communication **skills** 행동과 대화 능력을 배우다 a **skilled** performer, but not a star 스타가 아닌 숙련된 공연가	능력, 기술, 기량
36	**standards**** [stǽndərds]	**n** criteria, category Labor **Standards** Law 근로 기준법 questioned our **standards** 우리의 기준을 심사하다	표준, 기준
37	**surrender** [səréndər]	**v** submit, yield, renounce, relinquish **surrender** to the enemy 적에게 항복하다	항복하다, 투항하다
38	**sweeping** [swí:piŋ]	**a** broad, wide, extensive, comprehensive, wholesale, vast A epidemic flu is **sweeping** through Tokyo. 유행성 독감이 도쿄를 휩쓸고 있다. at one **sweep** 단번에, 단숨에	휩쓸어가는, 광범위한
39	**treat**** [tri:t]	**v** ① use, handle, wield, manage **treat** the tools with care 도구를 조심스럽게 사용하다 ② entertain, amuse, cheer **treat** my friends to a great show 내 친구에게 멋진 쇼를 보여주다 ③ nurse, doctor, minister, remedy **treat** the wound 상처를 치료하다 ④ finance, spend, fund **treat** the children to pizza 아이들에게 피자를 대접하다	① 사용하다 ② 즐기다 ③ 돌보다 ④ 자금을 공급하다, 대접하다,
40	**wholesale**** [houlseil]	**a** numerous, extensive, indiscriminate **wholesale** prices 도매 가격	도매의, 광범위한

01. English comedy enjoyed a period of extreme freedom during the reign of Charles II.
    A anarchy
    B government
    C monarchy
    D kingdom

02. Water vapor in the air also holds a tremendous amount of latent heat energy.
    A conductive
    B powerful
    C incomplete
    D inactive

03. Many species are killed by people who believe that the animals threaten their livelihoods.
    A circumstances
    B bread and butter
    C body
    D health

04. The space age opened in 1957 after Russia launched it's first artificial satellite to encircle the earth.
    A mediated
    B send-off
    C joined
    D avoided

05. The government drove state bank notes out of circulation by imposing a tax on their use.
    A immobile
    B impermeable
    C ordaining
    D imaginative

06. No one can avoid stress, but a person can do certain things to help lessen the dangers of becoming ill from it.
    A decrease
    B continue
    C occur
    D respond

07. The United States government has been taking a census on the American population every 10 years since 1790.
    A boom
    B increment
    C official survey
    D decrease

08. Many couples prefer a traditional religious ceremony, although some people depart from custom.
    A hate
    B ignore
    C accustom to
    D derivate from

09. Advertisers pay movie and TV stars, popular athletes, and other celebrities to endorse products.
    A improve
    B criticize
    C advertise
    D understand

10. Ice sheets which are vulnerable to periods of rapid disintegration have disappeared at least once in the past 600,000 years.
    A construction
    B breakup
    C freezing
    D floating

DAY 19

11. Bill Clinton, the 42nd president of the United States, was impeached in 1998 for perjury and obstruction of justice.
    (A) help
    (B) assist
    (C) impediment
    (D) increase

12. Gondwanaland began to break apart at around 140 million years ago, and Antarctica started drifting southward.
    (A) sailing fast
    (B) moving aimlessly
    (C) inflating
    (D) exploding

13. During the two months of campaigning, Grant refreshed his memory about the handling of troops and supplies.
    (A) believed
    (B) renewed
    (C) supported
    (D) eliminated

14. By the time the fighting ended, most of the Seminoles had surrendered or been captured and had been sent to the West.
    (A) resisted
    (B) rebeled
    (C) capitulated
    (D) shot

15. To prevent British forces from sweeping down from Canada into New York, the Continental Congress ordered an invasion of Canada.
    (A) battling
    (B) conveying
    (C) charging
    (D) discouraging

16. Sometimes governments intentionally devalued their money in an effort to increase foreign sales.
    (A) lowered the value of
    (B) increased
    (C) minted
    (D) withdrawal

17. Pohang is a leading city in the wholesale trade of machinery, and Kyeonggi province is a center for trade of agricultural products.
    (A) general
    (B) specific
    (C) mass
    (D) light

18. Adding to the gaiety of the play, is the broad humor of the talkative village constable, Dogberry, and his assistant, Verges.
    (A) value
    (B) society
    (C) extent
    (D) pleasure

19. Ptolemy's observations and theories are preserved in a 13-part work entitled *Mathematike Syntaxis*, or *Mathematical Composition*.
    (A) named
    (B) chosen for
    (C) including
    (D) starring

20. Americans tried to make equality a reality soon after the war by ratifying the 13th Amendment to the Constitution, which officially abolished slavery throughout the United States.
    (A) abolishing
    (B) amending
    (C) approving
    (D) disregarding

01. an avowed enemy
    - Ⓐ deadly
    - Ⓑ declared
    - Ⓒ discouraging
    - Ⓓ defeated

02. entreat them to leave
    - Ⓐ command
    - Ⓑ beg
    - Ⓒ demand
    - Ⓓ expect

03. eroded his determination
    - Ⓐ increased
    - Ⓑ wore away
    - Ⓒ explained
    - Ⓓ justified

04. choose an appropriate excerpt
    - Ⓐ topic
    - Ⓑ title
    - Ⓒ selection
    - Ⓓ leader

05. become a fugitive
    - Ⓐ criminal
    - Ⓑ runaway
    - Ⓒ jailer
    - Ⓓ victim

06. garnish a salad
    - Ⓐ eat
    - Ⓑ toss
    - Ⓒ prepare
    - Ⓓ decorate

07. gruesome details
    - Ⓐ delicious
    - Ⓑ novel
    - Ⓒ horrifying
    - Ⓓ unexpected

08. indulge the children
    - Ⓐ coddle
    - Ⓑ discipline
    - Ⓒ mistreat
    - Ⓓ feed

09. interrogate the witness
    - Ⓐ question
    - Ⓑ believe
    - Ⓒ punish
    - Ⓓ listen

10. a malignant growth
    - Ⓐ harmless
    - Ⓑ dangerous
    - Ⓒ ugly
    - Ⓓ unexplained

11. miscellaneous objects
    - Ⓐ worthless
    - Ⓑ expensive
    - Ⓒ various
    - Ⓓ similar

12. nomadic tribes
    - Ⓐ warlike
    - Ⓑ settled
    - Ⓒ migrant
    - Ⓓ peaceful

13. orthodox belief
    - Ⓐ accepted
    - Ⓑ heretical
    - Ⓒ interesting
    - Ⓓ puzzling

14. guilty of perjury
    - Ⓐ kindapping
    - Ⓑ stealing
    - Ⓒ killing
    - Ⓓ lying

15. a potential threat
    - Ⓐ possible
    - Ⓑ real
    - Ⓒ new
    - Ⓓ minor

16. preclude failure to deliver
    - Ⓐ anticipate
    - Ⓑ prevent
    - Ⓒ cause
    - Ⓓ reveal

17. sagacious remarks
    - Ⓐ nasty
    - Ⓑ humourous
    - Ⓒ kind
    - Ⓓ wise

18. tamper with the evidence
    - Ⓐ begin
    - Ⓑ impede
    - Ⓒ agree
    - Ⓓ cause

19. the uncertainty of the situation
    - Ⓐ doubtfulness
    - Ⓑ newness
    - Ⓒ strangeness
    - Ⓓ sureness

20. be ever vigilant
    - Ⓐ careless
    - Ⓑ timid
    - Ⓒ merciless
    - Ⓓ watchful

1	abound in	be full of, abound with	~이 풍부하다
2	accede to	agree to, consent	~에 동의하다, 응하다
3	account for	explain, illuminate	~을 설명하다
4	(be) acquainted with	informed about, be conscious of	~와 아는 사이이다
5	ahead of	in front of, before	~ 앞에
6	all over	everywhere, around	전체의
7	aloof from	separate from, apart from	~와 거리를 두는
8	arrive at	reach, come to	~에 도착하다, 닿다
9	as well as	in addition to, and	~에 더하여, 게다가
10	(be) at home	(be) comfortable, be well	편안함을 느끼다
11	at odds	in disagreement, dissension	불일치의, 다투어
12	at twilight	at dusk, candlelight, cockshut	황혼의 낮과 밤의 경계에
13	attribute to	identified as, be ascribed to,	~의 탓으로 돌리다
14	belong to	be members of, be part of, fall into	~에 속하다
15	break apart	split, divide	~으로 나누다
16	break out	began, burst out, erupt	발생하다, ~에서 달아나다
17	break up	separate, divide	분리하다, 부서지다
18	brief look	glance, cast, glimpse, dekko	짧은 응시
19	bring about	be caused by, result from	~을 유발 [초래]하다
20	bring out	introduce, present, recommend	~을 소개하다, 선물하다
21	by chance	accidentally, haphazard, incidentally	우연히, 뜻밖에
22	call for	require, need, demand	~을 요구하다, 부르다
23	call off	cancel, abolish, abrogate, annul	~을 취소하다, 철수시키다
24	clean out	empties, clean up, clear away	~을 깨끗이 하다, 치우다
25	clear away	move away, eliminate, get rid of, remove	~을 제거하다, 없애다
26	cling to	sticks to, adhere to, conglutinate	~에 집착하다, 고수하다
27	come through	receive, arrive	도착하다, 해내다, 회복하다
28	come to	regain consciousness, revival, come to oneself	~에 도달하다, 닿다
29	comply with	obey, abide by, how to, observe, stand by	~에 따르다, 지키다, 순응하다
30	concentrate on	focus on, centralize	~에 집중하다
31	conform to	meet, accord with, tally with	~에 따르다, 들어맞다
32	come up with	propose, advise, make suggestions	~을 제시하다, 찾아내다, 따라잡다
33	contrary to	in conflict with, oppose, reverse	~에 반해서
34	count on	trust, rely on, accredit	~을 믿다, 기대하다
35	(be) critical to	crucial for	~에 중요하다
36	cut down	reduces, abridge	~을 줄이다, (가격)을 깎다
37	deal with	concern, involve, relate to	~와 관련되다
38	(be) deflected	(be) deviated, be declined to,	편향되다
39	depend on	are determined by, cling to, rely on, tie to	~에 의존하다, ~을 믿다
40	be deterred from	be kept from, be prevented from	~을 단념하게 하다, 막다
41	devoid of	free of, lacking, absent	~이 결여된, 없는
42	(be) devoted to	reserved for	~에 전념하다, 헌신하다
43	dip in	immersed in	~에 빠지다, 몰두하다
44	dispense with	omit, avoid, do without	~을 필요없이 하다, ~없이 하다
45	dispose of	get rid of, remove	~을 처리하다, 없애다
46	dividing line	boundary, division	경계선
47	do away with	get rid of, throw away	~을 제거하다, 버리다, 죽이다

48	draw from	taken from, rooted from	~에서 끌어내다
49	dwell in	reside in	~에 살다
50	dwindle away	eventually disappearing, gradually, vanish, die away	점점 감소하다
51	engage in	carry on, undertake	~에 착수하다, 종사하다
52	except for	apart from, except	~을 제외하고, ~이외에
53	(be) excluded from	kept out of, be fought off, be ostracized, be kept out of	~로부터 소외되다, 제외되다
54	fail to	do not	~하지 않다
55	(be) fed up	disgusted, bored	~에 싫증나다, 물리다
56	feed on	eat	~으로 먹고 살다, 상식하다
57	fraught with	full of, permeated with, imbued with, abound with	~투성인
58	(be) free of	unhampered by	~에서 자유롭다
59	get over	recover from, heal	~을 극복하다, 회복하다
60	get rid of	discarded, cast away, abandon	~을 처리하다, 없애다
61	(be) granted to	given to, be awarded to	~을 수여하다
62	give in	yield to, concede to	~에 항복하다, 양보하다
63	give out	announce, pronounce, issue	~을 발표하다
64	gives way(rise) to	produce, breed, cause, create	~에 굽히다, 번식시키다
65	go awry	becomes faulty, tread awry	실패하다, 예측에서 어긋나다
66	hand in	submit, give in	제출하다, 인계하다
67	hand out	distribute, give out	분배하다, 제출하다
68	in a rage	outraged, hit the roof, get angry	화를 벌컥 내는
69	in abundance	in great quantities, full of	풍부하게, 다량으로
70	in fact	actually, as a matter of fact	실제로, 사실은
71	in general	usually, on the whole	보통, 대개, 전반적으로
72	in retrospect	looking back, backdate	돌이켜 생각해보면
73	insight into	understanding of	통찰력이 있는
74	instead of	replace, substitute	~ 대신에
75	interfere with	disrupt, hinder, obstruct	~을 방해하다, 막다
76	lead the way	pioneer	길을 안내하다
77	leap up	jump, bounce, vault	뛰다
78	(be) left out of	be excluded from, be fought off, be ostracized	~을 남겨두다, 제외시키다
79	(be) linked to	be related to	~와 관련되다
80	lodge in	deposit in, enter	~에 예치하다
81	look after	care for, see after, take care of	~을 돌보다, 후원하다
82	look over	inspect, checkup, examine	~을 조사하다
83	make do with	manage with	가까스로 ~해 나가다
84	make possible	allows	~할 수 있도록 하다, 허락하다
85	make up	constitutes, form	~을 이루다, 구성하다
86	make up for	compensate for, fetch up, offset, recuperate	~을 만회하다, 보상하다
87	makeshift	crude temporary	일시적인 방편, 임시변통
88	mix up	confuse, mix	~을 섞다,
89	oblivious to	unaware of, forgetful	~을 감지하지 못하는, 알지 못하는
90	of means	with money, rich, wealthy	재산을 가진, 부유한
91	off and on	now and then, ever and again	때때로, 가끔
92	on the wane	stabilizing, comedown, decline, dwindle	줄어드는, 시들해지는
93	on the whole	generally	전체적으로, 전반적으로
94	ought to	should, be supposed to	~해야 한다
95	owing to	due to, thanks to, because of	~ 덕분에
96	pertain to	associated with, be part of, belong to	~와 관계가 있다, 속하다
97	pick up	gathers, acquire	~을 집다, 알다
98	plague with	afflicted by, feazed, harassed	~로 귀찮게 하다, 괴롭히다
99	prior to	before	~이전에
100	pull off	tear away, remove, detach, tear off	~을 벗어나다, 제거하다

DAY 20

101	put off	postpone, delay, hang up	~을 연기하다, 미루다
102	put up	supply	~을 제공하다, 올리다, 붙이다
103	put up with	tolerate, stand	~을 참다, 견디다
104	react to	respond to	~에 반응하다
105	regardless of	whatever	~에 상관없이, 구애받지 않고
106	retreat from	withdraw from, secede	~로부터 후퇴하다
107	root in	base on, derive from	~에 기초를 두다
108	rule out	eliminate, remove	~을 제거하다, 제외시키다
109	run out	became depleted, exhausted, used up	~이 다 떨어지다
110	set apart	differentiate, asunder, detach	~을 구별하다, 따로 놓아두다
111	set forth	set apart, launch, embark, set afloat	~을 설명하다
112	set off	begin, leave, set out, start off	출발하다
113	set up	establish	~을 설립하다, 세우다
114	shed light on	explain	~을 밝히다, 해명하다
115	sit on	serve on, hold a post on	~의 일원으로 일하다
116	skip class	miss class, cut school, stay away from school	수업을 빼먹다
117	spell out	detail, expatiate, expound	~을 자세하게 설명하다
118	spring up	emerge, come into being, engender	갑자기 나타나다
119	spread out	radiate, diffuse, proliferate	(빛, 열) 발산하다
120	stand against	defiance of	~을 무시하다, 저항하다
121	stand for	represents	~을 나타내다, 상징하다
122	stem from	derives from, base on	~에서 유래하다, 기인하다
123	stick to	clings to, pasten	~을 고수하다, 집착하다
124	succumb to	yielded to, give in, submit to	~에 굴복하다
125	(be) suspicious of	be mistrustful of, be doubtful of	~을 의심스러워하다
126	take after	resemble, like	~을 닮다, 쫓아가다
127	take down	record, note down	~을 기록하다
128	take for	confused with	~으로 잘못 알다
129	take in	deceive, befool, cheat	~을 속이다
130	take off	depart, take wing	이륙하다
131	take on	assume, bear	~을 떠맡다, 처신하다
132	take place	occur, appear	열리다, 개최되다
133	take priority	be filled first, give preference to, take into account first	우선권을 얻다
134	take up	absorb	~을 흡수하다, 차지하다
135	teem with	swarm with, be full of, abound with	~이 바글거리다, 풍부하다
136	thrive on	do well on, flourish, prosper	~을 번성하게 하다
137	throw away	discard, chuck away, put off	~을 내던지다
138	tie up	hinder, baffle, block	~을 저지하다, 묶다
139	trade-in	exchange, sell	보상판매를 하다
140	turn down	reject, refuse, decline	~을 거절하다, 낮추다
141	turn into	become, turn to	~로 바꾸다
142	up to	able to make, as many as	~까지
143	usher in	introduce, fetch in, introduce into	안내하다
144	vie for	compete for, rivalize, strife	~와 경쟁하다
145	ward off	keep away from, avoid, evade	~을 피하다
146	wear away	erode, abrased, rub out	차츰 닳다, 부식되다
147	wear out	no longer usable, abrased	닳아 없어지다
148	whisk off	hurry away, take away suddenly	~을 쫓아내다
149	wind up	conclude, terminate, end	끝을 맺다, 마무리를 하다
150	wipe out	destroyed	~을 파괴하다

01. Plants are constantly being challenged by pathogens, but disease is rare.
    (A) confronted with
    (B) do away with
    (C) acquainted with
    (D) make possible

02. Magnetic instabilities that are analogous to earthquakes may account for the flares.
    (A) occurred in
    (B) remnants
    (C) witnesses to
    (D) parallel to

03. Many of the prokaryotes are surrounded by a rough wall rich in carbohydrates and amino acids.
    (A) protected
    (B) encircled
    (C) flooded
    (D) supplied

04. The oldest known fossils are one-celled plants that lived at least 3,100 million years ago.
    (A) finally
    (B) almost
    (C) at minimum
    (D) approximately

05. Streets are kept free from filth in which disease germs thrive.
    (A) complemented by
    (B) elucidated by
    (C) imprisoned by
    (D) unhampered by

06. When water reaches the boiling point, it is not immediately turned into steam.
    (A) altered into
    (B) resemble
    (C) disguise
    (D) cause

07. Both individual organisms and entire species must adapt to the environmental changes in order to survive.
    (A) protect
    (B) keep
    (C) adjust to
    (D) help

08. Decomposition means the breaking down of a substance into two or more parts.
    (A) collapse in
    (B) decrease in
    (C) reordering of
    (D) itemization of

09. Engineers who are called load dispatchers keep track of the current flow through the transmission network.
    (A) send
    (B) trace
    (C) show
    (D) maintain

10. Myofibrils are complex structures composed of filaments that are made up of special proteins called actin and myosin.
    (A) including
    (B) harming
    (C) removing
    (D) constituted of

11. George Washington along with other leaders wondered if the colonies had rebelled against the United Kingdom in vain.
    Ⓐ successfully
    Ⓑ barely
    Ⓒ seriously
    Ⓓ uselessly

12. Lincoln used the powers set forth in the article to free slaves during the Civil War (1861-1865).
    Ⓐ explained
    Ⓑ oracled
    Ⓒ read
    Ⓓ organized

13. To send messages, sailors fly hoists of one to five flags which include code meanings or spell out words.
    Ⓐ evaluate
    Ⓑ interpret
    Ⓒ support
    Ⓓ mention

14. Adaptation or evolution involves changes in genes, which are then passed on from generation to generation.
    Ⓐ transferred
    Ⓑ prepare for
    Ⓒ wait for
    Ⓓ miss

15. During the Dark Ages, many fierce barbarian conquests even threatened to wipe out civilizations in Western Europe.
    Ⓐ altered
    Ⓑ penetrated
    Ⓒ devalued
    Ⓓ destroyed

16. The process by which human beings can arbitrarily make certain things stand for other things may be called the symbolic process.
    Ⓐ replace
    Ⓑ reform
    Ⓒ represent
    Ⓓ restrict

17. Jazz was also partially rooted in black dance music, as well as in the brass band music played in New Orleans during funeral processions and parades.
    Ⓐ linked with
    Ⓑ removed by
    Ⓒ included by
    Ⓓ anchored in

18. Mitochondrias are tiny, numerous organelles that are bounded by two membranes with inner plate like folds called cristae which are associated with respiration.
    Ⓐ twisted by
    Ⓑ tied by
    Ⓒ related with
    Ⓓ connected with

19. In 1888, Riis's photographs of the slums of New York City shocked the public and helped bring about the abolition of one of the city's worst districts
    Ⓐ determined by
    Ⓑ initiated by
    Ⓒ caused by
    Ⓓ bring back

20. The microscope has and continues to have a profound effect on not only plant studies but on the whole of biological sciences and its related fields.
    Ⓐ continuously   Ⓑ partly
    Ⓒ slightly   Ⓓ entirely

01. mock another's hopes
   Ⓐ censure   Ⓑ barter
   Ⓒ ridicule   Ⓓ affirm

02. reach the zenith of prosperity
   Ⓐ pinnacle   Ⓑ justice
   Ⓒ basic part   Ⓓ wretchedness

03. a comprehensive survey
   Ⓐ lenient   Ⓑ violent
   Ⓒ extensive   Ⓓ disable

04. an innate instinct
   Ⓐ reflective   Ⓑ natural
   Ⓒ loud   Ⓓ fragile

05. surge ahead of the pack
   Ⓐ annoy   Ⓑ droop
   Ⓒ reprimand   Ⓓ increase

06. brittle tree branches
   Ⓐ requisite   Ⓑ precious
   Ⓒ fragile   Ⓓ conceived

07. an outburst of emotion
   Ⓐ device   Ⓑ explosion
   Ⓒ mount   Ⓓ ascend

08. the demolition of the old bridge
   Ⓐ ruin   Ⓑ inhibit
   Ⓒ explosion   Ⓓ hardship

09. keep a person in custody
   Ⓐ expedite   Ⓑ imprisonment
   Ⓒ tool   Ⓓ program

10. The secret oozed out.
   Ⓐ strewed   Ⓑ hindered
   Ⓒ seeped   Ⓓ infringed

11. an impulsive action
   Ⓐ dignified   Ⓑ proceeded
   Ⓒ emotional   Ⓓ intruded

12. flamboyant colors
   Ⓐ dignified   Ⓑ supernatural
   Ⓒ showy   Ⓓ irresponsible

13. the gaiety of nation
   Ⓐ joviality   Ⓑ expertise
   Ⓒ design   Ⓓ apprehension

14. ratify a treaty
   Ⓐ divert   Ⓑ reanimate
   Ⓒ suppose   Ⓓ endorse

15. a man of imposing appearance
   Ⓐ insulting   Ⓑ dwindling
   Ⓒ impressive   Ⓓ unyielding

16. decided to retreat
   Ⓐ convict   Ⓑ mollify
   Ⓒ withdraw   Ⓓ respect

17. He has many virtues.
   Ⓐ justices   Ⓑ apexes
   Ⓒ morality   Ⓓ pouches

18. a notable feature
   Ⓐ evidence   Ⓑ characteristic
   Ⓒ plan   Ⓓ instrument

19. endorse the new test
   Ⓐ divert   Ⓑ approve of
   Ⓒ move   Ⓓ predominate

20. depart from one's promise
   Ⓐ leave   Ⓑ validate
   Ⓒ account   Ⓓ underestimate

01. A market is commonly thought of as a place where commodities are bought and sold.
    (A) products
    (B) entrepreneurs
    (C) appropriations
    (D) motives

02. Through the centuries, people have gazed at the moon, worshiped it, and studied it.
    (A) prayed
    (B) scrutinized
    (C) exploited
    (D) stared

03. France's financial troubles helped bring on the French Revolution in 1789.
    (A) subsidies
    (B) breakdowns
    (C) dificiencies
    (D) problems

04. Consumer education provides people with the knowledge which is necessary when making intelligent decisions about buying various products.
    (A) value
    (B) assistance
    (C) learning
    (D) skill

05. An elephant may scare an enemy away by sticking its ears straight out and charging.
    (A) attract
    (B) affect
    (C) frighten
    (D) excite

06. In some parts of Africa and on many Pacific islands, people weave the stems of tall grass into houses.
    (A) leaves
    (B) fibers
    (C) textiles
    (D) stalks

07. Scrupulous proofreading can be lessened the errors in a paper.
    (A) increased
    (B) decreased
    (C) conceed
    (D) expanded

08. Steam engines cost too much to build and maintain, so the steam-powered car gradually disappeared.
    (A) powerful
    (B) increasing
    (C) vanished
    (D) interested

09. Roosevelt improved the merit system by establishing examinations for certain civil service jobs.
    (A) outcome
    (B) surplus
    (C) value
    (D) balance

10. People convicted of crimes were either whipped or given some other type of brutal remedial punishment.
    (A) light
    (B) illegal
    (C) vicious
    (D) ridiculous

11. The golden rule is a principle that states that people should treat others as they would like to be treated themselves.
    Ⓐ hurt
    Ⓑ released
    Ⓒ used
    Ⓓ considered

12. Some victims require surgery to remove the dead tissues and to repair their skin.
    Ⓐ heal
    Ⓑ peel
    Ⓒ wet
    Ⓓ cover

13. Global warming of the atmosphere threatens to raise the earth's average temperature by 2-5 degrees Celsius during the next thirty years.
    Ⓐ jeopardize
    Ⓑ distrust
    Ⓒ fierce
    Ⓓ impudent

14. Over a period of 4,000 years, Indian sculptors created powerful works characterized by spiritual content and technical brilliance.
    Ⓐ controversy
    Ⓑ confusion
    Ⓒ meaning
    Ⓓ examination

15. Because of the importance of weather, meteorologists have developed various ways to forecast weather conditions.
    Ⓐ impede
    Ⓑ divert
    Ⓒ diagram
    Ⓓ predict

16. Martha Graham did not invent American modern dance, but her name came to be synonymous with it.
    Ⓐ originate
    Ⓑ perfect
    Ⓒ publicize
    Ⓓ remember

17. The law required anyone who owned or operated an airplane within the state to register the plane and obtain a pilot's license.
    Ⓐ prove
    Ⓑ drive
    Ⓒ enroll
    Ⓓ board

18. In the 1800's, talented authors and illustrators began to create children's books that intended to entertain rather than just instruct.
    Ⓐ teach
    Ⓑ amuse
    Ⓒ advise
    Ⓓ stimulate

19. Doctors may prescribe drugs as a part of a weight control program for carefully selected patients who are seriously obese.
    Ⓐ chosen
    Ⓑ honored
    Ⓒ supported
    Ⓓ trained

20. Many Ottoman aristocrats were skilled in the arts, languages, and literature, and they set the standard for culture in the Muslim world.
    Ⓐ adept
    Ⓑ clumsy
    Ⓒ argued
    Ⓓ matched

01. Men and women in the US Navy may retire with a pension after 20 years' service.
   Ⓐ begin
   Ⓑ give up
   Ⓒ handle
   Ⓓ finish

02. Across the Appalachians, settlers could obtain a plot of fertile land for a fraction of the cost of land in the East.
   Ⓐ project
   Ⓑ maintenance
   Ⓒ land
   Ⓓ preparation

03. Some operate under unofficial cover, meaning they pose as a private citizen of the United States or of a foreign country.
   Ⓐ act
   Ⓑ violate
   Ⓒ reside
   Ⓓ expel

04. The goal of urban conservation is to make these places more attractive and pleasant to live in.
   Ⓐ enjoyable
   Ⓑ suitable
   Ⓒ useful
   Ⓓ precious

05. Taxation provides about 60 percent of the state government's general revenue.
   Ⓐ tax
   Ⓑ outcome
   Ⓒ income
   Ⓓ production

06. On March 1, 1781, Maryland became the last state to ratify the Articles of Confederation.
   Ⓐ revise
   Ⓑ propose
   Ⓒ affirm
   Ⓓ discuss

07. Henry M. Leland took charge of the Cadillac Automobile Company in the United States, and began building cars that used interchangeable parts.
   Ⓐ special
   Ⓑ equivalent
   Ⓒ separate
   Ⓓ different

08. Elephants are called pachyderms, a term that comes from a Greek word meaning thick-skinned, however, the elephant's skin is surprisingly tender.
   Ⓐ slippery
   Ⓑ gentle
   Ⓒ coarse
   Ⓓ glossy

09. Greek sculptors made columns in the form of clothed female figures called caryatids, which actually held up parts of the building.
   Ⓐ get down
   Ⓑ keep up
   Ⓒ float
   Ⓓ set up

10. Later, Thomas Cromwell supplanted Wolsey as chief minister, and from then on Henry took a greater part in running the country.
   Ⓐ designated   Ⓑ replaced
   Ⓒ surveyed   Ⓓ furnished

11. Because we know nothing, in this view, we should treat all things with indifference and make no judgments.
    A. critic
    B. argument
    C. harmony
    D. apathy

12. An imbalance of certain chemicals in the body or a lack of nutritious foods can delay or permanently damage the development of the nervous system.
    A. delicious
    B. filling
    C. common
    D. nourishing

13. During the previous year, King Louis XV of France had secretly transferred all of Louisiana west of the Mississippi to Spain, to compensate Spain for its military aid and territorial losses during the war.
    A. confront
    B. reimburse
    C. substitute
    D. allow

14. So-called multi-potent neural stem cells may split up periodically in the brain, giving rise to other stem cells and to the progeny which can grow up to be either a neuron or a support cell called the glia.
    A. dehydrating
    B. augment
    C. examining
    D. considering

15. In summer, continental tropical air mass with hot and dry surges over Texas and other parts of the American Southwest.
    A. rushes   B. increases
    C. avalanche   D. stirs

16. In nondemocratic countries, the internal security service often works with the police and other institutions to eliminate dissent and to imprison or kill dissenters.
    A. distraction
    B. consent
    C. rebuff
    D. disagreement

17. Using magic, Prospero creates a tempest that causes a ship carrying his enemies to be wrecked on the island.
    A. fell down
    B. shattered
    C. arrived
    D. expelled

18. Many people bought them from the church, hoping the indulgences would hasten the release of a dead person's soul from purgatory.
    A. identify
    B. access
    C. hurry
    D. secure

19. Wind and daily heating and cooling of the atmosphere produce pockets and swirls of warm and cool air.
    A. swaggers
    B. twists
    C. swindles
    D. spasm

20. Many young person are exposed to substance abuse, reckless driving, and health problems.
    A. careless
    B. senseless
    C. unrefined
    D. cautious

～의 탓으로 돌리다	- ascribe, assume to, be true of, attribute, refer
분해하다	- disintegrate
새롭게 하다	- refresh, freshen, enliven, reanimate
군림하다, 통치하다	- reign, rule, govern, prevail, predominate
즐겁게 하다	- entertain, divert, amuse, please
존경하다	- esteem, prize, value, respect
칭찬하다	- exalt, glorify, extol, acclaim, praise
급격히 오르다	- surge, increase, shift, skyrocket
침입하다	- trespass
정복하다	- subdue, conquer, defeat, suppress, subjugate
관련되다, 포함되다	- involve, include, embrace, contain, comprise, entail
간주하다	- deem, reckon, regard as
포괄적인	- comprehensive, exhaustive, inclusive, broad, extensive, sweeping
불안정한	- insecure, unsafe, untrustworthy, unreliable, unstable
안정된, 변화 없는	- stable, fixed, invariable, steadfast, unchangeable, uniform, consistent, unchanging
점성의	- gelatinous, viscous, gelatinous
부드러운	- tender, soft, delicate, fragile
숭고한	- noble, lofty, honorable, dignified, imposing
매우 귀중한	- invaluable, priceless, precious
가장자리에(～의 직전에)	- on the verge of, at the margin of, periphery, perimeter
유산	- legacy, tradition, culture, heritage, inheritance
증언	- testimony, evidence, statement
회복	- rehabilitation, recovery
장점	- merit, worth, virtue, excellence, value
맛, 풍미	- relish, taste, flavor, savor

Effects of biological control on native biodiversity

Biological control is a component of an integrated pest management (IPM) ❶ <u>strategy</u>. It is defined as the reduction of pest populations by natural enemies and typically involves an active human role. Keep in mind that all insect species are also suppressed by naturally occurring organisms and environmental factors, with no human interference. Natural enemies of insect pests are also known as biological control agents.

Biological control can ❷ <u>potentially</u> have positive and negative effects on biodiversity. The most common problems with biological control occur via predation, parasitism, pathogenicity, competition, or other attacks on non-target species. Often a biological control agent is imported into an area to reduce the competitive advantage of an exotic species that has previously ❻ <u>invaded</u> or been introduced there, the aim being to thereby protect the existing native species and ecology. However the introduced control does not always target only the intended species; it can also target native species. In Hawaii during the 1940s, parasitic wasps were introduced to ❼ <u>control</u> a lepidopteran pest and the wasps are still found there today. This may have a ❽ <u>negative impact</u> on the native ecosystem, however, host range and impacts need to be studied before declaring their impact on the environment.

Over the past 15 years with the rise in biological control interest there has become a greater focus on the non-target impacts that could occur. In the past many biological control releases were not ❸ <u>thoroughly</u> examined and agents of biological control were released without any consideration. When introducing a biological control agent to a new area, a primary concern is its ❾ <u>host-specificity</u>. Generalist feeders (control agents that are not restricted to preying on a single species or a small range of species) often make poor biological control agents, and may become invasive species themselves. For this reason potential biological control agents should be subject to ❹ <u>extensive</u> testing and quarantine before release into any new environment. If a species is introduced and attacks a native species, the biodiversity in that area can change ❺ <u>dramatically</u>. When one native species is removed from an area, ❿ <u>it</u> may have filled an essential ecological niche. When this niche is absent it may directly affect the entire ecosystem.

The word that Closest meaning to

1. strategy   Ⓐ approach   Ⓑ goal   Ⓒ progress   Ⓓ case
2. potentially   Ⓐ easily   Ⓑ possibly   Ⓒ somewhat   Ⓓ absolutely
3. thoroughly   Ⓐ carelessly   Ⓑ partly   Ⓒ completely   Ⓓ negatively
4. extensive   Ⓐ spacious   Ⓑ confined   Ⓒ plentiful   Ⓓ far-reaching
5. dramatically   Ⓐ energetically   Ⓑ drastically   Ⓒ periodically   Ⓓ irregularly

지방 고유의 생물 다양성^{native biodiversity}**에 미치는 생물적 방제의 영향**

생물적 방제^{biological control}는 종합적 해충방제 (IPM; integrated pest management) 전략^{strategy}의 한 구성요소이다. 이것은 천적으로 해충의 밀도를 감소^{the reduction of pest populations by natural enemies}시키는 것으로 정의할 수 있으며 대체로 적극적인 인간의 역할을 수반한다. 모든 곤충 종들은 자연적으로 발생하는 유기체^{naturally occurring organisms}와 인간의 간섭이 없는 환경에 의해 억제된다는 것을 기억해야 한다. 해충의 천적은 또한 생물적 방제제^{biological control agents}로 알려져 있다.

생물적 방제는 잠재적으로 생물 다양성에 긍정적인 효과와 부정적인 효과를 가지고 있다. 생물적 방제가 가진 가장 일반적인 문제들은 포식, 기생, 병원성, 경쟁이나 다른 비표적 생물 종에 대한 공격^{other attacks on non-target} species 등을 통해 일어난다. 종종 생물적 방제가 한 지역에 이전에 침입되었거나^{has previously invaded} 도입되어 온 외래종의 경쟁적 유리한 점을 감소시키고,^{to reduce the competitive advantage of an exotic species} 그렇게 함으로써 기존에 존재하는 그 지역 토착종과 생태를 보호하고자^{protect the existing native species and ecology} 하는 목적으로 수입되었다. 그러나 유입된 방제가 언제나 계획한 생물종뿐 아니라^{does not always target only the intended species} 지역 토착종도 목표로 삼았다. 1940년대 하와이에서는 기생성 벌을 나비목 해충을 방제하기 위하여 도입이 되었고 벌은 오늘날 그곳에서 여전히 발견되고 있다. 이것은 토착 생태계에 부정적인 영향을 준 것일지 모르나 숙주 범위와 영향에 대해서는 환경에 미친 그들의 영향력을 단언하기 전에^{before declaring their impact on the environment} 연구될 필요가 있다.

지난 15년 간 생물적 방제에 대한 관심의 증가로 비표적 생물에 일어날 수 있는 영향에 대해서 많은 관심이 집중되어 왔다^{has become a greater focus on the non-target impacts that could occur}. 과거에 많은 생물적 방제의 방사는 철저하게 검토되지 않았고^{were not thoroughly examined} 생물적 방제 행위자는 어떠한 고려도 없이 풀어주었다^{were released without any consideration}. 새로운 지역에 생물적 방제제를 도입하였을 때 첫 번째 고려사항은 숙주 특이성이다^{a primary concern is its host-specificity}. 잡식성으로 먹는 곤충^{generalist feeders}(방제제로서 단일 종이나 좁은 범위의 종만을 먹도록 한정하지 않는다)은 종종 바람직하지 못한 생물적 방제제가 되고^{often make poor biological control agents} 그들 자신이 침입종이 될 수도 있다. 이러한 이유로 잠재적 생물적 방제원은 폭넓은 심사를 받아야만 하며^{should be subject to extensive testing} 어떤 새로운 환경에 방사하기 전에 검역을 해야 한다^{quarantine before release into any new environment}. 만일 한 종이 유입이 되고 토착종을 공격한다면 그 지역에서의 생물 다양성은 급격하게 변한다. 한 토착종이 한 지역에서 제거되었을 때 유입된 종은 필수적인 생태적 지위를 채우게 될 것이다^{have filled an essential ecological niche}. 이런 생태적 지위가 없을 때 유입된 종은 전체 생태계에 직접적으로 영향을 줄 수도 있다.

1. Ⓐ   2. Ⓑ   3. Ⓒ   4. Ⓓ   5. Ⓑ   6. introduced or exotic   7. the reduction of pest populations
8. other attacks on non-target species   9. small range of species   10. Ⓑ

TOEFL 3
iBT [Finish-up]
정답 · 해설

TOEFL DAY 01

Daily Checkup 01

1. ⓒ	2. Ⓐ	3. Ⓐ	4. ⓒ	5. Ⓑ
6. ⓒ	7. Ⓑ	8. ⓒ	9. Ⓑ	10. Ⓓ
11. ⓒ	12. Ⓑ	13. Ⓐ	14. Ⓑ	15. Ⓓ
16. Ⓐ	17. ⓒ	18. Ⓑ	19. Ⓑ	20. Ⓓ

1. 사업을 진행하다
2. 돈은 나의 동기부여이다. / 나를 움직이는 것은 돈이다.
3. 활기찬 이른 아침의 수영
4. 환자의 고통을 완화시키다
5. 냉소적인 성명을 발표하다

6. 정기적으로 순찰을 도는 구역
7. 활동성이 없는 오랜 기간
8. 계획의 가시적인 성과
9. 전원 생활의 즐거움을 찾다
10. 슬픈 광경

11. 세계 여행을 계획하다
12. 그의 말과 행동은 일치하지 않는다.
13. 차량을 보호할 책임이 있는
14. 고대 이야기 모음
15. 실용적인 목적

16. 뻔뻔스런 젊은 악당
17. 그 클럽 가입에 불안감을 갖다
18. 매운 소스
19. 혈관을 수축하다
20. 나는 환경에 적응하려고 노력했다.

Practice Test 01

1. Ⓑ	2. Ⓓ	3. ⓒ	4. ⓒ	5. Ⓐ
6. ⓒ	7. Ⓐ	8. Ⓑ	9. Ⓐ	10. ⓒ
11. Ⓐ	12. Ⓓ	13. Ⓐ	14. Ⓐ	15. Ⓑ
16. Ⓐ	17. Ⓓ	18. ⓒ	19. Ⓓ	20. ⓒ

1. 물의 가격이 저렴했었기 때문에 사람들은 부주의하게 낭비해 왔다.
2. 셰익스피어는 특정 연기자의 능력에 맞춰 연극을 썼다.
3. 빛 파장이 흐려져 망원경이 흐릿한 영상을 만든다.
4. 지질학자들은 석유가 해저에 존재할 것이라는 증거를 발견했다.
5. 가설은 관찰된 무엇인가에 대한 단지 잠정적이며 증명되지 않은 설명이다.

6. 탄소의 원자량 12는 임의로 12 원자량에 설정됐다.
7. 초기 연구는 관련하여 네안데르탈인의 비효율적인 수렵 채집이 연달아 일어난 죽음의 원인이 되었을 것으로 암시했다.
8. 대부분의 식물세포와 대다수의 동물세포는 너무 작아서 육안으로 확인할 수 없다.
9. 파티에서 일부 학생들은 행동을 잘 한 반면에 다른 학생들은 무례한 행동을 했다.
10. 산은 다른 고도에서 다양한 조건들을 포함하기 때문에, 많은 종류의 동식물에 적합한 환경을 제공한다.

11. 또한, 암호와 키 카드와는 다르게 생체인식 식별자는 잃어버리거나 잊거나 위조할 수 없다.
12. 증가하는 스키 타는 사람들을 수용하기 위해 미국, 캐나다 및 유럽에서 많은 스키장과 리조트들이 확대되거나 개발되었다.
13. 많은 국가들이 자원봉사 선생님에 의존하는 문맹퇴치 프로그램을 실행하였다.
14. 비용 절감을 위해서, 회사들은 원자재를 편리하게 구할 수 있는 국가로 공장을 이전하는 경향이 있다.
15. 휴지 상태는 적절한 환경이 충족되더라도 종자, 꽃 봉우리 및 기타 식물이 성장이 활동하지 않는 기간이다.

16. 조각된 이미지에 대한 명상을 통해, 아시아 사람들은 신의 힘을 이해하기 위해 노력하며 영원히 하나가 되기를 바란다.
17. 삼색설 이론에 따르면 뇌에서 일어나는 색의 감각은 단순하며 직접적인 방법에서의 전자 신호와 일치한다.
18. 오늘의 많은 작품들 특히 「상복이 어울리는 일렉트라(1931)」는 애처로운 주인공과 우울한 분위기를 포함한다.
19. 개신교인들이 다른 국가에서 보다 많은 비율을 구성하지만 라틴아메리카의 전체 인구의 약 5%를 구성한다.
20. 현대판 셰익스피어(소설)은 셰익스피어가 일했던 시대의 사회 및 지적 배경의 고조된 인식을 보여준다.

Daily Checkup 02

1. ⑧	2. ⓒ	3. ⓒ	4. ⑧	5. ⑩
6. ④	7. ⑧	8. ⑩	9. ④	10. ④
11. ④	12. ⑩	13. ⑧	14. ⓒ	15. ⑩
16. ⑩	17. ④	18. ④	19. ⓒ	20. ⑧

1. 자신의 행위를 **변명하다** / 자신의 **옳음을 밝히다**
2. **위기**에 몰아넣다
3. **신중한** 남자
4. 관습에서 **벗어나다**
5. **인정**을 많이 받다

6. 대학에 **영광**을 더하다
7. (대학의) **중간** 시험
8. 침입한 **영상** 증거
9. **몸집**이 작은
10. 내 손의 **격렬한** 고통

11. 그의 부모에 대한 **애정**
12. 군중이 **창고**로 몰려들었다.
13. 강은 도시를 **침수시켰다.**
14. 감정을 **숨기다**
15. **담담한** 태도로 임하다

16. **견딜 수 없는** 더위
17. 분주한 **거리**
18. 우정의 **표명**
19. **악의로** 답변하지 않다 / 묵비권을 행사하다
20. **유복자** / 아버지 **사후에** 난 아이

Practice Test 02

1. ④	2. ⑧	3. ⑩	4. ⓒ	5. ⑧
6. ⑩	7. ④	8. ④	9. ⑧	10. ⓒ
11. ⑩	12. ⑩	13. ⑧	14. ④	15. ④
16. ⑩	17. ⓒ	18. ⑧	19. ⑩	20. ⑧

1. 새들이 음식이 있는 부분으로 아주 많은 수가 **모였다.**
2. 크로스컨트리 스키를 즐기는 사람들은 눈으로 덮힌 평평하거나 약간의 언덕 지형을 **미끄러지듯이** 스키를 탄다.
3. 철학자들은 참과 거짓 사이를 구분하기 위한 **기준**을 정의 내리려고 노력해왔다.
4. 해리슨은 사람들이 이미 존재하는 신비하거나 종교적인 의식을 **정당화하기** 위해 신화를 만들었다고 주장했다.
5. 조오지아 주의 사바나 시는 세계에서 가장 최신의 부두와 **창고** 시스템을 가지고 있다.

6. 상어 **가죽**은 비늘이 제거된 뒤에 더 고급스러운 가죽으로 만들어진다. (luxurious leather 사치스러운 가죽 the scale 비늘)
7. 성난 주민들이 송전철탑의 건설에 항의했다.
8. 이로퀴우스 **연맹**을 구성한 5개의 부족은 그들의 연합을 이끌기 위해 50명의 추장을 선택했다.
9. 지도자는 사람들에게 정리해고와 다른 희생을 받아들여 **위기**를 극복하자고 호소하였다.
10. 많은 다양한 라디오 주파수를 처리하는 동일한 **중간** 주파수의 사용은 라디오 디자인을 단순하게 한다.

11. 도시 중심지역에 폭탄이 터져 1명이 사망하고 50명이 넘게 부상을 당하여 경기가 **망쳐졌다.**
12. **아마추어** 천문학자가 이용하는 망원경은 육안의 100배 정도의 해상도를 가지고 있다.
13. 모험 이야기는 환상적인 상황에서 용감한 영웅과 교활한 **악당**에 관한 액션으로 가득 찬 이야기이다.
14. 종교적인 해석은 그림, 조각, 문학, 춤과 영화를 위한 **수많은** 재료를 제공했다.
15. 북미의 서부지역은 많은 화산이 **분출하였고**, 용암이 현재의 오리건 주와 워싱턴 주의 많은 부분을 덮었다.

16. 셰익스피어의 「베니스의 상인」에서 포티아는 바사니오에 대한 그녀의 **애정**을 잃었지만, 그 비밀을 누설하지 않기로 맹세하였다.
17. 적외선 광선을 반사하는 표면은 복사작용에 의해 열의 순환를 **단열할** 수 있다.
18. 역사학자들은 전체 역사의 **범위**를 고대, 중세, 근대 초기와 현대의 4개의 큰 기간으로 나눈다.
19. 바다 아래의 지진은 수마일을 거쳐 해안을 **물에 잠기게 하는** 쓰나미라고 하는 거대하고 파괴력이 강한 일련의 파도를 만들 수 있다.
20. 컬러 레이저 프린터는 **비싸지 않아** 이익이 많이 남지 않지만, 제조사들은 프린터 토너를 만들어 아직도 많은 수익을 낸다.

Daily Checkup 03

1. Ⓐ	2. Ⓒ	3. Ⓓ	4. Ⓓ	5. Ⓒ
6. Ⓑ	7. Ⓓ	8. Ⓑ	9. Ⓒ	10. Ⓒ
11. Ⓒ	12. Ⓑ	13. Ⓓ	14. Ⓑ	15. Ⓑ
16. Ⓓ	17. Ⓓ	18. Ⓒ	19. Ⓒ	20. Ⓐ

1. 역경과 싸우다
2. 앵무새는 인간의 말을 흉내 낸다.
3. 평판과 결합하여
4. 대통령을 암살할 음모
5. 눈을 깜박거리다

6. 8명의 범죄자를 석방하다
7. 참담한 생활 여건
8. 가난은 창피한 게 아니다.
9. 타고난 권리
10. 슬픈 결과를 얻다 / 실패하다

11. 두 팔을 벌리다
12. 보석으로 장식된
13. 무관심에 상처를 입다
14. (누구를) 버릇이 없어 꾸짖다
15. 죽은 듯이 고요함

16. ~에게 물건을 달라고 조르다
17. 그는 자신의 일에 열정을 느끼다
18. 당황하여 말문이 막히다
19. 기억에 남다
20. 실수로 잘못 대답하다

Practice Test 03

1. Ⓑ	2. Ⓓ	3. Ⓐ	4. Ⓒ	5. Ⓑ
6. Ⓐ	7. Ⓑ	8. Ⓓ	9. Ⓐ	10. Ⓒ
11. Ⓓ	12. Ⓓ	13. Ⓓ	14. Ⓐ	15. Ⓑ
16. Ⓐ	17. Ⓑ	18. Ⓒ	19. Ⓑ	20. Ⓓ

1. 동물의 일부 종들은 단순히 멸종되고 자손을 남기지 않는다.
2. 이 과학적 방법은 귀납적과 연역적 양쪽 조합이 필요하다.
3. 지구에서 물질은 3가지 형태인 고체, 액체와 기체로 존재한다.
4. 질산은이 영상에서 표백된 후에, 필름에서 투명해진다.
5. 형법을 위반한 사람은 경찰에 의해서 체포될 수 있으며 지역, 주 및 연방법에 따라 법정에 서게 된다.

6. 동요는 어린이를 즐겁게 하거나 진정시키는 율동적인 시이다.
7. 많은 사람들은 빠른 움직임과 급변화에 원활하게 익숙해져 있다.
8. 태양은 평온한 시기보다는 급격한 활동이 발생하는 시기에 X선 뿐만 아니라 자외선을 더 발산한다.
9. 제1차 세계대전 이후, 인종과 관련한 문제가 북부 도시에서 점점 더 긴박해졌다.
10. 모든 별들은 빛을 내는 에너지를 결국 소진할 것이다.

11. 언제라도 체포된 적이 있는 사람의 대략 2/3는 범죄 경력이 있다.
12. 많은 바다 생물들이, 다른 종을 잡는 그물망에 우연하게 (종이) 잡혀서 의도적이지 않게 감소해 왔다.
13. 아무도 지난 경제호황처럼 경기침체 시기의 생각을 받아들일 수 없었으며, 이해가 잘 되지 않았고 쉽게 통제가 되지 않았다.
14. 일본군은 항복이 치욕이라 믿었기에 연합군에게 생포되는 일은 거의 없었다.
15. 많은 환경운동가와 철학자들은 인간 이외의 생물도 생존을 하기 위한 고유한 권리가 있다고 믿는다.

16. 비극 「오셀로」에서 셰익스피어는 질투는 '찬사의 조롱이므로 녹색눈의 괴물이 먹이를 먹는 것 같다'고 표현하였다.
17. 완벽한 다이아몬드는 균열, 흠, 결점이나 흐린 모양의 외관상의 결함이 없어야 한다.
18. 베토벤은 아버지의 성격을 물려받지 않아 아버지에게 반항하였으며 큰 슬픔에 잠겼었다.
19. 보호론자들은 전세계에 멸종위기 종을 8,000종 이상으로 분류하여 왔는데, 개별적으로 연구되지 않아 온 많은 다른 종들도 똑같이 위험에 처해 있을 것이다.
20. 에코인섹트사는 천안시에 공장을 지어 곤충 밀도를 경제적 허용 수준 아래로 유지시켜 주는 효과적인 친환경 농자재의 제품을 주요 고객인 농민들에게 전달해왔다.

Daily Checkup 04

1. Ⓑ	2. Ⓐ	3. Ⓒ	4. Ⓑ	5. Ⓐ
6. Ⓐ	7. Ⓓ	8. Ⓒ	9. Ⓒ	10. Ⓑ
11. Ⓒ	12. Ⓑ	13. Ⓓ	14. Ⓐ	15. Ⓑ
16. Ⓒ	17. Ⓐ	18. Ⓐ	19. Ⓓ	20. Ⓑ

1. 국내와 국외에서
2. 선거 사기
3. 혁신을 위한 끊임없는 욕망
4. 실패를 두려워하는
5. 우는 아이를 달래려고 노력하다

6. 개혁의 선구자
7. 상품을 분류하다
8. 추로로 떨다
9. 연극을 재공연하다
10. 누구를 힘으로 능가하다

11. 대량 생산
12. 성장을 보장하지 않다
13. 폭동을 부추기려고 시도하다
14. 그의 방식은 조용하고 겸손하다
15. ~라는 뜻의 진술을 하다

16. 교수로 임용되다
17. 의견의 차이점
18. 그물로 운반하다
19. 비정상적인 행동
20. 참석자 없는 회의

Practice Test 04

1. Ⓑ	2. Ⓒ	3. Ⓒ	4. Ⓐ	5. Ⓑ
6. Ⓓ	7. Ⓓ	8. Ⓒ	9. Ⓒ	10. Ⓑ
11. Ⓐ	12. Ⓓ	13. Ⓒ	14. Ⓒ	15. Ⓑ
16. Ⓒ	17. Ⓓ	18. Ⓑ	19. Ⓐ	20. Ⓒ

1. 많은 야채재배 농부들이 농산물을 수확한 후 곧 시장으로 운송한다.
2. 동요는 어린이를 즐겁게 하거나 진정시키는 율동적인 시이다
3. 디자인과 실용적 편안함이 도입된 혁신적 기술은 문화의 확산을 더욱 쉽게 만들었다.
4. 대한민국에서 거의 10만 명의 재능 있는 학생들이 특별 언어 교육프로그램에 등록을 마쳤다.

5. 원시인들은 굶주리는 것이 두려워서 식량을 수집하는 일에 관심을 두었을 것이다.
6. 우주왕복선은 서비스뿐만 아니라 발사작업을 필요로 하는 인공위성을 복구할 수 있다.
7. 기본적인 '우주의 성분'은 물질이라 불리며 고체, 액체 및 기체의 형태로 존재한다.
8. 헌법은 언론, 종교 및 표현의 자유와 같은 권리들을 보장한다.
9. 동맥이 절단되면, 피는 심장의 규칙적인 반복운동에 따라 뿜어져 나온다.
10. 그레이엄은 1951년에 댄서인 에릭 호킨스와의 결혼에 실패하자 절망에 빠졌다.

11. 구리, 납, 니켈, 아연 등의 매장량이 확인된 광물질들은 100년 안에 고갈될 수 있다.
12. 더 좋은 식물 품종과 비료의 개발은 여러 주요 작물의 수확량을 두 배, 심지어 세 배로 늘리는 데 도움을 주었다.
13. 1944년, 김구 선생은 대한민국 임시정부의 주석으로 취임했다.
14. 1832년 말에 사우스캐롤라이나 주는 연방 관세법이 위헌이라 선언하였으며 항구에서 관세 징수를 거부했다.
15. 아기는 연령에 상관없이 목욕할 때 방치하지 말아야 한다.

16. 기후학자들은 특히 최근 온난화 경향과 관련하여 인간의 활동이 기후 변화에 영향을 끼쳐왔다는 것에 동의하지 않는다.
17. 그는 조용하고 겸손한 성격이어서 상당히 수줍어했고, 리더처럼 보이지 않았다.
18. 전통적인 관습에서는 개인이 아무리 엉뚱한(비정상적인) 행동을 한다고 하여도 대중의 행동보다는 더 놀랍지 않다.
19. 숲을 농지로 전환하는 것은 대기로부터 탄소를 흡수하고 온실효과를 감소시키는 나무를 제거한다.
20. 연극을 통해, 셰익스피어는 그의 대비극적 작품에서 어둠을 밝게 할 인간의 몇 가지 본질을 통해 인간의 최악의 상태를 묘사한다.

TOEFL DAY 05

Daily Checkup 05

1. ⑩	2. ⓐ	3. ⓐ	4. ⑧	5. ⓒ
6. ⓐ	7. ⑧	8. ⑩	9. ⓐ	10. ⑧
11. ⑧	12. ⓒ	13. ⑩	14. ⓐ	15. ⑩
16. ⓐ	17. ⑧	18. ⓐ	19. ⓒ	20. ⓒ

1. 동물에 대한 인도적인 치료
2. 현지 실사
3. 770페이지의 소설을 요약하다
4. 동기 없이
5. 그들의 이익이 침해되다.

6. ~에 대해 의심을 가지다
7. ~에 대해 분개하다
8. 머리를 혹사하다
9. 두려움에 떨다
10. 길을 비틀비틀 걷다

11. 누구의 몸을 망치다
12. 숙제를 늦장 부리며 하다
13. 다른 사람을 배려하다
14. 책의 부피
15. 자연보호 운동을 촉진하다

16. 정교한 비평
17. 달아난 말을 추적하다
18. 긴팔원숭이와 오랑우탄은 주로 나무 위에서 산다.
19. 즐거운 국내 환경
20. 다른 무엇보다도 먼저

6. 설탕은 물에 녹으며 물 전체를 달게 한다.
7. 어느 밤, 달은 은빛 지구본처럼 빛난다.
8. 섬유질은 대량으로 음식에 첨가되어 노폐물을 장(腸)을 통해 이동시킨다.
9. 많은 지역사회는 질병으로부터 사람을 보호하도록 돕는 예방접종 프로그램이 있다.
10. 에피쿠로스는 물을 마시지 않고 건조한 빵을 먹으면서 행복을 추구했다.

11. 개척자들은 도끼를 이용하여 덤불을 자르고, 나무를 잘게 자르고, 통나무를 대패질(손질)을 했다.
12. 그리스의 천문학자 프톨레마이오스의 이론은 태양뿐만 아니라 모든 행성이 지구를 중심으로 공전한다는 것이다.
13. 발생학은 생명의 가장 초기 단계에서 생명체가 발달하는 방법을 연구하는 학문이다.
14. 국립공원시스템은 국립공원, 국립기념비, 국립역사 및 국가적 역사 현장 등의 20개 유형의 지역으로 구성된다.
15. 모든 전자기기에서 회로는 전기 전류가 흐르는 기기에 경로를 제공한다.

16. 시와 주정부는 많은 도시재건 프로젝트를 계획하며 개인 투자자들에게 장려금을 제공한다.
17. 남북전쟁 후 「톰아저씨의 오두막」은 주로 책을 바탕으로 한 소설의 요약본과 연극을 통해 많은 사람들에게 잘 알려졌다.
18. 100년대의 로마제국은 지중해 주변의 모든 땅을 포함하며 영국 해협의 서쪽까지 제국을 넓혔다.
19. 630년대 비잔틴 영토는 몇 년 전에 먼저 설립된 종교인 이슬람의 깃발을 휘날리는 아랍 침입자들에 의해 공격당했다.
20. 학습장애는 집중, 조정, 언어, 기억 등 기본 기술의 발달에 지장을 줄 수 있다.

Practice Test 05

1. ⓐ	2. ⑧	3. ⑩	4. ⑩	5. ⓒ
6. ⑧	7. ⓒ	8. ⓐ	9. ⓒ	10. ⓒ
11. ⓒ	12. ⑩	13. ⑩	14. ⓐ	15. ⑧
16. ⓒ	17. ⓒ	18. ⑧	19. ⑩	20. ⑩

1. 국내 시장은 해외 시장보다 덜 위험하다.
2. 워터게이트 사건은 대통령에 관한 대중의 인식을 한층 더 악화시켰다.
3. 별이 반짝이는 동안 행성은 빛을 낸다.
4. 탐욕과 게으름은 현대문명에서 악으로 여겨지지 않는다.
5. 보살이란 미덕과 지혜의 삶을 살면서 부처가 되기로 맹세한 사람이다.

Exercise 01-05

1. ⑩	2. ⑧	3. ⓒ	4. ⑩	5. ⑧
6. ⑩	7. ⓒ	8. ⑧	9. ⑩	10. ⑩
11. ⑧	12. ⑧	13. ⓒ	14. ⑧	15. ⑩
16. ⑩	17. ⑧	18. ⑩	19. ⑧	20. ⑧

1. 긴장하고 있는 사람
2. 쓰레기를 제거하다
3. 특징이 잘 묘사되었다.
4. 동향을 따르다
5. 뜨거운 물이 뿜어 나왔다.

6. 무대를 떠나다
7. 시골지역을 황폐화시키다
8. 대량 생산
9. 세상을 품은 바다
10. 눈 깜짝할 사이에

11. 아마추어 프로그램 제작자
12. 여기저기 뒤져 책을 찾다
13. 일찍 잠자리에 드는 것에 익숙하다
14. 미국은 50개의 주를 포함한다
15. 임의로 선택하다

16. 자기의 재능을 썩히다
17. 악역을 맡다
18. 화산은 격렬하게 분출하였다.
19. 체스를 두며 놀다
20. 오점 없이

Practice Test 01-05

1. ⑩	2. ⓒ	3. ⓒ	4. ⑩	5. ⓒ
6. ⓒ	7. ⑩	8. ⑧	9. ⑧	10. ⑧
11. ⓒ	12. ⑧	13. ⑧	14. ⓒ	15. ⑧
16. ⓒ	17. ⑩	18. ⓒ	19. ⑧	20. ⑩

1. 비록 과학자들은 제너의 백신이 효과적이라는 것을 깨달았지만, 왜 그런지 이유는 알지 못했다.
2. 여우는 종종 교활하고 올빼미는 현명한 것으로 묘사되었다.
3. 식민지 시대에는 많은 라틴아메리카의 화가들이 유럽 스타일을 모방하였다.
4. 셔먼은 끔찍한 파괴가 전쟁을 계속하려는 적의 의지를 꺾을 것으로 희망했다.

5. 이탈리아에서는 로마 사제 및 더 높은 성직자들이 세속적인 황태자처럼 살았다.
6. 거칠고 부자연스러운 소리의 조화는 불협화음이다.
7. 카우보이 모자는 눈을 가릴 수 있는 넓은 챙이 있었다.
8. 인간의 몸이 올바르게 기능하려면 다양한 영양소가 필요하다.
9. 이신론에 따르면 신은 자연을 통제하여 기계적으로 지속되게 하였다.
10. 일반적으로 다이아몬드는 그 어떤 다른 보석보다 단단하고 광택이 뛰어나기 때문에 가장 가치 있는 보석이다.

11. 여러 로마가톨릭 선교사들 특히 바르톨로메 데 라스 카사스 주교는 원주민들에 대한 보다 인간적인 처우를 호소했다.
12. 심리학자들은 개인 인성의 표현으로 이러한 시험에 대한 응답을 해석할 수 있다.
13. 작가는 소설과 장편의 비소설에서 적절한 자료를 발췌할 수 있다.
14. 2000년대 한국은 휘발유와 난방유 가격의 상승으로 인한 주기적인 연료 부족을 경험하였다.
15. 그들은 동물의 가죽 및 털로 옷을 만들고 은신처를 짓기 위해 나뭇가지와 다른 자연 재료를 이용하였다.

16. 할로윈 기간에 맞춰, 젊은 배우 겸 영화감독인 오슨 웰스는 주간 라디오 프로그램 '실시간 머큐리 연극' 방영을 위해 소설을 각색하였다.
17. 그 역할을 잘하기 위해서 연기자는 사람의 감정, 태도 및 동기에 대해 익히 알고 있어야 한다.
18. 전문적인 생물학자가 되기 위한 최소한의 교육 자격조건은 대학에서 과학 학사학위이다.
19. 워싱턴의 초상화는 1달러짜리 지표와 25센트 동전에 나타난다.
20. 조련사는 최상의 상태와 완벽하고 다치지 않은 깃털을 가진 새를 선택한다.

Intensive Practice 01-05

1. ⑩	2. ⑧	3. ⑩	4. ⑧	5. ⓒ
6. ⑧	7. ⓒ	8. ⑧	9. ⑧	10. ⑩
11. ⑧	12. ⓒ	13. ⑧	14. ⑧	15. ⑩
16. ⑧	17. ⑧	18. ⓒ	19. ⑧	20. ⑧

1. 광물의 광택은 표본마다 다를 수 있다.
2. 남성 생식세포는 동물과 식물 유기체간에 형태와 모양이 상당히 다양하다.
3. 그리스 최고 수학자 중 한 명인 유클리드는 기원전 300년경에 원소에 관해 저술했다.
4. 보석은 보석류 및 기타 장신구에 사용되는 무기질이거나 다른 형태의 물질이다.
5. 많은 경우에 일부 약물은 세포매개 면역뿐만 아니라 항체 반응도 감소시킨다.

6. 집에서 사는 것은 **애정을** 느끼는 사람들과 가까이 지내도록 해준다.
7. 역선택필터는 분자를 **분해하여** 필터 소재 내로 들어간 다음 확산되도록 한다.
8. 일부 사람들은 현실과는 확연히 차이가 나는 세상의 행복을 **추구한다.**
9. 배가 바람을 가로질러 항해할 때 **옆으로** 미끄러지지 않기 위해서는 무언가가 있어야 한다.
10. 많은 바다 생물들이 다른 생물을 포획하기 위한 그물에 **우연히** 잡혀서 숫자가 감소해 왔다.

11. 푸에블로 인디언인 마리아 마티네즈는 남서부 푸에블로 부족들 사이에서 도자기 제작을 예술로 **부활시켰다.**
12. 이 이야기는 세상에서 자기가 가장 똑똑한 탐정이라고 믿고 있는 **활발하고** 재치 있는 여우에 관한 이야기이다.
13. 오리부리 공룡으로 알려진 하드로사우르스는 강한 뒷다리가 있고 꼬리가 뻣뻣하게 **뻗어** 지면과 평행을 이룰 수 있다.
14. 국립공원관리공단은 공원 내 그 어떤 동물들에게도 먹이를 주거나 **괴롭히거나** 만지지 말라고 방문객들에게 지속적으로 안내를 했다.
15. 4대 유인원 중의 한 부류(나머지 셋은 고릴라, 침팬지와 보노보 원숭이)인, 퐁고 피그미우스는 서남아시아 보르네오와 수마트라 섬의 숲에 **절묘하게** 적응하였다.

16. 작가는 항상 **신뢰할 수 있는** 근거 자료를 사용해서 기사가 정확한 정보를 제공하도록 해야 한다.
17. 단백질이 만들어질 때, 단백질은 리보솜(세포 안의 RNA와 단백질의 복합체)으로부터 **분리되어,** ER 시스터네(긴 세포)를 통해 부드러운 ER(리보솜이 없으며) 안으로 이동한다. 단백질은 나중에 변형이 될 수 있다.
18. 톨스토이의 유명한 걸작, 「죄와 벌(1866)」에서 작가는 두 번의 살인을 저지른 학생의 **고뇌에 찬** 마음을 파헤쳤다.
19. 강수량의 대략 75%가 다시 바다로 흐르며, 나머지는 대지로 **스며들어** 육지 상수도가 된다.
20. 전문가들은 이 시스템이, 다른 사람의 목소리를 모방하는 **재주**가 있는 사람이라도 실제 사람의 목소리를 단지 피상적으로만 비슷하게 모방할 수 있기 때문에, 상당히 신뢰할 수 있다고 말한다.

Daily Checkup 06

1. Ⓑ	2. Ⓑ	3. Ⓐ	4. Ⓒ	5. Ⓒ
6. Ⓒ	7. Ⓐ	8. Ⓒ	9. Ⓑ	10. Ⓓ
11. Ⓑ	12. Ⓑ	13. Ⓒ	14. Ⓒ	15. Ⓑ
16. Ⓒ	17. Ⓑ	18. Ⓐ	19. Ⓓ	20. Ⓑ

1. **위생**의 이유로
2. 어떤 일이 사실이라고 **주장하다**
3. 누구에게 비밀을 지킬 것을 **맹세하다**
4. 금속의 **용해**
5. **완전히 다 자란** 식물

6. **겉면**의 측정
7. **구두** 약속(언약)
8. 홍수로 인하여 생긴 손실을 **파악하다**
9. **구어체**를 사용하다
10. **성급한** 약속

11. **작은 충돌**이 확대되어 큰 전쟁이 된다.
12. **하품을** 하면서
13. 호수의 **잔잔한** 물결
14. 학교에서 개인 주도성을 위한 넓은 **시야(영역)**의
15. **건장한** 체력

16. 그의 비디오 카세트를 **탐내다**
17. 예술과 역사의 **욕심 많은** 수집가
18. 난민을 **대피시키다**
19. 자신이 한 말을 **삼키다(취소하다)** / 잘못을 인정하다
20. **자화자찬하다**

Practice Test 06

1. Ⓑ	2. Ⓑ	3. Ⓒ	4. Ⓐ	5. Ⓐ
6. Ⓐ	7. Ⓒ	8. Ⓐ	9. Ⓑ	10. Ⓒ
11. Ⓑ	12. Ⓐ	13. Ⓓ	14. Ⓒ	15. Ⓓ
16. Ⓑ	17. Ⓓ	18. Ⓒ	19. Ⓒ	20. Ⓑ

1. 청소년기는 '성장하는' 기간을 말하며, 엄격히 말하면 태어나서부터 **완전한 발달**까지 적용해야 한다.
2. 요오드의 부족으로 갑상선이 **확장된** 병인 갑상선종을 일으킬 수 있다.
3. 보상 부서는 발명의 **범위**를 결정하고 준비할 시간이 오래 걸릴 수 있다.
4. 봄에는 화려한 분홍색과 흰색 벚꽃이 나무마다 전체에 **핀다.**

5. 즐겁고 편한 활동은 몸의 긴장을 풀고 신체를 **튼튼하게** 하는 데 도움을 준다.

6. 에너지는 광합성과정에서 식물 내에 **모이게 되고** 화학적 화합물로 저장된다.

7. 의회의 개정은 기도로 시작되고 법원 증인은 성경에 선서를 **맹세한다.**

8. 대부분의 광산 기술직은 대학에서 공학학위를 **필요로 한다.**

9. 1966년 대법원은 주와 지방선거에서 투표세(인두세)의 사용을 **불법화하였다.**

10. 버지니아 민병대는 1776년도의 여러 **전투** 후에 식민지에서 던모어 총독을 몰아냈다.

11. 오페라를 즐기는 사람들은 생생하고, 사실적인 인물을 묘사한 피가로의 결혼 오페라를 **칭찬하였다.**

12. 오랜 기간 동안 다이아몬드가 어떻게 형성되는지 알지 못하는 신비한 과정으로 남았었다 / 사람들은 다이아몬드를 **원했지만** 어디서 왔는지 알 수 없었다.

13. 전파 탐지기, 전파 천문장비, **탐사** 우주선이 금성을 탐사하는 데 사용되어왔다.

14. 1776년 3월 영국이 보스턴에서 **철수한** 직후, 호위 장군은 캐나다에서 미국 식민지로 복귀하기 위한 계획을 시작했다.

15. 스키 점프는 고도의 전문화된 스키 기술이며, 스키 선수가 가파른 길을 따라 내려와 끝부분의 **단상**에서 날아오른다.

16. 지하광산에서의 폭발은 광산이 정상적으로 **환기되지** 않는다면 위험한 수준의 이산화탄소가 생성될 수 있다.

17. 1951년 키파우버 심리에서, 에스티 키파우버 미국 상원위원과 상원위원회는 조직범죄에 대한 폭력 **혐의**에 대한 심리가 방송되었다.

18. 두 물리학자 한스 베스와 칼 본 바이츠제커는 태양이 열 핵 **융합**으로 분출하는 충분한 에너지가 태양을 수백만 년 동안 밝게 할 수 있다는 것을 보여주었다.

19. 공중보건당국은 적절한 **위생**, 예방접종 및 검역을 강화하여 질병을 예방하고 통제하는 임무를 수행한다.

20. 안면인식시스템을 개발한 회사는 컴퓨터 프로그램이 외모의 **인위적인** 변형으로 속지 않을 만큼 똑똑하다고 주장한다.

TOEFL DAY 07

Daily Checkup 07

1. Ⓐ	2. Ⓓ	3. Ⓑ	4. Ⓒ	5. Ⓒ
6. Ⓑ	7. Ⓑ	8. Ⓑ	9. Ⓒ	10. Ⓐ
11. Ⓓ	12. Ⓐ	13. Ⓒ	14. Ⓐ	15. Ⓑ
16. Ⓒ	17. Ⓐ	18. Ⓓ	19. Ⓓ	20. Ⓒ

1. 상을 **주다**
2. 창백한 **색깔**
3. 은혜에 보답하다
4. 눈이 **녹고 있다.**
5. 밧줄을 **꽉 붙잡다**

6. 조사를 **방해하다**
7. 군대 **규율**
8. 신세를 **한탄하다**
9. **열렬한** 천주교도
10. 살인죄로 **처형하다**

11. **튼튼한** 몸
12. 누구를 **찔러** 죽음에 이르게 하다
13. 연결 **역**
14. 계곡을 3피트까지 **침수시키다**
15. 저임금에 **항의하다**

16. 지식을 **흡수하다**
17. 그들은 지도자를 **아주 좋아한다.**
18. 해충을 **박멸하다**
19. 구매하기에 **비싸다**
20. 결과에 **무관심하다**

Practice Test 07

1. Ⓐ	2. Ⓐ	3. Ⓐ	4. Ⓓ	5. Ⓒ
6. Ⓓ	7. Ⓐ	8. Ⓐ	9. Ⓐ	10. Ⓒ
11. Ⓒ	12. Ⓓ	13. Ⓒ	14. Ⓒ	15. Ⓐ
16. Ⓐ	17. Ⓑ	18. Ⓓ	19. Ⓓ	20. Ⓐ

1. 언론기자는 전달할 사건의 모든 부분을 정확하게 전달해야 **책임**이 있다.
2. 음모와 **사기**로 리골레토의 사랑하는 딸이 살해됐다.
3. 캘리포니아의 민간 지도자들과 기업가들은 중국 노동자의 첫번째 도착을 기쁘게 **환영했다.**
4. 전자레인지는 냉동 식품을 **해동하고** 국, 채소 및 남은 음식을 데우는 데 특히 유용하다.
5. 조각예술은 힘들고 시간이 오래 소요되는 과정이며, **고가의** 재료로 조각가의 돈을 속박한다.

6. 일부 **민첩한** 포식자들은 튼튼한 뒷다리나 가끔은 네 발로 먹잇감을 추격한다.

7. 돌고래는 좋은 시야를 가졌으며, 전체 몸에는 **예리한** 감각기관이 있다. (the sense of touch 촉각)

8. 1970년대 초반까지, 대부분 국가의 정부들은 자국의 **통화** 환율을 지정하였다.

9. 모든 **독실한** 무슬림들은 무하마드의 탄생지인 메카로 성지순례를 하고 싶어 한다.

10. 디프테리아균이 분비하는 물질은 인간에게 가장 치명적인 **독** 중의 하나로서 1밀리그램의 독은 3.5톤의 기니아피그를 죽이기에 충분하다.

11. 작가가 고객을 찾은 후에는 작가는 전체 크기의 조각을 **만든다.**

12. 일본 조각상은 아시아 본토에서 발달된 스타일을 **개선한 것이다.**

13. 모든 유형의 태양 활동은 흑점주기 단계에서 **최고조**가 된다.

14. 빈곤, 범죄, 절망은 빈민가라 불려졌던 흑인 사회를 **괴롭혔다.**

15. 대부분의 서사시는 전투에서 영웅의 행적이나 인간과 자연 또는 **신**과의 대결을 묘사한다.

16. 유교는 사람들이 보다 좋고 보람 있는 인생을 위해 **규율**과 교육을 통해 인생의 올바른 목적으로 살게 도와준다.

17. 전쟁의 초기, 버지니아 정부는 하퍼스 항에서 미국 무기와 병기를 **몰수하려고** 준비했다.

18. 스위스 제네바에 위치한 국제표준기구(ISO)는 상품과 서비스의 전 세계적인 교역을 쉽게 하기 위해 **균일한** 크기와 기타 세부기준 수립을 위해서 노력한다.

19. 사냥꾼들은 아프리카의 블라우복, 얼룩말 같은 콰가, 스텔러 바다암소 등의 포유류를 **멸종시켜 왔다.**

20. 단극성 신경에서는, 한 쪽은 감각수용기에 연결되며 다른 한 쪽은 신경 접합부라는 특수 **연결 부위**에 다른 신경세포로 연결된다.

Daily Checkup 08

1. ⓑ	2. ⓐ	3. ⓓ	4. ⓐ	5. ⓒ
6. ⓐ	7. ⓐ	8. ⓓ	9. ⓐ	10. ⓒ
11. ⓓ	12. ⓐ	13. ⓑ	14. ⓑ	15. ⓑ
16. ⓒ	17. ⓐ	18. ⓐ	19. ⓒ	20. ⓒ

1. 누구를 **결혼시켜 넘겨주다** / 누구를 며느리(사위)로 주다(삼다)
2. **간단한** 연설을 하다
3. **정상에** (노력해서) 오르다
4. 희소식을 듣고 **기뻐하다**
5. **거주** 외국인

6. 클럽의 규칙을 **개정하다**
7. 연료의 **부족한** 공급
8. **기적적인** 일대 사건
9. 친구에게 **솔직하다**
10. 고열을 **발산하다**

11. 그는 건강을 **회복했다.**
12. 그는 그들의 비웃음으로 **굴욕**을 당했다.
13. **해독하기** 어려운 필체
14. 전화로 **주문하다**
15. 누군가가 비밀을 **공개하여** 왔다.

16. 요즈음 한국은 **복잡하고** 어려운 상황이다.
17. **압도적인** 승리를 거두다
18. **잠수함**
19. **먼** 나라의 사진
20. **위험을 무릅쓰다**

Practice Test 08

1. ⓐ	2. ⓒ	3. ⓒ	4. ⓑ	5. ⓒ
6. ⓑ	7. ⓑ	8. ⓓ	9. ⓓ	10. ⓑ
11. ⓑ	12. ⓐ	13. ⓐ	14. ⓓ	15. ⓑ
16. ⓓ	17. ⓒ	18. ⓐ	19. ⓓ	20. ⓐ

1. 비만은 심장질환과 같은 생명을 위협하는 다양한 **질환**의 위험을 증가시킬 수 있다.
2. 남극 대륙으로 **위험을 무릅쓰고** 간 과학자들은 혹독한 자연 환경에 자주 접한다.
3. 목과 목구멍은 노래를 부르는 데 필요한 **울림**을 제공한다.
4. 영양실조는 좋지 않은 음식, 영양이 **충분하지 않은** 음식이 원인이다.
5. 식물은 수액의 흐름과 같은 **내부의** 움직임을 수행한다.

6. 바다에 사는 생물 중 단지 25만 종만이 확인되었다.
7. 중력 침식은 상당한 양의 바위나 토양이 흐르는 것으로, 산사태나 토양이 흐르는 특징이 있다.
8. 그 회동은 소련과 미국의 정상 간의 첫 정상 회의였다.
9. 많은 독일인들은 제1차 세계대전의 패배와 베르사이유 조약에 따라 부과된 가혹한 취급으로 굴욕을 느꼈다.
10. 바이러스 학자(바이러스를 연구하는 학자)는 1900년대 초에 바이러스가 동물에서 암을 발생시킬 수 있다는 것을 증명했다.

11. 성지순례는 기적적인 치유의 힘이 있는 신성한 물체나 장소로 떠나는 여행이다.
12. 많은 사진 작가들이 사진이 찍히는 줄 모르게 자연스럽게 사람들을 찍기 위해서 스냅사진을 이용한다.
13. 중성미자가 얼음에서 원자와 충돌할 때, 푸른 빛을 발산하며 뮤온이라는 다른 아원자가 생성된다.
14. 최근에 100개 이상의 인공 언어가 만들어졌어도, 세 가지 언어가 기타 다른 언어들보다 훨씬 더 많이 알려지고 사용된다.
15. 형사처럼 천문학자들도 은하수 사이에 존재하는 기체에 대한 이야기를 밝혀내기 위해 간접적인 단서를 모으고 조심스럽게 조각을 맞춘다.

16. 혼자 사냥하는 포식자는 일반적으로 먹잇감에 은밀히 접근하여 숨으며, 대부분의 포식자들은 주위 환경과 어우러진 털 가죽이 있다.
17. 공기가 산맥 반대편 아래로 하강하면서 온도가 상승하고, 상대적으로 습도가 감소하며 구름이 가늘어지거나 사라진다.
18. 기형의 한 가지로 추정되는 원인은 자외선 방사선에 과도하게 노출되면서 기형적인 형태를 찾을 수 있었기 때문이다.
19. 이제 인간 유전자가 해독되면서, 과시적 환경에서 우리 세포 안에 있는 유전적 '청사진'으로 불리는 단백질의 완전체인 단백질 유전정보로 관심이 이동하였다. (proteome 단백질 유전정보)
20. 이집트 수학자들은 범람 후 지역을 측정하거나, 피라미드를 건설할 때 필요한 복잡한 계산을 하는 등 많은 실용적인 수학적 발견을 했다.

TOEFL DAY 09

Daily Checkup 09

1. Ⓐ	2. Ⓐ	3. Ⓐ	4. Ⓒ	5. Ⓑ
6. Ⓓ	7. Ⓐ	8. Ⓓ	9. Ⓐ	10. Ⓑ
11. Ⓑ	12. Ⓑ	13. Ⓒ	14. Ⓓ	15. Ⓐ
16. Ⓑ	17. Ⓐ	18. Ⓐ	19. Ⓒ	20. Ⓑ

1. 필요한 자금을 조달하다
2. 인디언의 악명 높은 학살
3. 책의 부분 요약
4. 의무를 회피하는 계약을 하다
5. 삶의 다양한 측면

6. 절세미인
7. 전염성 병동
8. 우리 조직의 올바른 회원
9. 유기체적 생명 / 생물
10. 변함없이 충성을 다하다

11. 정신적 고통을 겪다
12. 소심한 새로운 학생
13. 방에 있는 모든 사람을 매혹시키다
14. 비타민으로 식단을 보충하다
15. 공기가 압축될 것이다.

16. 하늘을 밝게 하다
17. 시끄러운 소란
18. 단단한 사암에(암석) 박혀 있다
19. 자유시장 정책을 지지하다
20. 그녀의 발레 교육에 대한 저항

Practice Test 09

1. Ⓐ	2. Ⓒ	3. Ⓒ	4. Ⓐ	5. Ⓐ
6. Ⓓ	7. Ⓑ	8. Ⓒ	9. Ⓑ	10. Ⓓ
11. Ⓒ	12. Ⓓ	13. Ⓑ	14. Ⓑ	15. Ⓑ
16. Ⓒ	17. Ⓑ	18. Ⓒ	19. Ⓐ	20. Ⓑ

1. 국제연맹 및 국제연합은 군축 감소를 옹호했다.
2. 월레스는 원자폭탄 개발로 이어지는 의사결정에 참여하였다.
3. 쿼크-글루온 플라즈마는 충돌이 핵을 압축 시킬 때 일반적인 크기의 조각으로 생성된다.
4. 대부분의 특허법들은 특허가 개발자와 사회 사이의 계약이라는 원칙을 준수한다.
5. 물리 치료사는 마비된 뇌졸증 환자의 근육이 경직되지 않고 움직일 수 있게 도와준다.

169

6. 아기는 괴로우면 훌쩍이고 무서우면 소리를 지른다.
7. 존슨은 저속하다고 생각하는 많은 웃기는 성적인 구절에 반대했다.
8. 고릴라는 가끔 걷거나 뛰기 위해 시끄러운 소리를 낸다.
9. 대통령 임기 초기 루즈벨트 대통령은 기업의 일에는 간섭하지 않겠다고 기업가들을 설득하려 노력했다.
10. 많은 육군 장교들이 정부에 대항하여 봉기했다.

11. 부채가 쌓여가서 사업을 접어야만 했다.
12. 한 신사는 예배드릴 때 진실되게 경건했으며 그의 아버지와 지도자를 존경하는 사람이었다.
13. 나폴레옹 전쟁 당시, 중남미 국가들은 스페인 통치에 저항했다.
14. 1603년 스코틀랜드 왕 제임스 6세는 영국의 제임스 1세가 됨에 따라서 영국과 스코틀랜드의 왕위를 통일하였다.
15. 역사학자, 전쟁 종군기자, 전기작가로서 처칠 경은 영어를 독보적으로 구사한다는 것을 보여주었다.

16. 디프테리아와 백일해와 같은 전염성 질병은 사람과 사람 사이에 빠르게 확산된다.
17. 역사를 통해 조각품은 건축과 밀접하게 연결되어 있는데, 부분적으로 유사한 물질과 기술이 두 분야에 사용되었기 때문이다.
18. 스마트카드는 이용자의 은행 거래내역 및 구매내역에 대한 정보를 저장하는 하나 또는 몇 개의 내장된 컴퓨터칩이 있다.
19. 인간이 다른 영장류와 구별되는 많은 육체적 특징은 사람은 똑바로 서고 두 다리로 걸을 수 있는 능력과 관련이 있다.
20. 기차가 고장이 났을 때, 일부 승객은 버스로 일부는 차로 집으로 갔고 그리고 남은 사람들은 기차에서 밤을 지새웠다.

Daily Checkup 10

1. Ⓐ	2. Ⓑ	3. Ⓐ	4. Ⓑ	5. Ⓒ
6. Ⓓ	7. Ⓐ	8. Ⓑ	9. Ⓓ	10. Ⓐ
11. Ⓐ	12. Ⓐ	13. Ⓒ	14. Ⓑ	15. Ⓓ
16. Ⓐ	17. Ⓐ	18. Ⓓ	19. Ⓑ	20. Ⓒ

1. 의견을 수정하다
2. 그 소식은 그녀를 놀라게 하였다.
3. 그것은 내 운명이다.
4. 불모지
5. 광대한 대륙을 탐험하다

6. 포커 치는 사람처럼 뻔뻔한
7. 신념을 준수하다
8. 권위가 있음을 환기시키다 [언급하다]
9. 원기를 내게 하다
10. 연극에서의 대화

11. (난처해서) 머리를 긁다
12. 신뢰를 깨다 / 배임
13. 소음을 줄이려고 노력했다
14. 나는 뱀에 대해 반감을 가지고 있다. / 나는 뱀을 질색한다.
15. 낯선 사람을 비웃다

16. 심판에게 항의하다
17. 다년생의 꽃
18. 잔인한 말
19. ~으로 스스로를 위로하다
20. 어떤 프로그램들은 서로 충돌했다.

Practice Test 10

1. Ⓑ	2. Ⓒ	3. Ⓐ	4. Ⓒ	5. Ⓓ
6. Ⓑ	7. Ⓑ	8. Ⓑ	9. Ⓑ	10. Ⓐ
11. Ⓑ	12. Ⓐ	13. Ⓒ	14. Ⓑ	15. Ⓓ
16. Ⓒ	17. Ⓐ	18. Ⓓ	19. Ⓐ	20. Ⓓ

1. 미국은 전시 생산량으로 세계를 놀라게 했다.
2. 구타와 경멸을 당했지만 돈키호테는 여전히 영웅적 운명을 믿었다.
3. 동물의 일생은 식물이 먹이로서 이용 가능해진 후 진화하고 번성할 수 있었다.
4. 히말라야는 여러 개의 병렬 산맥으로 이루어졌다.
5. 의사와 치과의사를 정기적으로 방문하세요. 그래야 의사와 치과의사가 건강을 지켜줄 수 있습니다.

6. 외항선은 구조와 **인양** 작업에 참여한다.
7. 달의 외부 표면은 **딱딱하고** 강한 것 같지만, 달의 내부는 아직 많이 알려지지 않았다.
8. 처음부터 퀘이커 교인들은 특정한 **교리**보다는 내면의 영적 경험을 강조하였다.
9. (책의) 자매편은 현대적인 작품으로 심혈을 기울여 제작되었고 조각가와의 면담을 통해 **새롭게 태어났다**.
10. 노예해방론자들과 흑인 지도자들은, 전쟁은 노예제도를 폐지하기 위해서 싸워야 한다며 **종용하였고** 흑인 부대가 전쟁에 참가하기를 요구하였다.

11. 가구제작자는 캐비닛 문과 나무처럼 보이지만 쉽게 청소할 수 있고 **휘지** 않는 탁상을 제작할 때 플라스틱을 사용한다.
12. **직업** 고등학교 졸업생들은 대학교에 들어가기 전에 1년간 특별 교육을 이수해야 한다.
13. 형이상학은 현실과 존재에 대한 **근본적인** 특성 및 만물의 본질에 대한 학문이다.
14. 전통적인 아시아 조각은 주로 **종교적** · 정치적 이상, 종교 의식과 소통하고 통치자를 영화롭게 하기 위해 만들어졌다.
15. 학생들은 금요일 밤에 마이클 김 교수님의 강의와 토론에 참석하기를 **열망했다**.

16. 이 개정안은 헌법에 **유효한** 일부가 되기 전에 선거나 상원의 임기에 영향을 미치도록 해석하면 안 된다.
17. 우리처럼 복잡한 사회에서 수많은 충돌적인 전통과 이론이라도, 대부분 윤리적인 결정은 우리를 **진퇴양난**에 빠뜨리지 않는다.
18. 남극 환경에 대한 국제협력과 관심으로, 얼어붙은 대륙은 지구의 과거, 현재 및 미래에 대한 정보의 어마어마한 **보물**을 지속적으로 제공할 것이다.
19. 특정 요소를 **강조함**으로써, 화가는 그의 작품을 이해하기 쉽고 특별한 분위기나 주제로 만들 수 있다.
20. 스위스 제네바에 위치한 국제적십자위원회는 국가간 **충돌** 시 전쟁 희생자의 보호를 위해서 중립적인 중재기구의 역할을 수행한다.

Exercise 06-10

1. ⑩	2. ⑧	3. ⑧	4. ⑧	5. ⑩
6. ⓒ	7. ⓐ	8. ⓐ	9. ⓒ	10. ⑩
11. ⓐ	12. ⓐ	13. ⓒ	14. ⓒ	15. ⑩
16. ⑩	17. ⑧	18. ⑧	19. ⓒ	20. ⑩

1. **확대한** 사진
2. 자금의 출처를 **조사하다**
3. 우리 마음에 공포가 **엄습했다**.
4. **재빠른** 동작
5. 믿는 도끼에 발등 찍힌다. / 믿음은 속임수의 어머니이다.

6. ~의 손을 **붙잡다**
7. 답변을 **공개하다**
8. 학생의 관심을 **최대에** 이르게 하다
9. 가벼운 **병**
10. 이 이야기의 줄거리는 매우 **복잡하다**.

11. 시야에서 **사라지다**
12. 개별 고객들과 **협상하다**
13. 공포로 **마비가** 되다
14. 이 상황에서 문제점을 **강조하다**
15. 사무실을 **이용가능하게** 만들다

16. 공포로 **비명을** 지르다
17. **저속한** 언어
18. 불에서 몇 가지를 **구하다**
19. **딜레마**에 빠지다
20. 첫 홈런의 기억을 **소중히** 여기다

Practice Test 06-10

1. ⑩	2. ⓐ	3. ⓐ	4. ⓒ	5. ⑩
6. ⑧	7. ⓐ	8. ⓒ	9. ⓒ	10. ⑩
11. ⓐ	12. ⑧	13. ⑩	14. ⓒ	15. ⓒ
16. ⓐ	17. ⑩	18. ⓐ	19. ⓐ	20. ⑧

1. 많은 미국인들이 전통적인 **결혼** 방식을 무시한다.
2. 조종사는 외부 온도와 계기판을 확인하여 실제 속도를 **측정**할 수 있다.
3. 공간이 넓은 많은 차량은 냉동 및 **냉장** 식품을 가열하기 위한 시설이 있다.
4. 라틴 아메리카 소설은 **전례 없는** 국제적인 관심을 받았다.
5. 1400년대 이전에 **대다수**의 유럽인들은 문맹이었다.

6. 자동차 사고는 전 세계적으로 죽음과 부상의 주요 원인이었다.
7. 소크라테스의 생각과 방법에 대한 우리의 지식은 그의 제자인 플라톤이 작성한 대화록에서 대부분 나온다.
8. 가장 단단한 무기물은 유리에 흠집을 낼 수 있다.
9. 당신의 지적 배경과 언어적 기억은 독서경험에 따라 변하고 같이 성장한다.
10. 스미소니언 박물관의 이름들은 소장품의 기록을 강조하여 제작된 것으로 유명하다.

11. 세포생물학의 대부분은 특수세포의 구조와 기능에 대한 연구에 전념한다.
12. 1982년 마가렛 대처 수상은 아르헨티나와의 충돌을 결정적으로 처리해서 찬사를 받았다.
13. 대부분의 경주장은 모든 경주 참여자에게 개방되며, 우승자에게 우승 상금이 수여된다.
14. 이와 옴진드기는 둘 다 피부를 가렵게 하며 전염성이다.
15. 전이라는 과정을 통해 악성종양은 주위 조직을 침범하여 순환계를 통하여 몸의 먼 부분으로 확산한다.

16. 일반 라디오 뉴스처럼, 일일 TV 뉴스 프로그램도 단지 몇 가지 간략한 사건에 대한 뉴스를 제공한다.
17. 사람이 충분한 리보플라빈을 섭취하지 못하면, (구강점막세포의) 변성이 입가 피부에 생길 수 있다.
18. 정보통신의 현대적인 방법이 너무 빠르기 때문에 수천 마일이나 멀리 떨어져 있는 구매자조차도 생산자가 요구하는 가격을 알 수 있다.
19. 거래가 특정지역으로 제안되더라도, 딜러는 먼 곳에 있는 고객을 대신해서 대리인으로 전체나 부분적으로 참여할 수 있다.
20. 컴퓨터 예술가는 작품의 제작단계에서 카메라 초점 및 투명성 조정 등의 시각적 효과를 흔히 조정한다.

Intensive Practice 06-10

1. ⑧	2. ⑩	3. ⓒ	4. ⑧	5. ⑧
6. ⓒ	7. ⑩	8. ⑧	9. ⓐ	10. ⑧
11. ⑩	12. ⓒ	13. ⑩	14. ⑧	15. ⓒ
16. ⑧	17. ⑧	18. ⑧	19. ⓐ	20. ⑩

1. 단색 구성표는 여러 가지 음영처럼 표현할 수 있는 색의 변화를 이용한다.
2. 회로에서 소재원자의 충돌은 열을 통해 일부 에너지 손실을 발생하는 원자의 흐름을 방해한다.
3. 물질의 일부는 남아서 성운이 되어 천체를 회전하며 수축하였다.
4. 많은 자원봉사자들이 인명구조와 구조작업에 참여한다.
5. 각각의 색상은 색조, 밝기와 채도의 정도로 다른 모든 것들과 다르다.

6. 가축 소유자는 가축의 무리에 위험하다고 생각하는 야생 동물을 총으로 쏘거나 덫으로 잡거나 독살할 수 있다.
7. 많은 학생들은 집안일이 공부에 방해되지 않는다고 느낀다.
8. 세포의 세계는 상당히 복잡하고 다양하다.
9. 파렴치한 죄는 죽음이나 구금하여 처벌해야 한다.
10. 어느 전공이든지 학위가 있고 3년의 경험이 있는 사람은 자격이 된다.

11. 아프리카계 흑인과 미국 인디언 집단 사이에서, 전통 춤은 즐거운 오락의 형태 뿐만 아니라 종교의식의 중요한 부분으로 남았다.
12. 혁신적인 사진과 재치 있는 문장은 기존의 이야기를 재미있게 다시 만들어낸다.
13. 기절은 짧은 시간 동안 뇌에 피가 부족하게 공급이 되면 일어날 수 있다.
14. 1815년 나폴레옹의 몰락 이후, 군주제는 스페인에서 부활되었으며, 신성동맹은 스페인의 식민지를 회복시키려 했을 것이다.
15. 기근, 전염병 및 자연재해는 인구의 급격한 감소를 초래했다.

16. 동일한 숫자를 양쪽 등식에서 빼게 되면, 새로운 숫자는 같게 된다.
17. 당뇨와 콩팥 질환 같은 일부 만성질병은 유산과 관련이 있다.
18. 저자가 원고를 준비할 때, 그는 2줄 공간으로 만들고 모든 페이지의 상단, 하단, 측면에 여백을 둔다.
19. 돈키호테의 주인공은 과거 기사에 대한 소설을 읽으면서, 소설이 사실이며 정확하다고 믿으면서 단조로운 삶에 활력을 넣고 싶은 스페인의 지주이다.
20. 1800년대 초반의 대부분의 화학자들은 유기화학 물질은 식물과 동물에 존재하는 생명의 힘으로만이 생성될 수 있다고 믿었다.

Daily Checkup 11

1. ⓒ	2. ⓓ	3. ⓐ	4. ⓑ	5. ⓑ
6. ⓑ	7. ⓒ	8. ⓒ	9. ⓐ	10. ⓒ
11. ⓒ	12. ⓐ	13. ⓓ	14. ⓓ	15. ⓐ
16. ⓓ	17. ⓒ	18. ⓑ	19. ⓓ	20. ⓑ

1. 학위를 수여하다
2. 우리 역사의 이정표를 기념하다
3. 공기는 소리의 매개체이다.
4. 난처하게 여기다
5. 부부 사이를 갈라놓다

6. 솔직한 진술을 피하다
7. 주의 깊은 청중
8. 자연 치유
9. (모든) 경쟁자를 물리치다
10. 폐를 팽창시키다

11. 개인적인 평가
12. 자연(폭풍우)의 분노
13. 감춰진 음모
14. 결정을 미루다
15. 절대적으로 부적절한 의견

16. 해변을 따라 산책하다
17. 관계없는 사항
18. 그녀의 이야기로 흥미로워했다
19. 일본과 모든 관계를 단절하다
20. 그녀의 목소리가 떨렸다.

Practice Test 11

1. ⓑ	2. ⓒ	3. ⓐ	4. ⓑ	5. ⓑ
6. ⓒ	7. ⓓ	8. ⓐ	9. ⓑ	10. ⓑ
11. ⓒ	12. ⓒ	13. ⓐ	14. ⓐ	15. ⓓ
16. ⓒ	17. ⓑ	18. ⓑ	19. ⓑ	20. ⓒ

1. 6인용 자동차는 의자 아래의 배터리로 구동된다.
2. 서부전선은 격렬한 전투에도 불구하고 3년 반 동안 거의 이동되지 않았다.
3. 필라델피아에서 링컨대통령은 암살 음모의 보고를 받았다.
4. 제국주의 힘은 지배 지역의 소중한 자원을 약탈하여 모을 수 있었다.
5. 캐츠킬 지역의 저수지는 뉴욕시민들에게 물을 제공한다.

6. 군복을 입지 않은 남자와 여자는 가슴에 오른쪽 손을 올려 경례를 한다.
7. 국제협약의 준수를 위해 군사력을 이용하는 것은 정당하다.
8. 매년 음악페스티벌이 이 행사의 기념일을 기념하기 위해 열린다.
9. 1600년대까지 연금술은 화학 지식의 중요한 원천이었다.
10. 인플레이션은 생산성을 능가하는 임금상승에 기인한다.

11. 1900년 초에 소개된 디지털 카메라는 거의 순식간에 사진을 만들 수 있다.
12. 섬광은 대기권으로 많은 빛을 내뿜어 우주인들은 태양을 배경으로 사진을 촬영할 수 있다.
13. 워싱턴은 선거 기간에 녹스 장군을 공개적으로 칭찬하였고, 녹스 장군은 준장으로 승진되었다.
14. 「베니스의 상인」에서 셰익스피어는 희극적 줄거리를 증오와 욕망의 생생한 묘사로 결합시켰다.
15. 원시적 조건에서 일에 대한 즉흥적인 관심은 그것과 관련된 다수의 사회적 가치에 의해 강화되었다.

16. 사춘기에 신체의 다른 부분들이 각기 다른 속도로 변화하기 때문에 많은 청소년들은 일시적으로 어색하게 느낀다.
17. 1835년에서 1836년 겨울에 텍사스 주민들은 멕시코 정부에 대한 불만으로 멕시코와 단절하기로 결정했다.
18. 생존한 나무와 죽은 나무의 나이테를 분석하여, 과학자들은 험난한 날씨로부터 상대적으로 좋은 날씨를 구별할 수 있다.
19. 일부 장애를 가진 아이들은 다른 아이와 어울리는 데 어려움이 있으며, 그로 인해 아이는 부적절하게 행동할 수 있다.
20. 동방정교회는 17세기 말에 서양의 영향에 압도되었다.

DAY 12

Daily Checkup 12

1. ⓒ	2. ⓑ	3. ⓓ	4. ⓓ	5. ⓒ
6. ⓐ	7. ⓑ	8. ⓓ	9. ⓒ	10. ⓐ
11. ⓐ	12. ⓒ	13. ⓒ	14. ⓐ	15. ⓑ
16. ⓑ	17. ⓓ	18. ⓒ	19. ⓓ	20. ⓐ

1. 실력 있는 사람
2. 한가한 목수
3. 논리 부족 / 어불성설
4. 신뢰할 수 있는 정보에 의하면
5. 그의 영향력은 서서히 감소하였다.

6. 리더십의 다른 종류
7. 권력의 쇠퇴
8. 인구가 희박한 지역
9. 망각으로부터 그의 연극을 구하다
10. 무자비한 처리

11. 화난 고객들을 진정시키다
12. 파티를 중단하기를 원했다
13. 생물과 무생물
14. 사무실을 가로질러 가다 / 직권을 거부하다
15. 우뚝 솟은 산들

16. 위급한 위험
17. 농약 잔류
18. 하늘의 무수한 별들
19. 야망이 좌절되다
20. 폐업 신고를 하다

Practice Test 12

1. ⓒ	2. ⓐ	3. ⓐ	4. ⓐ	5. ⓓ
6. ⓒ	7. ⓑ	8. ⓒ	9. ⓐ	10. ⓒ
11. ⓐ	12. ⓒ	13. ⓒ	14. ⓑ	15. ⓓ
16. ⓑ	17. ⓒ	18. ⓑ	19. ⓒ	20. ⓑ

1. 도시들은 성장하고 공장들이 생겨난다.
2. 전자 현미경은 사물의 영상을 확대하기 위해 전자 광선을 사용하는 기구이다.
3. 일부 지주들과 관리자들은 권력을 올바르게 사용하지만, 다른 이들은 무자비한 독재자처럼 행동했다.
4. 집합이론은 수학과 논리의 문제를 해결하는 방법이다.
5. 쌍둥이자리에서 태어난 사람은 말이 많거나 재치 있는 사람으로 추정된다.

6. 율리시스는 신뢰할 수 있는 사람이어서, 그의 아버지는 그를 종종 출장을 보냈다.
7. 영국의 소설가 조나단 스위프트의 소설 「걸리버 여행기(1726)」는 환상적인 여행 이야기를 사회적 비판과 결합하였다.
8. 사기업들은 캘리포니아에 새로운 제품의 연구와 테스트를 위한 수백 개의 연구소를 보유하고 있다.
9. 가봉에서 벌목은 국가의 두 번째로 큰 수익 원천이며 노동력의 1/4 이상을 고용하고 있다.
10. 23년이 지난 후 노예제도가 사회적으로 큰 문제가 되었을 때, 링컨은 대통령직에 임명되었다.

11. 소련의 달 착륙 시도는 위대한 N-1 추진로켓의 계속되는 실패로 좌절되었다.
12. 깨진 화강암은 미국의 중북부 지역과 동북부 지역에서 생산된다.
13. 더 많은 종이 멸종위기에 처함에 따라, 생태환경이 불안정해지고 결국 붕괴되고 있다.
14. 최초의 척추동물들은 바다 밑이나 민물에서 죽은 동물의 작은 조각이나 아주 작은 생명체를 먹고 살았을 것이다.
15. 1800년대 중반 전통적인 아시아의 사회제도는 증가하는 사회적 문제에 대응하기에는 비효율적이었음이 증명되기 시작했다.

16. 출생 시, 코끼리는 성장함에 따라 털갈이를 할 수 있는 드문드문 난 갈색, 검은색 또는 붉은 갈색털로 덮여 태어난다.
17. 길리안 크로스가 쓴 「Roscoe's Leap(1987)」에서 12살 한 소년이 쇠퇴해가는 저택에서 이상한 비밀과 직면한다.
18. 20세기 말이 지나기 전 아프리카, 아시아 및 미국의 많은 언어들은 어떤 능력 있는 언어학자들이 이 언어들을 기록하지 않는다면 완전히 잊혀질 수도 있다.
19. 포크너의 「소리와 분노(1929)」와 다른 소설에서 그는 남부귀족 집안의 몰락과 전통적인 행동 양식의 붕괴를 다루었다.
20. 많은 식물들은 초기의 빠른 성장과 그 후의 부피가 증가하는 잠깐의 성장과, 마지막으로 성장의 멈춤이나 조직의 파괴 후 완전한 중단으로 이어지는 죽음의 일반적인 성장과정을 겪는다.

Daily Checkup 13

1. ⓓ	2. ⓐ	3. ⓑ	4. ⓒ	5. ⓓ
6. ⓐ	7. ⓑ	8. ⓐ	9. ⓓ	10. ⓓ
11. ⓑ	12. ⓒ	13. ⓑ	14. ⓐ	15. ⓒ
16. ⓑ	17. ⓑ	18. ⓐ	19. ⓐ	20. ⓐ

1. 전쟁의 참사
2. 이 길은 되돌아갈 수 없는 길이다.
3. 향기로운 향수
4. 그 행사에 적합한 의류
5. 터널을 뚫다

6. 사회 · 정치 개혁을 착수하다
7. 적에게 복수하다
8. 지독한 거짓말쟁이
9. 판매 가격을 계산하다
10. 명백하게 대답하다

11. 건전한 환경
12. 찰리는 다수의 학생들을 돌보아야 했다.
13. 봉투를 찢어 열다
14. 따로 떨어진 구름 조각
15. 시험 응시생들이 사고 때문에 늦어졌다.

16. 성심성의껏 최선을 다하다
17. 나는 그를 문까지 바래다줬다.
18. 권력 집중
19. 대칭적인 창문
20. 누구에게 지불을 면제하다

Practice Test 13

1. ⓐ	2. ⓓ	3. ⓒ	4. ⓐ	5. ⓒ
6. ⓒ	7. ⓐ	8. ⓑ	9. ⓒ	10. ⓓ
11. ⓒ	12. ⓓ	13. ⓑ	14. ⓒ	15. ⓓ
16. ⓑ	17. ⓒ	18. ⓑ	19. ⓒ	20. ⓑ

1. 등록된 많은 영양사들이 학교, 요양원과 식당의 음식 서비스를 관리한다.
2. 카터 대통령 센터는 애틀랜타 도심을 내려다보는 언덕 위에 위치한다.
3. 일반적인 현미경으로 볼 수 있는 가장 작은 점도 100억 개 이상의 원자가 있다.
4. 원시사회에서 잔치가 열리면 음식을 만든 사람들은 음식의 가장 좋은 부분을 가져간다.

5. 일부 문화에서, 결혼은 신랑 또는 신부의 가족이 다른 가족에게 선물을 주는 것을 포함한다.
6. 대부분의 노예는 결혼해서 죽을 때까지 같은 배우자와 살았다.
7. 모든 사람은 임의적으로 감금되거나 구속당하지 않을 권리가 있다.
8. 해초는 광합성의 부산물로 방출되는 산소를 바다 동물에게 제공한다.
9. 원시사회에서 대부분의 경제적 노력은 음식 생산에 집중된다.
10. 오페라의 마지막 부분에서 마가레타는 죽고 천사의 합창이 그녀를 하늘로 호위한다.

11. 미국의 경우, 최근 연구는 성인의 1/4 정도가 비만이라는 것을 보여준다.
12. 1950년, 척 쿠퍼는 보스턴 셀틱스와 입단 서명을 한 NBA 역사상 첫 흑인 선수가 되었다.
13. 물이 장기적으로 부족한 장소에서 식물은 성장이 느리고, 잎은 작고 비정상적인 색과 일부분은 괴사상태가 될 수도 있다.
14. 아무도 얼마나 온도가 높게 올라가는지 알지 못하며 가장 뜨거운 별의 내부 온도는 수백만도이다.
15. 많은 에이전트는 편집자 또는 전문작가로부터 추천 받은 작가와만 일을 한다.

16. 상원의원은 단순한 동의를 통해서 의안을 상정하거나 누구의 반대도 없는 만장일치로 법안을 표결한다.
17. 1910년 이후, 많은 사진작가들은 수정을 하지 않은 사진은 다른 예술작품에 비교할 수 없는 아름다움과 우아함을 지녔다고 믿었다.
18. 약을 끊을 때 분리현상이 반대로 되고, 섬유상과 과립상 구성물이 산재된다.
19. 지미 헨드릭스의 경험이나 에릭 크랩톤의 크림밴드가 연주한 음악은 종종 현대적인 록음악으로 분류된다.
20. 온실효과의 결과인 지구온난화 현상은 바다, 토양 및 식물에서 수분을 증발시켜 대지를 바싹 마르게 한다.

Daily Checkup 14

1. ⑧	2. ⑧	3. ⑩	4. ⑩	5. ⑧
6. ⓒ	7. ④	8. ⓒ	9. ⑩	10. ⑧
11. ⑩	12. ⓒ	13. ⑧	14. ④	15. ⓒ
16. ⓒ	17. ⑧	18. ⑩	19. ⑧	20. ⑩

1. 전기를 발생시키다
2. 혼란 상태에 있다
3. 수은은 가열하면 팽창한다
4. 곱셈의 원리를 공부하다
5. 예상치 못한 보상을 받다

6. 지불할 돈을 충당하다
7. 장미 향기
8. 실로 천을 짜다
9. 은행에 예금하다
10. 곤충의 종류를 분류하다

11. 주권
12. 내 발언을 강조하다
13. 내 의견의 다양한 이유
14. 본성과 양육
15. 다루기 힘든 가방

16. 편안한 마음
17. 경기를 부양하다
18. 동물을 올가미로 잡다
19. 시스템을 통해 침투하다
20. 일상생활의 슬픔

Practice Test 14

1. ⓒ	2. ⓒ	3. ⓒ	4. ⑧	5. ④
6. ⓒ	7. ⑩	8. ⑧	9. ④	10. ④
11. ⓒ	12. ⓒ	13. ⓒ	14. ⑧	15. ④
16. ⓒ	17. ④	18. ⑧	19. ⓒ	20. ⑩

1. 지구에는 충분한 양의 물이 있지만, 고르지 않게 분배된다.
2. 지구에서 가장 높은 곳은 에베레스트 정상이며 해수면 8,848 미터에 이른다.
3. 열이 눈송이의 정돈된 형태를 정리되지 않은 형태로 바꿨다.
4. NBA 선수들은 1992년 올림픽게임에 출전할 자격이 주어졌다.
5. 이 상징적인 과정은 인간 삶의 가장 원초적이면서도 가장 문명이 발달한 수준으로 확산된다.

6. 인물사진 작가들은 사진 모델이 자세를 취하고 사진을 찍기 위한 편안한 환경을 만들 수 있어야 한다.
7. 최저음 가수는 특히 낮은 음성이 있으며, 웅장하고 진지한 역할을 맡는다.
8. 만일 학생이 시험 문제를 틀리게 대답하였다면, 그 답안 디스크는 자동적으로 올바른 정보를 제공한다.
9. 외심막과 심낭 사이의 미끄러운 체액은 심장에 윤활유 역할을 하여 편안하게 수축할 수 있게 한다.
10. 원시사회에서 사람이 노동을 해서 얻은 보상의 원칙은 인정이 되지 않는다.

11. 스페인 사람이 양을 남서부에 소개한 후, 푸에블로는 옷을 만들기 위해 양털로 천을 짰다.
12. 프리미엄(할증금) 영화 채널과 같은 특정 채널은 월 기본 케이블 서비스 비용에 추가하여 특별 비용을 소비자에게 부과한다.
13. 가톨릭 신자들은 사람은 하나님의 은혜를 통한 믿음과 자신의 선행을 통해서 구원을 얻을 수 있다고 믿는다.
14. 호수는 바다로 흐르는 자연 유출구가 차단되거나, 물이 후진하여 강이 토사를 퇴적하면 만들어질 수 있다.
15. 색상을 설명하거나 맞추는 문제를 해결하기 위해, 색상 전문가들은 색상을 분류하는 다양한 시스템을 개발하였다.

16. 연구자들은 일반적으로 후각계와 연결된 기체 색층 분석법을 통해 커피콩 볶는 향기를 분석한다.
17. 정부는 상업용 배들이 해외무역 및 국가보호를 위해 중요한 역할을 하기 때문에 보조금을 지원한다.
18. 멘델브로트는 이러한 도형의 분열되고 불규칙한 본질을 강조하기 위해 라틴어 fractus(조각)로부터 '차원 분열도형'이란 용어를 만들었다.
19. 어린이 도서를 위해 추천되는 대부분의 책 목록은 월간 또는 연간 단위로 팸플릿의 형태로 출판되지만, 단지 일부만이 책의 형태로 출판되어 가끔 수정될 수 있다.
20. 산 빙하로부터 녹은 물은 지난 100년 동안 5센티미터 정도 해수면을 상승시켰으며, 이러한 지속적인 빙하의 유입은 미래에 더 빠르게 해수면을 높일 것이다.

Daily Checkup 15

1. ⓓ	2. ⓑ	3. ⓓ	4. ⓓ	5. ⓒ
6. ⓐ	7. ⓒ	8. ⓐ	9. ⓑ	10. ⓓ
11. ⓑ	12. ⓒ	13. ⓐ	14. ⓑ	15. ⓐ
16. ⓒ	17. ⓑ	18. ⓐ	19. ⓒ	20. ⓓ

1. 갑자기 뒤돌아서다
2. 진지한 얼굴
3. 축축한 공기
4. 즐거운 저녁을 보내다
5. 자연 자원을 보호하다

6. 인구 밀도가 낮은 외곽 지역
7. 몹시 화난 군중
8. 극렬한 저항
9. 한 번의 타격으로 방패를 쪼개다
10. 순종적인 말

11. 법적 절차
12. 어려운 일
13. 변경할 수 없는 규칙
14. 순진한 신입생 때문에 즐거워했다
15. 그는 몇 단어에 말을 더듬었다.

16. 특사를 보내다
17. 아주 적은 시간
18. 정치적 변화를 위한 리더
19. 부모를 대신할 사람은 없다.
20. 영양실조는 확실히 환자를 약하게 만들었다.

Practice Test 15

1. ⓒ	2. ⓒ	3. ⓐ	4. ⓒ	5. ⓑ
6. ⓒ	7. ⓓ	8. ⓓ	9. ⓒ	10. ⓑ
11. ⓓ	12. ⓐ	13. ⓒ	14. ⓓ	15. ⓒ
16. ⓒ	17. ⓑ	18. ⓒ	19. ⓒ	20. ⓓ

1. 파피루스는 습한 기후에 쉽게 부패하는 식물성 물질이었다.
2. 많은 국가들이 자원봉사 선생님에게 의존하는 문맹퇴치 프로그램을 실행하였다.
3. 대부분 큰 공항은 중심도시의 외곽에 위치한다.
4. 영양실조는 세계 보건의 또 다른 문제점이다.
5. 가정에서나 상업적으로 만든 제품은 어머니의 모유를 대신할 수 있다.

6. 곡물의 과잉 생산은 사람들이 필요로 하는 식품보다 더 많기 때문에 가격을 낮춘다.
7. 라디오 및 TV 방송국은 뉴스를 방영하기 위해 언제든지 정규프로그램을 중단할 수 있다.
8. 행복의 전체 주제는, 내 생각에 너무 엄숙하게 다루어진 것 같다.
9. 영국의 차에 부여한 세금은 아담과 그의 동료 식민지 주민들을 분노하게 했다.
10. 조각예술은 예술가가 고가의 재료에 돈이 묶여 있는 힘이 많이 들고 오랜 시간이 걸리는 과정이다.

11. 쥐는 3만 개의 유전자를 가지고 있으며, 그중 99%가 인간 DNA와 상응한다.
12. 허리케인은 미국 매사추세츠 해안을 때때로 강타한다.
13. 예를 들어, 해면동물은 정지한 상태에서 먹이 조각들이 가득한 물을 순환시킨다
14. 진주만 폭격 이후, 일부 미국인들은 일본계 미국인들에게 분노를 표출했다
15. 실수(實數) 직선은 공간을 정의하고, 깊이와 거리의 착각인 원근을 만드는 데 도움을 준다.

16. 긍정적으로, 논리적으로, 건전하게 생각한다면 당신은 더 즐겁고 성공적인 삶을 만드는 데 도움이 될 것이다.
17. 유럽인들이 인디언 원주민들을 더 척박한 땅으로 밀어냈기에 먹을 음식이 예전보다 충분하지 않았다.
18. 칼훈은 국가는 헌법을 위반한 의회의 법률은 무효화시킬 수 있다고 주장한다.
19. 당뇨병은 많은 국가에서 '조용한 살인자'로 알려졌으며, 중국인들의 주요 만성질환으로 빠르게 자리잡았다.
20. 공기는 마찰의 가장 빈번한 원인 중의 하나이며, 자동차와 항공기는 유선형으로 만들어 공기를 뚫고 쉽게 이동을 할 수 있다.

TOEFL DAY 11-15

Exercise 11-15

1. ⓓ	2. ⓐ	3. ⓓ	4. ⓑ	5. ⓑ
6. ⓐ	7. ⓑ	8. ⓒ	9. ⓒ	10. ⓒ
11. ⓑ	12. ⓒ	13. ⓐ	14. ⓑ	15. ⓐ
16. ⓐ	17. ⓐ	18. ⓑ	19. ⓑ	20. ⓒ

1. 마틴은 위엄 있게 경례했다.
2. 합법적인 정부
3. 사방팔방으로 펴지다
4. 그녀의 우수한 성적을 칭찬하다
5. 가차없이 벌을 주다

6. 불안정한 정부
7. 무능한 관리자
8. 광고 수입
9. 만장일치의 박수갈채로
10. 현대 사회의 부산물

11. 불규칙한 심장 박동
12. 당신은 회원이 될 자격이 있다.
13. 규칙적으로 기계에 윤활유를 바르다
14. 고르지 못하게 분배한
15. 최고로 중요한 문제

16. 전류를 차단하다
17. 계약을 무효화하다
18. 추가 자료
19. 서유럽의 상대
20. 만성 스트레스의 원인

Practice Test 11-15

1. ⓒ	2. ⓑ	3. ⓓ	4. ⓓ	5. ⓑ
6. ⓐ	7. ⓑ	8. ⓓ	9. ⓒ	10. ⓒ
11. ⓐ	12. ⓒ	13. ⓑ	14. ⓒ	15. ⓑ
16. ⓓ	17. ⓑ	18. ⓒ	19. ⓓ	20. ⓐ

1. 모직은 거칠거나 부드러운 직물로도 상당히 튼튼한 옷으로 제작이 가능하다.
2. 상품 가격과 부동산 가치가 부풀려졌다.
3. 구조분석이라는 단어인식 전략으로, 독자들은 단어의 의미를 추측하기 위해 단서를 사용한다.
4. 자유 국가들은 언론에게 정부의 관여 없이 뉴스나 의견을 표현할 권리를 부여한다.
5. 몸은 새로운 조직을 만들고 오래되어 닳아 없어지는 조직을 재생한다.

6. 일부 화학비료의 과도한 사용은 부엽토를 부식시키고 영양분을 자연스럽게 생산하는 세균의 능력을 감소시킬 수 있다.
7. 기자들 사이에서의 경쟁은 많은 독자를 끌어 모으기 위해 계산된 선정적인 뉴스 보도를 종종 낸다.
8. 소비자는 더 많은 플라스틱 용기를 사용하며, 더 많은 플라스틱 쓰레기가 만들어진다.
9. 식물들은 수주 동안 비가 없으면 확실히 생기를 잃게 될 것이다.
10. 농업과학과 교육은 1900년 이후에 더 전문적인 지식과 기술의 수요에 대응하기 위해 확장되었다.

11. 황금률은 상대방에게 대우를 받으려면 상대방에게 좋은 대우를 해야 한다는 원칙이다.
12. 현대차와 같은 자동차 회사들은 합리적인 가격에 편안하고 멋이 있고 속도 나는 조립차를 생산하여 제공했다.
13. 과학자들은 특정한 깊이에서 지진파의 속도와 방향이 갑자기 변하는 것을 발견했다.
14. 브리스톨대학교 존 R. 파크스와 동료들은 해저 퇴적물에 서식하는 다소 높은 고밀도 집단인 미생물을 발견했다.
15. 영국은 아일랜드를 수세기 동안 지배하였고, 아일랜드 사람들은 영국의 지배를 싫어했다.

16. 화석을 연구하면서, 고생물학자는 지구 초기의 다양한 시기에 어떠한 생명체들이 존재하였는지 연구한다.
17. 언어를 사용하면서, 인간은 논리적이고 다른 동물들보다 더 고차원적으로 문제를 해결할 수 있는 능력을 발전시켜 왔다.
18. 많은 신고전주의 비평가들은 셰익스피어는 아리스토텔레스가 드라마 작성을 위한 특정 기준을 정한 것을 준수하지 않은 것에 불쾌해했다.
19. 효소 치료는 비용이 많이 들고, 효소가 단백질이기에 구강으로 소화되면 분해될 수 있기 때문에 반드시 정맥으로 전달되어야 한다.
20. 미국의 공장과 증기발전소는 매일 6백만 리터의 물을 우물, 강, 호수로부터 끌어온다.

Intensive Practice 11-15

1. ⓓ	2. ⓑ	3. ⓒ	4. ⓓ	5. ⓐ
6. ⓓ	7. ⓐ	8. ⓑ	9. ⓒ	10. ⓒ
11. ⓒ	12. ⓒ	13. ⓒ	14. ⓓ	15. ⓐ
16. ⓑ	17. ⓓ	18. ⓐ	19. ⓒ	20. ⓐ

1. 야생에서 캠핑하는 사람들은 공원관리자들에게 캠핑 계획을 알려야 한다.
2. 많은 과학자들이 달에서 특정 화학물질들이 발견되어 지구에 생명체들이 어떻게 탄생하였는지에 대한 단서를 제공하기를 기대했다.
3. 방송산업은 노골적으로 폭력적이거나 성적인 내용에 프로그램 등급을 표시한다.

4. 모차르트의 작곡은 의심의 여지가 없는 세계에서 가장 위대한 작곡들이다.
5. 과학소설의 기본 주제는 시간여행, 공간여행, 놀라운 발명 또는 발견, 다른 세상의 생명체 및 외계인의 지구 침공을 다룬다.

6. 일반적으로, 아동도서는 성인도서에 비교하여 삽화를 상당히 많이 강조한다.
7. 인생은 결과적으로 이해할 수 없이 난해했고, 역설적인 상황을 공부하면서 즐거움을 찾을 수 있었다.
8. 열과 압력은 일부 바위를 대리석이나 석판과 같은 변성암으로 변형시킨다.
9. 제국주의 권력은 소중한 자원의 종속된 지역을 약탈하여 부를 축적할 수 있었다.
10. 다른 에너지의 원천이 개발되기 전까지, 국가는 최대한 공급이 충분할 수 있도록 화석 연료를 보전하여야 한다.

11. 일부 문화에서 조상은 사악한 영혼으로 간주하여, 영혼을 달래는 의식을 행한다.
12. 물이 강, 호수 및 바다로부터 증발될 때, 물은 대기 중에 떠 있으며, 구름이 생긴다.
13. 주택을 지을 때, 건설 노동자들은 먼저 건물의 최하위층에 기반을 다지기 위해 도랑이나 구멍을 판다.
14. 아이들은 부모에 대한 순종을 배우며, 아이들과 어른은 연장자에 대한 존경심이 보이기를 기대한다.
15. 1895년에 상황을 더 악화시킨 불경기일 때, 혁명이 재발하여 끝이 보이지 않을 정도로 지속적으로 위협하였다.

16. 작물을 수확한 후, 농부는 토양 아래에 파묻기 전에 토양을 덮을 작물의 잔재물을 버린다.
17. 1776년 독립선언 이후, 각각의 영국 식민지는 주권 확립을 위해 스스로를 국가로 불렀다.
18. 산업용 등급의 다이아몬드는 불완전하게 형성되거나, 기타 여러 결함이나 색결함이 있는 돌을 포함한다.
19. 미세소관은 가지가 없고 가늘고, 속이 비었으며, 단백질로 구성된 관처럼 생긴 구조이다; 미세소관은 크기가 다르며 크기는 지름 15~25나노미터 정도이다.
20. 보건 전문가들은 어린이, 청소년, 임산부, 운전을 하려는 사람, 약을 복용한 사람, 음주의 양을 조절할 수 없는 사람들을 포함한 특정 사람들은 알코올 섭취를 전적으로 피해야 한다고 권유한다.

Daily Checkup 16

1. Ⓑ	2. Ⓒ	3. Ⓓ	4. Ⓐ	5. Ⓐ
6. Ⓐ	7. Ⓓ	8. Ⓑ	9. Ⓑ	10. Ⓓ
11. Ⓑ	12. Ⓒ	13. Ⓒ	14. Ⓑ	15. Ⓑ
16. Ⓐ	17. Ⓓ	18. Ⓐ	19. Ⓒ	20. Ⓓ

1. 의장직을 맡다
2. 잔인한 사람
3. 빛을 억누르다
4. 긴장하여 / 노력하여
5. 모기 때문에 망쳤다

6. 단어를 정확하게 발음하다
7. 행동을 비난하다
8. 우리는 숲을 보존해야 한다.
9. 맹렬한 비 / 폭우
10. 남에게서 은신처를 찾다 / 남에게로 도피하다

11. 누구를 더 높은 관직으로 승진시키다
12. 이 발명품은 최박사님이 발명했다고 한다.
13. 토지 매입
14. 자기 장점을 살려 / 자기 실력으로
15. 긴 실은 얽히기 쉽다.

16. 불안전한 숨을 곳
17. 안경을 쓰고 사람의 얼굴을 뜯어보다
18. 당신의 충고를 존중합니다.
19. 그는 병 때문에 일을 할 수 없었다.
20. 교환 가능한 부품

Practice Test 16

1. Ⓑ	2. Ⓒ	3. Ⓓ	4. Ⓒ	5. Ⓒ
6. Ⓐ	7. Ⓒ	8. Ⓒ	9. Ⓑ	10. Ⓓ
11. Ⓒ	12. Ⓒ	13. Ⓓ	14. Ⓓ	15. Ⓒ
16. Ⓑ	17. Ⓓ	18. Ⓓ	19. Ⓒ	20. Ⓑ

1. 단지 길들여진 동물들만 일반적으로 가축으로 여긴다.
2. 많은 폭력범죄가 피해자와 안면이 있는 사람들에 의해 저질러 진다.
3. 결혼의 전통을 조롱하는 것처럼 디킨슨은 매일 하얀 정장을 입었다.
4. 고대사회는 오늘날 대부분의 사람들이 비난할 수 있는 다양한 가족관습을 허용했다.
5. 혹동고래의 가장 큰 특징은 유난히 긴 지느러미인데, 그것은 몸의 3분의 1정도로 길다.

6. 유고슬라비아는 모든 빨치산 운동에 가장 효과적인 저항운동을 했었다.
7. 많은 작물들이 빨리 상하는 경향이 있어서 농부는 수확 후 작물들을 가능한 한 빨리 시장으로 운반한다.
8. 어떤 홍조류는 실험실에서 세균을 배양하는 데 사용하는 젤리와 비슷한 물질인 한천의 원천이 된다.
9. 대부분 암컷 포유류의 유두는 배 위에 있는 육아낭이라 불리는 주머니에 위치해 있다.
10. 남부는 전쟁 중에 필요한 것들을 얻기 위해 노력했지만, 경제상태가 거의 한계에 이를 정도로 무리를 했다.

11. 어떤 뇌우는 상당히 심각하여 해일, 폭풍우 또는 강한 바람을 일으킬 수 있다.
12. 영국함대가 보급로를 위협하자 군대는 캐나다로 다시 후퇴하였다.
13. 기억, 공동의 경험 및 국가의 역사 기록을 보전하는 것이 언어이다.
14. 1850년대 후반과 1860년대 초기의 미국 원주민들은 일부 포장 마차대에서 농작물과 들소고기를 담배와 술과 쇳조각으로 교환하였다.
15. 성자는 미덕과 종교적 미덕을 실천하여 모범이 됨으로써 종교적으로 영웅이 된 신성한 사람이다.

16. 주정부 도서관은 네덜란드 초기 식민지 지배자들의 기록을 포함한 광범위한 뉴욕의 역사를 보관한다.
17. 발광은 종을 분별하거나 인식하며 잠재적 먹잇감을 유혹하고, 포식자를 놀라게 하며 동료에게 위험을 알리는 다양한 목적으로 수행된다.
18. 많은 독일인들은 자국의 영토와 자원을 포기하고 재건비용을 부담하게 하는 베르사이유조약에 자국의 경제적 어려움을 비난했다.
19. 매년 수백만의 바다새, 거북, 물고기, 해양동물들이 플라스틱 쓰레기에 걸려서 죽거나 섭취하여 죽는다.
20. 서양세계에 '위대한 술레이만'이라 불리는 술탄 술레이만 I세 시기에 제국은 부와 권력의 최고조에 이르렀다.

Daily Checkup 17

1. Ⓐ	2. Ⓐ	3. Ⓒ	4. Ⓓ	5. Ⓓ
6. Ⓒ	7. Ⓑ	8. Ⓐ	9. Ⓒ	10. Ⓓ
11. Ⓐ	12. Ⓑ	13. Ⓒ	14. Ⓓ	15. Ⓒ
16. Ⓑ	17. Ⓒ	18. Ⓑ	19. Ⓒ	20. Ⓑ

1. 새로운 장치를 발명하다
2. 사람의 얼굴을 응시하다
3. 근거 없는 추측
4. 서로가 협력하는
5. 그는 모든 일에 나를 끌어들인다.

6. 사실을 알고 있다
7. 정부 지출을 삭감하다
8. 남에게 폐를 끼치다 / 귀찮게 하다
9. 친구 간의 불화
10. 원대한 소망

11. 지식의 풍부한 유산
12. 경찰에게 군중을 해산하도록 명령하다
13. 생각에 잠긴 눈
14. 인생에 필요한 물건들
15. 사람을 꾸짖다

16. 안정적인 관계
17. 상품 무역
18. 정당의 골치 아픈 사안
19. 시든 나뭇잎
20. ~에게 증거를 제출하다

Practice Test 17

1. Ⓒ	2. Ⓒ	3. Ⓒ	4. Ⓒ	5. Ⓑ
6. Ⓑ	7. Ⓓ	8. Ⓒ	9. Ⓓ	10. Ⓐ
11. Ⓑ	12. Ⓒ	13. Ⓓ	14. Ⓐ	15. Ⓑ
16. Ⓒ	17. Ⓒ	18. Ⓐ	19. Ⓓ	20. Ⓑ

1. 어떤 동물들은 현화식물의 씨앗들을 흩뿌린다.
2. 철학자 로크는 타고난 발상은 없으며, 즉 사람들은 발상과 함께 태어나지는 않는다고 주장했다.
3. 합성수지로 만든 비행기 창문은 유리보다 가볍고 더 잘게 부서진다.
4. 공해농도는 바닷가도 안전하지 않은 곳으로 만든다.
5. 예를 들어, 빙하기에서 간빙기 사이에 메탄은 각각 50%에서 75%로 급격히 증가했다.

6. 칼날이 앤드류의 손을 뼈가 보일 정도로 그었고, 머리도 심하게 베어냈다.
7. 많은 사람들에게 종교란 믿음, 의식, 관행의 체계적인 제도이며 전능한 신을 숭배하는 것이다.
8. 뇌졸중은 혈관이 파열되어 피가 뇌 또는 주변 조직으로 흐를 때 발생한다.
9. 폭탄이 집, 공장, 교통 및 통신수단을 파괴했다.
10. 삽화는 교육과정 및 정보를 제공하는 데 상당히 중요하다.

11. 구애과정 중에, 고래는 지느러미로 서로를 어루만질 수 있다.
12. 라디오의 인기는 제2차 세계대전(1939 -1945) 이후 TV의 인기가 호황이 시작되기 전까지 대략 20년 동안 치솟았다.
13. 인쇄 발명의 결과 중의 하나는 15세기 단어의 철자를 불변하도록 만든 것에 있었다.
14. 단백질의 아미노산에서 NH2 및 COOH기는 구성 요소이고 체인을 형성하기 위해 결합한다.
15. 일부 세포는 6면의 박스 형태이지만, 다른 세포는 세포의 위치와 기능에 따라 다양한 형태의 모양을 취한다.

16. 1965년 8월에 로스앤젤레스 흑인 빈민가인 왓츠에서의 폭동으로 34명의 사람이 죽었고 거의 900명이 부상당했다.
17. 시끄러운 소리나 갑작스런 동요에 의해 놀라게 되면, 경악반사라고 불리는 반사행동으로 팔과 다리를 갑자기 움찔린다.
18. 육군은 다양한 전문가 또는 전쟁을 수행하거나 폭약 작업 등 위험한 임무를 수행하는 군인들에게 특별수당을 지급한다.
19. 자동차 배기가스의 오염 물질을 줄이기 위해서, 정유회사들은 자동차 제조사와 협력하여 무연 휘발유를 생산한다.
20. 그 선언문은 독립선언문을 사례로 이용하여 '우리는 이러한 진리가 옳다는 확신을 가지고 있으며, 모든 사람은 평등하다'고 선언한다.

TOEFL DAY 18

Daily Checkup 18

1. Ⓐ	2. Ⓐ	3. Ⓒ	4. Ⓒ	5. Ⓓ
6. Ⓒ	7. Ⓓ	8. Ⓒ	9. Ⓐ	10. Ⓐ
11. Ⓒ	12. Ⓒ	13. Ⓓ	14. Ⓑ	15. Ⓓ
16. Ⓒ	17. Ⓒ	18. Ⓒ	19. Ⓐ	20. Ⓑ

1. 그랜드캐년에는 많은 작은 협곡이 있다.
2. 군중 속으로 사라지다
3. 증거를 입증할 수 있는 / 사실임을 입증할 수 있는
4. 최선의 노력을 다하다
5. 난폭 운전

6. 할 일이 산더미처럼 쌓였다
7. 밧줄을 팽팽하게 늘리다
8. 출입 금지.
9. 선명한 색으로 칠해진
10. (맛) 충분히 음미하며

11. ~의 자랑스런 후계자
12. 우리는 그녀가 정직하다고 생각한다.
13. 민족 문화의 회복
14. 우울한 색으로 색칠했다
15. 고의적인 잔인한 행동

16. 다수의 관점과 의견이 다르다
17. 손가락을 움직이다
18. 출발을 서두르다
19. 협정을 승인하다
20. 프리즘은 태양광을 다양한 색으로 분해한다.

Practice Test 18

1. Ⓓ	2. Ⓒ	3. Ⓑ	4. Ⓒ	5. Ⓓ
6. Ⓐ	7. Ⓒ	8. Ⓐ	9. Ⓒ	10. Ⓓ
11. Ⓒ	12. Ⓑ	13. Ⓑ	14. Ⓑ	15. Ⓒ
16. Ⓓ	17. Ⓓ	18. Ⓒ	19. Ⓒ	20. Ⓒ

1. 염증성 피부는 딱딱해지며 고름이 나올 수 있다.
2. 천일염 작업은 증발을 촉진하기 위해 뜨겁고 건조한 기후를 필요로 한다.
3. 과도한 사냥 때문에 고래의 몇몇 종들은 멸종 위기에 처했다.
4. 설탕이 가열되면 탄소와 물로 분해된다.
5. 전두엽전피질은 과잉행동을 억제하는 역할을 할 수 있다.

6. 그의 공직생활에서의 중요한 결정에서 보면, 역사는 그가 옳고 **상대방**이 틀렸다는 것을 증명해왔다.
7. 1792년 8월, 파리의 시민들은 루이 16세와 그의 가족을 **구금하고** 감옥에 가뒀다.
8. 이슬람에서 무하마드는 신의 최후의 메신저이며, 선지자들의 진실된 가르침을 **확인하기 위해** 보내졌다고 여긴다.
9. 이탈리아 군대는 기관총, 탱크, 비행기를 이용하여 에티오피아의 형편없는 장비를 갖춘 군대를 **압도하였다.**
10. 많은 지방자치단체와 공기업은 거대한 공공건설 프로그램에 **무모하게** 예산을 낭비했다.

11. 블루그래스는 노래할 때 복잡한 발성과 기계적인 솔로 및 정교한 호흡을 **보여준다.** (bluegrass 미국 남부의 백인 민속음악에서 유래된 컨트리음악을 말함)
12. 적십자사는 재난 구호와 **재건**을 위해 1960년대에 1억 4천 6백만 달러의 구호자금을 사용했다.
13. **충동적인** 장군들은 때때로 노예해방을 위한 성명서를 발표하였지만, 링컨 대통령은 기각했다.
14. 카시미르 플라스키는 미국 독립전쟁 시 미국을 위해 싸운 폴란드의 **귀족**이었다.
15. 가설이라 불리는 공리는 사실로 믿어지는 주장이며, 그러므로 **증거** 없이 받아들여진다.

16. 리처드 페니맨의 활기차고 **화려한** 무대공연은 공연자들이 따라가야 할 모델로 제공됐다.
17. 많은 사람들이 점성술이나 심령술과 같은 초자연적인 가르침의 **신비스러운** 방식에 매료된다.
18. 비행과 위험에 대한 **긴밀한 구성의** 이야기는 기술을 회피하고 미신이 넘치는 미래의 영국에서 발생했다.
19. 의회와 대법원은 대통령의 권한을 넘는 권력을 **남용하는** 어떠한 행위라도 제한하거나 정지해야 한다.
20. 작가는 작품의 시기와 작품의 **생생한** 감정을 창조하기 위한 서술적 묘사와 대화를 사용하여 전기를 작성하기 시작했다.

Daily Checkup 19

1. Ⓐ	2. Ⓒ	3. Ⓐ	4. Ⓐ	5. Ⓒ
6. Ⓒ	7. Ⓒ	8. Ⓑ	9. Ⓒ	10. Ⓑ
11. Ⓑ	12. Ⓒ	13. Ⓐ	14. Ⓒ	15. Ⓓ
16. Ⓒ	17. Ⓒ	18. Ⓓ	19. Ⓒ	20. Ⓑ

1. ~ 일을 시작하다
2. 적에게 **항복하다**
3. 새로운 **기술을** 배우다
4. 그의 기억을 **새롭게 하다**
5. **잠재적인**, 표현하지 않은 적대심

6. 다소 **관대한** 관점
7. 다과를 **대접받다**
8. 길을 **막다**
9. 유행을 **지배하다** / 유행을 **이끌다**
10. 그는 연금을 받을 **자격이 있다.**

11. 높은 **경의**를 가지다 / 누구를 **존경**하다
12. **편견** 없이
13. **어수룩한** 사람
14. 비용이 얼마나 들지 **알아내다**
15. ~대한 **완강한** 저항

16. **대담한** 야심
17. 도시로 사람들이 **이동하다**
18. 배는 **산산조각 났다.**
19. 미래에 대해 **두려워하다**
20. 겨울에 **동면하다**

Practice Test 19

1. Ⓒ	2. Ⓓ	3. Ⓑ	4. Ⓑ	5. Ⓒ
6. Ⓐ	7. Ⓒ	8. Ⓓ	9. Ⓒ	10. Ⓑ
11. Ⓒ	12. Ⓑ	13. Ⓑ	14. Ⓒ	15. Ⓒ
16. Ⓐ	17. Ⓒ	18. Ⓓ	19. Ⓐ	20. Ⓒ

1. 영국 희극은 찰스 II세의 **재임 기간** 동안 상당한 자유를 누렸다.
2. 대기 중의 수증기는 엄청난 양의 **보이지 않는** 열에너지를 보전한다.
3. 많은 동물들이 **생계**를 위협한다고 믿는 사람들에 의해 피살됐다.
4. 우주시대는 1957년 러시아가 첫 인공위성을 **발사한** 후에 지구 위를 공전하면서 시작됐다.
5. 정부는 국영은행권에 세금을 **부과함**으로써 국영은행권이 유통되지 않게 했다.

6. 누구도 스트레스에서 벗어날 수 없지만, 스트레스로 인한 질병의 위험을 **감소시킬** 수 있는 일들을 할 수 있다.
7. 미국 정부는 1790년 이후 10년을 주기로 미국의 **인구조사를** 실시하고 있다.
8. 일부 사람들이 전통적인 결혼 방식을 **깨뜨리지만**, 다수의 많은 연인들은 전통적인 종교의식의 결혼을 선호한다.
9. 광고주들은 영화와 TV 스타, 유명한 스포츠 스타 및 기타 유명인사들과 광고계약을 **맺는다**.
10. 급속한 **붕괴**의 시기에 취약한 대륙 빙하는 지난 6십만 년 동안 최소한 한 번은 사라졌다.

11. 미국의 제42대 대통령인 빌 클린턴은 1998년 위증과 재판 **방해**로 탄핵되었다.
12. 곤드와나랜드는 대략 1억 4천만 년 전에 분리가 시작되어, 남극이 남쪽으로 **표류하기** 시작했다.
13. 2개월의 작전기간 동안 그랜트 장군은 그의 군대와 물자의 운영을 어떻게 할지에 대해 기억을 **되살렸다**.
14. 전쟁이 끝나자, 세미놀족(아메리카 원주민의 하나)은 **항복**하거나 인질이 되어 서부로 이주됐다.
15. 영국군이 캐나다에서 뉴욕으로 **돌격하는** 것을 방지하기 위해, 대륙의회는 캐나다 침공을 명령했다.

16. 가끔 정부는 해외 매출을 증가하기 위한 노력으로 고의적으로 통화가치를 **하락시킨다**.
17. 포항은 기계류의 **도매무역**에서 일등 도시이며 경기도는 농산물 무역의 중심이다.
18. 연극의 **즐거움**에 더하여, 말 많은 지방 경찰관 도그베리와 그의 조수 베지스의 폭넓은 유머가 있다.
19. 프톨레미의 관찰과 이론은 13장에 Mathematike Syntaxis 또는 수학적 정리의 **제목으로** 보전되었다.
20. 미국인들은 공식적으로 미국 전역에 노예제도를 폐기한다는 헌법의 제13조항을 **수정하여** 전쟁 종료 후 평등을 현실로 하기 위해서 노력했다.

Daily Checkup 20

1. ⓑ	2. ⓑ	3. ⓑ	4. ⓒ	5. ⓑ
6. ⓓ	7. ⓒ	8. ⓓ	9. ⓐ	10. ⓑ
11. ⓒ	12. ⓒ	13. ⓐ	14. ⓓ	15. ⓐ
16. ⓑ	17. ⓓ	18. ⓑ	19. ⓐ	20. ⓓ

1. **공공의** 적
2. 그들에게 떠나라고 **간청하다**
3. 그의 결단을 **약화시켰다**
4. 적절한 **발췌를** 선택하다
5. **도망자가** 되다

6. 샐러드에 **고명을** 얹다
7. **섬뜩한** 내용
8. 아이를 **배불리** 먹이다
9. 증인을 **심문하다**
10. **악성** 종양

11. **다양한 물체 / 잡동사니** 물건
12. **유목하는** 민족
13. **전통적인** 믿음
14. **위증** 죄
15. **잠재적** 위협

16. 배달사고를 **예방하다**
17. **현명한** 발언
18. 증거에 **손대다 / 증거를 조작하다**
19. 시국의 **불확실성**
20. 아주 **신중하다**

Practice Test 20

1. ⓐ	2. ⓓ	3. ⓑ	4. ⓒ	5. ⓓ
6. ⓐ	7. ⓒ	8. ⓐ	9. ⓑ	10. ⓓ
11. ⓓ	12. ⓐ	13. ⓑ	14. ⓐ	15. ⓓ
16. ⓒ	17. ⓓ	18. ⓑ	19. ⓒ	20. ⓓ

1. 식물은 병원균들로부터 항상 **도전을 받고 있지만** 병은 드물게 일어난다.
2. 지진과 **유사한** 자석의 불안정성은 폭발에 대하여 설명할 수 있을 것이다.
3. 많은 원핵생물들이 탄수화물과 아미노산이 풍부한 울퉁불퉁한 벽에 의해 **둘러쌓여 있다**.
4. 가장 오래된 것으로 알려진 화석은 **적어도** 31억년 전에 살았던 단세포로 된 식물이다.
5. 거리에는 질병 병원균이 번창할 수 있는 오물이 **치워졌다**.

6. 물이 비등점에 도달할 때, 즉시 증기로 **변하지** 않는다.
7. 개별 유기체와 전체 종 모두 생존하기 위하여 환경 변화에 반드시 **적응해야 한다.**
8. 분해는 한 물질이 두 개 이상의 부분으로 **부서지는** 것을 의미한다.
9. 급전사령이라 불리는 기술자들이 전송 네트워크를 통해서 전류 흐름을 **추적한다.**
10. 근원 섬유는 액틴과 미오신이라 부르는 특별한 단백질로 **만들어진** 필라멘트로 구성된 복잡한 구조이다.

11. 조지 워싱턴과 다른 지도자들은 만일 식민지가 영국에 대항하여 모반을 했는지를 **부질없이** 궁금해했다.
12. 링컨은 남북전쟁(1861-1865) 동안에 노예를 해방하기 위한 조항을 **발표하기 위해** 무력을 사용했다.
13. 메시지를 보내기 위해 선원들은 의미를 암호화하거나 단어를 **판독하는** 것을 포함하는 깃발을 한 개에서 다섯 개까지 높이 게양한다.
14. 적응 또는 진화는 한 세대에서 다음 세대로 **전해지는** 유전자의 변화를 포함한다.
15. 암흑기 동안에 많은 잔인한 야만인들의 정복은 서유럽의 문명을 **없애도록** 더욱 위협했다.

16. 인간이 다른 사물을 마음대로 **표현할 수 있는** 과정을 상징적 과정이라고 부른다.
17. 재즈는 뉴올리언스에서 장례식이나 퍼레이드에서 연주되는 브라스밴드 음악과 같은 흑인의 춤추는 음악에 일부 **뿌리를 두고 있다.**
18. 미토콘드리아는 작고 수많은 미세소기관으로 호흡과 연관된 내막(cristae)이라 불리는 안쪽의 층모양의 겹을 가진 두 개의 막에 의해 **둘러쌓여 있다.**
19. 1888년에 리스의 뉴욕시 빈민가 사진은 대중에게 충격을 주었으며, 그 도시에서 가장 열악한 지역 중 하나를 없애는 **결과를 가져오도록** 도왔다.
20. 현미경에는 식물 연구뿐만 아니라 생물학과 그 관련 분야 **전체에** 심원한 효과를 갖게 하고 계속하게 한다.

TOEFL DAY 16-20

Exercise 16-20

1. ⓒ	2. Ⓐ	3. ⓒ	4. Ⓑ	5. Ⓓ
6. ⓒ	7. Ⓑ	8. Ⓐ	9. Ⓑ	10. ⓒ
11. ⓒ	12. ⓒ	13. Ⓐ	14. Ⓓ	15. ⓒ
16. ⓒ	17. ⓒ	18. Ⓑ	19. Ⓑ	20. Ⓐ

1. **조롱하다** / 다른 사람의 기대를 **저버리다**
2. 부의 **최고조에** 도달하다
3. **광범위한** 조사
4. **타고난** 본능
5. 무리 앞에 **갑자기 밀려들다**

6. **잘 부러지는** 나뭇가지
7. 감정의 **폭발**
8. 오래된 다리의 **파괴**
9. 사람을 **감금시키다**
10. 비밀이 **새어 나왔다.**

11. **충동적인** 행동
12. **화려한** 색상
13. 국민의 **즐거움**
14. 조약을 **비준하다**
15. **멋들어진 풍채의** 남자 / **인상 깊은** 모습의 남자

16. **후퇴하기로** 결정하다
17. 그는 **선행을** 많이 하는 사람이다.
18. 현저한 **특징**
19. 새로운 시험을 **지지하다**
20. 약속을 **어기다**

Practice Test 16-20

1. Ⓐ	2. Ⓓ	3. Ⓓ	4. ⓒ	5. ⓒ
6. Ⓓ	7. Ⓑ	8. ⓒ	9. ⓒ	10. ⓒ
11. Ⓓ	12. Ⓐ	13. Ⓐ	14. ⓒ	15. Ⓓ
16. Ⓐ	17. ⓒ	18. Ⓑ	19. Ⓐ	20. Ⓐ

1. 시장은 일반적으로 **상품을** 사고파는 장소로 여겨진다.
2. 수세기 동안, 사람들은 달을 **관찰했으며** 경배하고 연구해왔다.
3. 프랑스의 재정적인 **어려움은** 1789년 프랑스혁명을 초래했다.
4. 소비자 교육은 사람들이 다양한 제품을 구매하는 경우 현명한 결정을 할 수 있도록 필요한 **지식을** 제공해준다.
5. 코끼리는 귀를 쫑긋 세우고 앞으로 돌진하여 적을 **위협하여** 쫓아낸다.

6. 아프리카와 많은 태평양 섬들의 일부 사람들은 큰 식물의 **줄기**를 집을 만드는 데 사용한다.
7. 세심한 교정은 논문의 실수를 **줄일 수 있다.**
8. 증기엔진은 차를 만들고 유지하는 데 비용이 많이 들어서, 증기엔진 자동차는 점점 **사라졌다.**
9. 루즈벨트 대통령은 특수 민간공무원이 되기 위한 시험을 만들어 **성과** 시스템을 개선하였다.
10. 범죄를 저지른 사람들은 태형에 처하거나 일부 **잔인한** 교정적 처벌을 받는다.

11. 황금률의 원리는 다른 사람들로부터 **대우를 받으려면** 똑같이 대우해야 한다는 것이다.
12. 일부 피해자들은 죽은 조직을 없애고 피부조직을 **재생하는** 외과수술이 필요하다.
13. 대기의 지구온난화는 앞으로 30년 동안 지구의 온도를 2~5도 정도 상승시킬 **조짐을** 보인다.
14. 4천 년 동안에 걸쳐, 인도 예술가는 영적인 **내용**과 기술적인 우수성으로 표현되는 강한 작품을 만들었다.
15. 날씨의 중요성 때문에, 기상학자들은 기상 상태를 **예측하기** 위한 다양한 방법을 개발해왔다.

16. 마사 그레이엄은 미국의 현대 춤을 **고안하지** 않았지만, 그녀의 이름은 현대 춤과 동의어로 사용된다.
17. 연방법은 누구든지 주에서 비행기를 소유하고 운행하기 위해서, 비행기를 **등록하고** 면허를 획득할 것을 요구했다.
18. 1800년대에 재능 있는 작가들과 화가들이 단순한 교육용이 아닌 **즐거움을 위한** 아이들의 동화책을 제작하기 시작했다.
19. 의사들은 고도 비만인 환자를 신중하게 **선택하여** 체중 감소 프로그램의 일부분으로 약을 처방할 수 있다.
20. 많은 오투만 군주들은 예술, 언어, 문학에 **능통하여,** 무슬림 사회의 문화의 기준을 세웠다.

Intensive Practice 16-20

1. ⓓ	2. ⓒ	3. ⓐ	4. ⓐ	5. ⓒ
6. ⓒ	7. ⓑ	8. ⓑ	9. ⓑ	10. ⓑ
11. ⓓ	12. ⓓ	13. ⓐ	14. ⓑ	15. ⓐ
16. ⓓ	17. ⓑ	18. ⓒ	19. ⓑ	20. ⓐ

1. 미국 해군에 복무하고 있는 남녀는 20년 복무 후 연금을 받고 **제대할 수 있다.**
2. 애팔래치아 산맥을 넘어, 정착민들은 동부 대지의 일부 비용으로 비옥한 **땅을** 얻을 수 있었다.
3. 몇몇 사람들이 비공식적으로 **활동하며,** 이는 미국시민이나 외국인으로 활동하는 의미이다.
4. 도시 보전의 목적은 더 매력적이고 **살기 좋은** 장소로 만드는 것이다.
5. 조세는 대략 주 정부 일반 **수익**의 60%를 제공한다.

6. 1781년 3월 1일, 메릴랜드 주는 연합헌장을 **승인하는** 마지막 주가 되었다.
7. 헨리 M. 리랜드는 미국의 캐딜락 자동차 회사를 인수하여, **호환 가능한** 부품을 사용하는 차를 생산하기 시작했다.
8. 코끼리는 그리스 어원으로 두꺼운 피부라는 용어로 후피동물이라 부르지만, 코끼리의 피부는 놀라울 정도로 **부드럽다.**
9. 그리스 조각가들은 여인상으로 불리는 옷을 입은 여인의 형상으로 만들어진 기둥을 제작하여 실제로 건물을 **지탱할 수** 있게 한다.

10. 나중에, 토마스 크롬웰은 울지를 장관으로 **대체하여,** 그 후로 헨리가 국가를 통치하는 데 큰 영향을 주었다.
11. 우리가 아무것도 알지 못하기 때문에, 모든 일들을 **편견 없이** 대해야 하며 판단을 해서는 안 된다.
12. 우리 몸의 특정 화학물질의 불균형이나 **영양이 풍부한** 음식의 부족은 신경조직의 발달에 장애를 주거나 영구적인 피해를 줄 수 있다.
13. 그 전년에, 프랑스의 루이 15세는 전쟁 중에 스페인으로부터 군사적인 도움과 영토 손실을 **보상하기 위해** 미시시피의 루이지아나 서부의 모든 지역을 비밀리에 스페인에게 넘겼다.
14. 다양한 인간 줄기세포로 불리는 세포는 뇌에서 주기적으로 분할되어 다른 줄기세포를 **생기게 하며,** 자손을 낳아 신경세포로 자라게 하는 지원세포인 교질세포로 불린다.
15. 여름에는 대륙성 따뜻하고 건조한 열대기단이 텍사스와 미국 남부의 일부 지역에 **밀어닥친다.**

16. 비민주주의 국가에서는 내부 보안기관이 **반대 의견을** 없애거나 반대 세력을 투옥시키거나 죽이기 위해 종종 경찰과 다른 기관들과 함께 일한다.
17. 마술을 이용하여 프로스페로가 그의 적들을 나르는 배를 그 섬에서 **난파되도록** 한 폭풍우를 만든다.(Prospero 셰익스피어의 작품 The tempest에 나오는 인물로 추방된 Milan의 공작, tempest = storm 폭풍)
18. 많은 사람들이 면죄부가 연옥으로부터 죽은 사람의 영혼의 해방을 서둘러 줄거라 희망하며 교회로부터 면죄부를 받는다.
19. 바람과 대기의 일상적인 가열과 냉각이 온냉기류의 **소용돌이**와 수직하강기류를 만든다.
20. 많은 젊은이들이 약물 남용, **무모한** 운전, 건강 문제에 노출되어 있다.

IELTS 급상승 Actual Test 1
[Reading &Writing] (Academic Module)

James H. Lee 저 | 210*280mm | 316쪽 | 16,800원

IELTS 급상승 Actual Test 2
[Listening & Speaking]

James H. Lee 저 | 210*280mm | 284쪽 | 16,800원

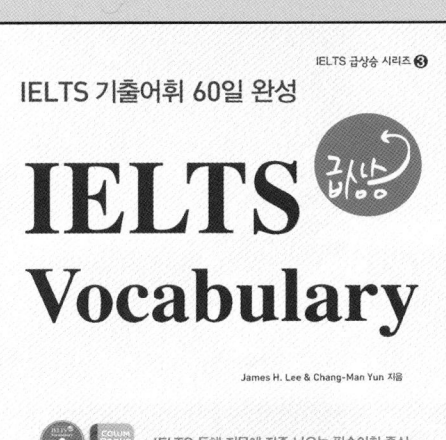

IELTS 급상승 Vocabulary

James H. Lee, Chang-man Yun 저 | 188*258mm | 440쪽 | 16,800원(mp3 무료 제공)

IELTS 급상승
기초다지기
시리즈

IELTS 급상승 Grammar 기초다지기
김재한 저 | 188*258mm | 172쪽 | 15,000원

IELTS 급상승 Writing 기초다지기
[Academic Module]
김재한 저 | 188*258mm | 320쪽 | 16,800원

IELTS 급상승 Reading 기초다지기
[Academic Module]
이수용 저 | 188*258mm | 248쪽 | 15,000원

IELTS 급상승 Listening 기초다지기
이수용 저 | 188*258mm | 224쪽 |
15,000원(mp3 파일 무료 제공)

IELTS 급상승 Speaking 기초다지기
이수용 저 | 188*258mm | 284쪽 |
15,000원 (mp3 파일 무료 제공)